All Glory to the
Only Good God

All Glory to the Only Good God

Reformed Spirituality

❖

HERMAN HOEKSEMA

Edited by
David J. Engelsma

Reformed Free Publishing Association
Jenison, Michigan

© 2013 Reformed Free Publishing Association
All rights reserved
Printed in the United States of America

Scripture cited is taken from the King James (Authorized) Version
Psalter numbers cited are taken from *The Psalter with Doctrinal
Standards, Liturgy, Church Order, and added Chorale Section,*
reprinted and revised edition of the 1912 United Presbyterian
Psalter (Grand Rapids, MI: Wm. B. Eerdmans Publishing
Company, 1927; rev. ed. 1965)

Reformed Free Publishing Association
1894 Georgetown Center Drive
Jenison, Michigan 49428

Cover and interior design by Gary Gore Book Design
ISBN 978-1-936054-28-2
LCCN 2013910580

Contents

Part IV: God's Goodness to His Chosen People: Generally

Part V: God's Goodness to His Chosen People: Specifically

Preface

This third volume in the series of the Reformed spirituality of Herman Hoeksema (and, in this way, of the Protestant Reformed Churches in America) has as its theme the end, or goal, of true Reformed spirituality in the glory of the God of all goodness.

In this respect genuinely Reformed spirituality distinguishes itself from much that passes for Reformed spirituality in our day. Reformed, biblical spirituality does not end in the sanctified sinner and his experience. It certainly does not end in the unrelieved doubt of his own salvation on the part of the member of a Reformed church, as though such doubt is normal for professing Reformed Christians, indeed as though such doubt is commendable experience. Persistent doubters are gross sinners against the gospel of Jesus Christ, which they profess to believe. Doubters cannot glorify the only good God. Doubt is the antithesis of Christian and Reformed experience.

But neither does genuinely Reformed spirituality end in the joy and holiness of the elect believer.

Genuinely Reformed spirituality ends in glorifying God as the God of all goodness, both in himself and in all his dealings with the elect believer. Reformed devotion is experience and life that are devoted to God.

The title of this volume expresses the theme of the meditations that make up the book: *All Glory to the Only Good God*. Reformed spirituality gives *all* glory to God because the Reformed faith, which this book confesses in a devotional manner, ascribes *all* of salvation to God and his goodness. "Only" in the title especially modifies "good." God is only good, both in himself and in all his dealings with the elect believer.

The first meditation in the *Standard Bearer*, in which all the meditations making up this volume originally appeared, was that on Psalm 145:9, 20, "Jehovah's Goodness" (*Standard Bearer* 1, no. 1 [October 1924], 1–2). Since the meditation was the front page of the magazine, the words "Jehovah's Goodness," were the first to be seen by the reader of the new magazine. There can be no doubt that this was deliberate on the part of the editors. This meditation is also first in this book.

As with the content of the preceding two volumes in this series, the devotional writing of Herman Hoeksema in this book is faithful, penetrating interpretation of Scripture. The reader therefore is instructed and moved by the word of God.

Devotional writing for Hoeksema did not mean the deliberate avoidance of sound doctrine. Spirituality is born of sound doctrine, for spirituality is the work of the Holy Spirit upon the heart and soul of the child of God. And the Spirit works no otherwise than by sound doctrine. The shallow devotional writing so popular in our day, avoiding sound doctrine like the plague, is mere emotionalism.

There is also in this unique, Reformed spirituality exposure and condemnation of error that wages war against the precious experience of the believer. The exposition of Psalm 119:32, "When Thou Shalt Enlarge My Heart," exposes the theology of doubt of the Puritans and the resultant lack of assurance and careless life of multitudes of their disciples in certain streams of the Reformed tradition: "sickly souls."

Repeatedly Hoeksema observes and insists on the particularity of the goodness, grace, and blessing of God that lies on the surface of Holy Scripture, against the prevalent error that makes his goodness a common thing and therefore hardly the reason for the believer's glorifying God.

Some of the meditations date themselves. The devotional on Psalm 33:22, "Thy Mercy, O Lord," identifies itself as having been preached on New Year's morning 1940 and published soon thereafter. World War II had just begun, in September 1939, with Hitler's invasion of Poland. The preacher and author took note of this world-shaking event in order to demonstrate the right attitude of church and believer toward such earthly calamities. Although dated, the message is not outdated.

The style of the writing makes plain that the author himself experienced the work of the Spirit that he taught and exhorted on the reader. Certain of the meditations leave the poignant impression that Hoeksema, although faithfully explaining and applying the text, was at the same time baring his own soul. This is particularly true of his insightful description of Moses in the mount with God, when God called him to lead Israel out of Egypt. The meditation "I Am That I Am" is on Exodus 3:14. Whereas forty years earlier Moses had been confident of his ability to deliver Israel, of course with the help of God, now he is, in his own estimation, "a small Moses." Hoeksema's application, strained through his own experience as a deliverer of the people of God, is, "Our own glory must always be cast into the dust, so that we learn to glory in the Lord."

We take delight in sending out another volume of genuinely Reformed spirituality by the notable theologian, courageous churchman, marvelous preacher (all the meditations in this volume were originally preached to the large congregation of the First Protestant Reformed Church in Grand Rapids, Michigan), and believing, experiential child of God, Herman Hoeksema.

—David J. Engelsma

PART I

God's Goodness
in Himself

1

Jehovah's Goodness

"The Lord is good to all...but all the wicked will he destroy."—Psalm 145:9, 20

ACCORDING to the Hebrew original, the poet who is the inspired author of this psalm puts it emphatically: "Good is Jehovah."

The Lord is goodness essentially.

Apart from any relation to his creatures, conceived all by himself, in himself, and for himself, as the absolutely self-existent, self-sufficient, independent one, the Lord is good. His essence is goodness; his eternally adorable divine being is only good. Could we enter into the amazing profundity and explore the fathomless depths of his infinite being, the deepest depths of the incomprehensible divine essence would reveal nothing but goodness.

He is the light, and there is no darkness in him. He is truth, righteousness, holiness, purity, love, grace, mercy, eternal life, and there is no lie, unrighteousness, defilement, corruption, or death in him.

He is *Summum Bonum*, the highest good, not in a mere superlative sense, not in a sense that would compare him with other goods or goodnesses that might be conceived as existing next to him, although in a far inferior degree, but in the sense that he is the sole good, that there is no good apart from him or without him. He is the ultimate and absolute criterion of all good. He is not good in the sense that he answers to a certain standard of goodness that might be applied to him, but he himself is the only standard of all that is called good.

He is good because he is God.

Very perfection in all his adorable virtues.
Good is Jehovah!

❖

The Lord is good.

Because the being of his adorable Godhead is goodness, the divine nature in all the glorious attributes thereof is purest perfection and immaculate goodness. Neither is there any reason of want in God that he would need an object unto which to reveal and upon which to lavish his goodness, for as the triune God he lives from everlasting to everlasting the perfect life of infinite goodness in and through himself. Never there arises from the unfathomable depths of his perfect essence the slightest thought that is not good, perfect, and true. Never the faintest thrill of imperfection there is in the will of Jehovah. Never the most imperceptible discord there is in his divine feeling. Never the tiniest ripple of evil there is on the stream of life flowing from his divine heart.

No shadow of darkness ever bedims the light of life, perfect and infinite, of the divine family. Father, Son, and Holy Ghost, each eternally subsisting in the unchangeable essence of limitless goodness, thinking in the perfect mind, willing with the perfect will, are living in absolute self-sufficiency an uninterrupted divine life of purest goodness, dwelling in a light that is never bedimmed.

Yea, good is Jehovah!

Everlastingly, solely, unchangeably good.

Because the Lord is good, the absolute good in himself, he is also good to all his creatures.

Good is Jehovah to all.

❖

Jehovah is the overflowing fount of all good.

All the good his creatures receive is solely from him and is only good because he is good, and he assumes an attitude of goodness to them. He is full of richest benevolence, which he lavishes in profuse abundance upon the whole creation. His goodness propels the silvery luster throughout the starry heavens and arranges their marvelous harmony night upon night. His goodness bedecks the sun with the glorious attire of wondrous gold day after day. His goodness adorns the lily of the field with the purest beauty such as Solomon never possessed and clothes the royal cedars of Lebanon with strength and majesty. His goodness causes the royal eagle to renew its strength as it sweeps the firmament with powerful wing and fills the mouth of the young raven crying to him for food. His goodness remembers the roaring lion and the chirping sparrow on the housetop. His goodness clothes the meadows in velvety green and covers the fields with golden grain. His goodness made man a little lower than the angels, adds keenness to his mind, strength to his arm, and fills his heart with gladness.

Surely all the works of Jehovah's hand speak of his goodness. Good is Jehovah to all!

❖

Nor is this the last word about Jehovah's goodness.

It may be the last word in the estimation of natural religion that knows of no sin and speaks of no grace.

It might be the last word had paradise not been lost. There in the midst of that Edenic virgin beauty of creation, in that original state of unmarred perfection, where sin had not dropped its strain, misery had not left its scar, and the groan of the sufferer was not heard—there God's goodness displayed itself simply as goodness, overflowing riches of benevolence, poured upon every creature according to the measure of its capacity.

The single light-beam of Jehovah's goodness had not resolved into the many-colored rays of his grace, tender mercy, and loving-kindness in contrast with his holy wrath and faultless justice.

But sin entered, and in the wake of sin came death. With death followed suffering in all its awful forms—agony of soul and body, pain, sorrow, grief, and fear. The curse of God was pronounced upon the creature and subjected it to vanity; the chilling breath of a good God, maintaining himself in his goodness over against a sinful world, caused the whole creation to groan and travail together in pain. Even thus the creature made subject to vanity and man in his guilt, bending under the cruel scourge of suffering and death, are testimonies that Jehovah is good and that there is no evil in him.

But more must be said.

Suffering creation, sin and guilt, misery and death, and all the

thick darkness from hell only became the occasion for God to manifest his goodness more abundantly. Darkness was employed by
him as a prism through which to resolve the pure white beam of his
goodness into wonderful rays of manifold perfection. On the occasion of sin and suffering, there is the beautiful and rich manifestation of God's wonderful mercy and loving-kindness. His tender
mercies are over all his works.

Radiating from the cross of God's beloved Son, this tender
mercy beams its warm glory first upon his chosen people whom
he loved with love everlasting, with a love that is always first. Upon
them he lavishes his tender mercy in the blood pouring from the
heart of his only begotten, and in these streams of mercy he cleanses them from guilt, heals them from sin, redeems them from the
power of death, comforts them forever for their misery, and makes
them heirs of an unspeakable glory, of a life incomparably richer,
fuller, and deeper than the first paradise ever knew. They taste his
loving-kindness and tender mercy, speak of it and sing of it, showing forth the praises of him who called them from darkness into his
marvelous light.

But even as the awful darkness of sin and misery spread from
the first Adam until it enshrouded an entire groaning creation in its
horrors, so that glad light of redemption radiates from the second
Adam and falls first upon the elect, thence to spread again over the
whole creation. Remembering his groaning creature with bowels of
mercy and compassion, Jehovah stretches the rainbow of an everlasting covenant over all. His tender mercies are over all his works.

The creature is made subject to vanity. It is subject to the yoke of
bondage. It is travailing in pain together until now.

But in hope!

The whole creation will be liberated from the bondage of corruption and be made to partake of the glorious liberty of the children of God.

Bowels of mercy! The Lord is good to all. His tender mercy is
over all his works.

❖

Good is Jehovah.
But all the wicked will he destroy.

Seemingly there is irreconcilable conflict here. The Lord is good, and yet he destroys. Many a sinful mind will not have it so. Many would dream of goodness without righteousness, of grace without justice, and of benevolence without holy wrath. Yet upon closer investigation this apparent conflict disappears and dissolves into the most sublime harmony. He will destroy all the wicked because he is good. The destruction of the wicked, God's wrath upon them, is another aspect of his perfect goodness.

The wicked are the vessels of wrath fitted unto destruction. They love iniquity and hate righteousness. God is not in all their thoughts. They say within their hearts, express in their words, and reveal in their ways that there is no God. They are God's enemies and children of their father the devil. They dwell in darkness and love it. They crucify Christ and persecute his people. They make the measure of their iniquity full.

So are all the wicked.

But the Lord is good. And because he is good and there is no evil in him, because he is a light and there is no darkness in him, his soul loves the righteous and loathes the wicked. His face beams with tender mercy upon those who love him, but burns with fierce wrath upon those who love iniquity. He preserves the righteous, but destroys all the wicked.

Jehovah is good. Therefore there are in him bowels of mercy and consuming fires of holy wrath.

Hallelujah!

2

I Am That I Am

"And God said unto Moses, I AM THAT I AM; and he said, Thus shalt thou say unto the children of Israel, I AM hath sent me to you."—Exodus 3:14

I AM THAT I AM!

This is my name.

Such was the answer the man of God received in the mount of God when he inquired after the name of him who sent him, Moses, to the people of Israel to deliver them out of their bondage.

A very small and humiliated Moses it was who met the Lord through the revelation of the burning bush, a revelation as comforting and assuring as it was marvelous. Moses here stood in trembling reverence on holy ground, having learned deeply to feel his own insignificance, unworthiness, and incapability to accomplish what the Most High had ordained and to which he now called him.

Forty years ago he had felt so entirely different.

Then he had made his choice, and his choice had been right and well-pleasing to the Lord, the fruit of God's gracious and efficacious call in the heart of the man of God. Then he had disdained to be called the son of Pharaoh's daughter; he had forsaken the treasures of Egypt that were freely offered him; he had chosen rather to suffer affliction with the people of God. Then he had set out to fight for their cause, to defend them against the cruel oppression of the Egyptian overseers, and he had slain him who would whip his brethren.

But he had not realized that the work of defending and delivering the brethren must be solely the Lord's: that the Most High had in Egypt the vessels of wrath fitted unto destruction, in whom not the power and wrath of Moses but the glory of the Almighty must be revealed, and the vessels of mercy through and upon whom the Lord of all would manifest his alone-glorious grace and the mercies of his covenant. Moses had then been full of zeal to deliver the people from bondage and confident that with the Lord's help and the people's rallying around the banner of insurrection, he would meet with success.

How different had been the outcome!

The people had not responded, but had spurned his zeal and threatened to turn against him; the Lord had not revealed his power from heaven; and a miserable Moses had been compelled to flee from the wrath of the king.

Forty years had passed. Forty years of solitude for the man of God, spent in quiet seclusion behind the flock of his father-in-law Jethro; years of inactivity, radically different from the first period of his life, when in Pharaoh's court he had been educated and trained; years apparently calculated to make him forever unfit to accomplish the superhuman task unto which he had been ordained from before the foundation of the world; yet years of invaluable training to prepare him as an instrument for the manifestation of the Lord's glory. During those years of quiet shepherd life, no doubt given to much meditation upon the Lord's ways and promises, Moses had not regretted his choice; he had never longingly looked back to the pleasures that might have been his, nor had he ceased to look forward to the realization of the Lord's promises and to pray for the deliverance of his brethren. But the last vestige of self-confidence had surely been obliterated from his heart and mind. He had learned to look upon the attempt of forty years ago, upon the zeal of his youth, as folly; he had been made to see that only the wondrous power of the Most High could deliver the people of Israel from the house of bondage, and more and more his impotence and insignificance had become clear to his consciousness.

As is evident from his attitude at the mount of God when the Lord calls him to deliver his people, he feels himself totally unfit for the Lord's work.

He has become a very small Moses.

Who am I that I should go to Pharaoh?

Who am I that I should deliver the children of Israel?

I am unfit. I have no prestige. The people will not believe me. I am not eloquent, but slow of speech; Lord, send whom thou would, but not me, for of all men I am the most incapable.

Apparently he had been spoiled by the forty years of solitude; he had lost his zeal and courage.

Yet it was not so. He had only learned to know himself and acknowledge his own incompetence. He had become a small Moses, and because of it, he had become a fit medium for the revelation of the glory of the Lord.

Our own glory must always be cast into the dust, so that we learn to glory in the Lord.

Before we will anxiously ask, "Who art thou, what is thy name, Lord?" we must in self-abasement cry out, "O Lord, who am I?"

Before we reach out for the rock of our salvation, we must know that in ourselves we are perishing in the waves. Then our soul will reach out for him. Then we will ask, "What is thy name?" And always the answer will come, "I AM THAT I AM."

❖

Lord, thy name!

It is the outcry of Moses' soul.

He does not express it thus. Rather, he puts the question in the mouths of the people to whom he must go. They will ask him for the name of the one who sent him.

Yet in the question Moses expresses the need of his soul to draw near to the being of his sender and the deliverer of his brethren. Not to distinguish the Lord from other gods does he ask the question, neither to become acquainted with the sound of the name Jehovah, for the fathers had long called upon him by that name. But Moses' humble soul, filled with a sense of weakness and helplessness, would reach out for the heart of God.

What is his name?

The name of God is his being. It is himself revealed to us.

Such is the significance of a name in general. With us—dead through sins and trespasses, darkened spiritually, and having only a small remnant of our once-glorious gifts—the name no longer has that meaning. Names for us have become mere sounds. Through sin we have lost that intuitive knowledge we once possessed in the state of original righteousness, through which we were able to discern the names of created things. But this does not alter the fact that everything has its own name, and that this name is essentially the manifestation of its being. For the Most High made all things by the Word, and without the Word nothing was made that was created. Creation is the embodiment of the thoughts of God. Every creature is one of his words, and that word of God is the creature's name. In the state of righteousness man possessed the power to read these words of God and know his thoughts.

God has a name, not in the sense of a distinguishing mark according to which he can be compared with or distinguished from other beings in the same order. For God is one. The Most High is God alone, and there is no God beside him. There was neither God before him, nor will there be a God after him. He stands alone, he cannot be compared, neither needs he a name to distinguish himself from other gods.

But in his name is his being, the revelation of his glorious divine nature. Essentially his name is the Son, the eternal Logos, the Word, the everlasting effulgence of his glory, the express image of his eternal substance, the name that is known and expressed in the divine fullness of infinite glory by himself alone. But there is also a name of God by which we can know him and apprehend him and have fellowship with him. For he revealed himself in all his works—in creation, in history, in his boundless grace, and centrally in God incarnate, Immanuel, the Lord Jesus Christ. And he was pleased to give himself names, sounds of human language, by which we can know him, stand face-to-face with him, address him, speak of him, and glorify him.

Always the name is the being, the revelation of God to us.

Hence we have the frequent identification of the name of God with himself. The Scriptures say that God's name is near, meaning that he himself is with us. They speak of trusting in his name, of believing in his name, of calling upon his name, of praising his holy name, which are the same as trusting and believing in him, calling upon him, and praising his glorious being.

Thus Moses' purpose in asking for the name becomes clear.

A tremendous task is placed upon his shoulders. And who is he? A trembling, wretchedly weak, and insignificant worm, a nonentity, devoid of all power and wisdom and courage in himself.

Will not the people to whom he is sent feel as he?

He cannot stand alone. He is totally incapable of going in his own name and power.

He reaches out for the Rock so his soul can cling to him.

He would find in God that of which he knows himself to be void.

Lord, reveal thyself. Let me cling to thee.

Draw near to me in the power of thy being.

Thy name, Lord.

I AM!

❖

I AM THAT I AM.

Of all the names of God there is no name like unto this name, no name that more fully and centrally expresses the divinity of the divine than *the* name.

I AM. Jehovah. The name he reveals again and in all the blessedness of sovereign and sure mercies in the name Jesus: Jehovah-salvation!

It reveals the Most High to us; in it he draws near to us in his eternal self-existence, self-being. No creature can say as he: My name is I *am*. I can say, I am what I am determined to be, I am what I am made, I am as I am born, I am what others make of me, what circumstances make of me, what rain and sunshine, climate and circumstances, friends and enemies, sickness and health, riches and poverty, peace and war, prosperity and adversity, and a thousand other agencies over which I have not the least control make of me. I am not, I became. I am not, I exist. I am not, for the source of my being is outside of me. I am not, for I am flitting away like a shadow. I was not what I am, I will not be what I am. As soon as I say I am, I am no more. I am but an atom, an infinitesimally small part of a whole, on that whole dependent, and without that whole not able to be. Lord, what stinking pride, what detestable conceit, what abominable folly it must be in thy sight when I, a mere worm, a flitting shadow, an inexpressibly insignificant dust particle, trust in self and exalt myself against thee!

But God is.

His name is I AM.

He is the self-existent.

He is such in his being. No cause had he outside of himself. Nothing caused him, nothing formed him, and he is the sole cause of all. Nothing bears him up, and he bears all. He is the uncaused cause of all, the unsustained sustainer of all, the unconceived conceiver of all, the unwilled will of all. He is what he is. Though all else disappears into nothingness, he still is; though all else collapses, he still stands. He alone is independent. There are no powers and forces, no incidents or circumstances, no agencies or influences that determine him. He alone determines all things with most absolute sovereignty. He is such in all his life, his will, his wisdom, his counsel, the alone unnecessitated necessity of all. His will alone is free, his counsel alone is uncounseled, and his own being is the sole reason for all God ever wills and does.

He is the immutable, the eternal.

He is that he is! He is fully all that he is forever and ever, the eternally perfect one. With perfect fullness he lives the infinite perfection of his divine life continuously. Therefore he is eternally the same. To infinite perfection you cannot add. From infinite perfection you cannot subtract. Infinite perfection cannot grow and increase, nor can it decrease and be diminished. What he is, that is he, now and forevermore and before the world was.

Jehovah, I AM THAT I AM.

The everlasting rock.

O blessed God of my salvation, only adorable Jehovah, thy name, please, let me know. Draw near unto my wretched and sinful soul, weak and helpless, and let me know thee. Stamp thy name by almighty grace indelibly upon my sin-stained mind, upon my proud heart, that all my imagined freewill and self-will, my conceit and abominable haughtiness, may be rooted out and abased before thee and I can always know that I am only dust of the balance, a drop of the bucket. Let me taste the sweet consolation of clinging with all the grace-wrought tendrils of my heart to thee.

Speak to my soul: I, Jehovah, the immutable, eternal, self-being, sovereign, faithful I AM, will be with you.

Then I will not be afraid.

Then I will go and face the terrible tyrant of Egypt and proclaim before him thy name, honor before him thy sovereign will, and confidently demand of him that he let thy people go. Then I, a mere worm, will not fear the stubbornness of a stiff-necked people, but will face them and speak to them of thy everlasting covenant. Thou and I. No, thou through me. I nothing, thou all. Then I will go and do thy will. Lord, what is thy name? Come near and let my soul reach out for the everlasting rock.

Thou through me.

Then call me, in the midst of a sinful, hostile world, to be thine, to be of thy party, over against the powers of darkness, sin, the devil, and the host of spiritual wickedness in high places. Call me, as thou callest thy people, to come out of them, to have no fellowship with them, to declare thy name and extol thy virtues before them.

Thou with me…

And I shall not be afraid.

For I know that thou lovest me with an independent love, for reasons of thine own. I know that thy sovereign love is immutable. I know that thou can and surely will deliver me.

Jehovah!

Rock of my salvation!

3
The Name

"And the LORD passed by before him, and proclaimed, The LORD, The LORD God, merciful and gracious, longsuffering, and abundant in goodness and truth, Keeping mercy for thousands, forgiving iniquity and transgression and sin, and that will by no means clear the guilty."—Exodus 34:6–7

AWFUL Sinai!

Mount that could be touched, yet might not, on penalty of death for man or beast.

Mount that rumbled with the voice of judgment, that burned with fire, and that was enveloped in blackness and darkness, and around whose rugged peak the terrible tempest raged.

Mount of the ever-blessed God, revealing himself in all the majesty of his Godhead to a sinful, stiff-necked people, who for a while stood trembling at the mountain's base, hearing the sound of the trumpet and the voice of words, entreating that the word should be spoken to them no more.

Mount of Jehovah.

There Moses, the mediator of the old dispensation, stood in the presence of the eternal glory, the reflection of which glittered with dreadful beauty in his face, without, however, seeing him who is invisible. There the Most High, God who is God, spoke directly with his servant, who mediated for his people in the valley, as the law was imposed upon the promise and the covenant was clothed in the form of precepts, every tittle and iota of which must be fulfilled before the freedom of faith and justification could come. There before Moses' wondering eyes, Jehovah engraved upon rock tablets the ten words that were to be hidden in the ark of the covenant and covered by the mercy seat.

Mount of God's covenant, from whose dreadful darkness the people of God would throughout the old dispensation look forward to the everlasting light of Mount Zion.

There a stiff-necked and rebellious people violated the covenant of God. In the sight of the smoking and quaking mount and the terrible darkness, when the echo of that dreadful voice they begged to speak to them no more had hardly died away in the stillness of the wilderness, they gladly stripped themselves of their gold in order to make a god of their own imagination, and they danced around the golden calf in drunken abandonment. In the very presence of the living God they chose the vanity of the heathen; to the awful God of the terrible voice they preferred a god upon whom they could impose their own will; definitely and ultimately they violated the covenant. The awful mount would pursue them, destroy them in the desert, harass them in the promised land, chase them into captivity, seal their damnation when they crucified the Lord of glory, scatter them among the nations, and assign them their place in lowest hell. For the God they would not serve will by no means clear the guilty.

Dreadful Mount Sinai.

There Moses, the servant of the Lord, the meekest man on the face of the earth, yet who lacked sufficient meekness to lead the people of God into the promised inheritance, thus pointing to and waiting for the meeker than the meek, pleaded with the Lord of Sinai not to execute his awful threat to destroy this rebellious people, beseeched him rather to blot out Moses' name from the book of life, pleaded on the basis of Jehovah's immutable covenant and unchangeable glory.

And there Jehovah, the I AM, the immutable rock, repented.

There the faithful, covenant God renewed his promise that he would send his angel before them and realize his every promise to his people Israel. But there he also taught his servant to understand that he would show mercy to whom he would show mercy and would be gracious to whom he is gracious.

There the servant of Jehovah and mediator of the old covenant, hardly knowing what he asked for, uttered in the presence of the invisible the awful prayer, "Show me now thy glory."

And there the Lord heard even this prayer.

There he hid Moses in the cleft of the rock and passed by his servant, hiding him with his own hand, so that seeing God Moses would not perish.

And there the Lord announced his name.

Dreadful Mount Sinai!

❖

The name.

The Lord, the Lord God.

Merciful and gracious, longsuffering, and abundant in goodness and truth.

Keeping mercy for thousands, forgiving iniquity and transgression and sin.

And that will by no means clear the guilty.

The name of the ever-blessed God, full of hope and blessing, yet apparently hopeless; announcing never-failing forgiveness, yet threatening with never-bending justice; forgiving, yet imputing sin; opening vistas of life, yet shutting them off by the darkness of death; taking a sinful people into the everlasting glories of heaven, yet casting them down to lowest hell; forgiving iniquity and transgression and sin, yet who will by no means clear the guilty.

Blessed name, glorious name of the Lord, the Lord God.

Awful name, dreadful name of the wholly other.

Paradoxical name, which immediately causes us to look for still another name under heaven by which the paradox can be solved.

The name!

❖

Blessed name.

Merciful and gracious.

Gracious is the Lord, for he is in himself the perfection of beauty, and in his right hand there are pleasures forevermore. All that is in him is pleasant to behold, to know, to experience, to taste. He is gracious absolutely in himself, apart from any relation to his creatures, and as the triune God he knows and contemplates himself eternally in all the beauty and attraction of his infinite perfection. He delights in himself with divine pleasure. He is gracious to his people and looks with everlasting favor upon Zion, the perfection of beauty, and causes his people to delight in him, to taste his grace, and to acknowledge that his loving-kindness is better than life. In the knowledge of him, in the experience of his favor and loving-kindness, they are blessed in his fellowship forever.

To bless them with himself, his presence and fellowship, with life eternal, is his everlasting purpose, for he is merciful.

His mercy is his will to bless, the eternal will to lead his people into the highest possible glory in his tabernacle. In relation to himself he is also merciful, for he is the ever-blessed God who wills to be blessed as the highest good. His eternal purpose is to reveal himself, to make himself known, to cause himself to be experienced and to be acknowledged by his people as the only and ever-blessed God in whose presence and communion there is fullness of joy. Hence he longs with an eternal longing to lift his people from their present misery of sin and death into the everlasting glory of heavenly perfection. In his mercy he is tenderly affected toward them and gently cares for them until they are perfectly delivered.

And he is longsuffering over them.

Slow to anger.

When they sin he does not immediately strike them down in wrath, but he remembers his mercy that he eternally purposed to reveal in Jesus Christ. Patiently he bears with them. He chastises them in his love, as a father chastises his children, to correct them. After they have been exercised, they reap the fruits of righteousness. When they suffer, he is long of passion and, rather than take them out of this present misery and woe, he patiently waits until all things have been fully prepared.

For abundant in goodness is he.

Zealous he is over his people to do them good. He loves them with all the love of his infinite being, constantly, eternally; and he burns with zeal to bestow upon them all the blessedness of his covenantal friendship.

Nor can his mercy fail. For he is also abundant in truth. He is the amen. The rock. He is as he is immutably. Everlastingly. And he reveals himself as he is. His promises are yea and amen.

This God is our God, forever and ever.

He will be our guide even unto death.

The Lord, the Lord God.
Blessed name!

❖

Amazing paradox.

Keeping mercy to thousands, forgiving iniquity, yet never and in no wise clearing the guilty.

He keeps mercy. He never forgets his mercy to his people. Neither does he ever fail to reveal his mercy to them. His mercy is not spasmodic, nor is the revelation of his mercy periodic. It is constant, for it is everlasting. He keeps it to thousands, that is, from generation to generation, even until the end.

And in his mercy he forgives. For his people commit iniquity and transgression and sin.

By nature they are perverse, a rebellious people, inclined to oppose God's yes by their foolish and wicked no. Upon their own no, in opposition and denial of God's yes, they are inclined to act, and they transgress his commandment and violate his holy law. Thus they sin. They miss the mark, God's purpose, and trample underfoot the holiness of his glorious name. They become worthy of his wrath and everlasting damnation in themselves. But he forgives. He dismisses their iniquities, their transgressions, their sins from his mind and heart. He never remembers them as sins, so they never provoke him to anger and displeasure with regard to his people. He does not impute sin unto them, so that he does not execute his wrath upon them. Rather than cast them down into lowest perdition, of which they are worthy, he lifts them up into the heavenly glory and crowns them with blessed and eternal life.

Oh, the blessedness of the man to whom the Lord does not impute iniquity.

Yet he never clears the guilty, for righteousness and justice are the foundation of his throne.

If any man sins, God will never pronounce him guiltless. If a man transgresses God's commandment, he will never justify that man in his transgression. If a man misses the mark and falls short of the glory of God, never will he forget or forgive, never will he excuse him who tramples his glory underfoot.

For God will not give his glory to another. He will demand the last farthing.

He forgives, yet never clears the guilty.

Astounding paradox!

❖

Adorable mystery.

He who never clears the guilty forgives all our iniquities, our transgressions, and our sins.

The paradox is solved in the profound mystery of the cross, in the moment when awful Sinai and blessed Zion meet on Golgotha. When the righteousness and the mercy, the justice and the grace, the terror and the blessedness, the death and the life, the hell and the heaven of the awful name of the blessed God, meet in sweetest harmony in the only name given under heaven whereby man can be saved.

Jesus.

The Lord. The Lord God.

Immanuel. God with us forever and ever.

The Lord, merciful and gracious, yet righteous and just; forgiving iniquity and transgression and sin, yet by no means clearing the guilty.

For such is Golgotha.

Mount Sinai must be superimposed upon Zion, the law upon the promise, righteousness upon grace, justice upon goodness, wrath upon mercy, until he came who would do what the children of the promise themselves could never do: fulfill the law, satisfy righteousness, bear the wrath of God, and lift Sinai that genders to bondage from the top of Zion that is free, lift death from life, and liberate Zion's children forever!

Marvelous grace and mercy.

Perfect righteousness and justice.

No, he never clears the guilty, yet he mercifully forgives all our transgressions.

The mercy of God is not that he winks at sin and allows his word to be set aside, his law to be violated, and his glory to be trampled underfoot. The wonder of God's everlasting goodness and grace is not that he loves the ungodly, blesses them, and makes them the objects of his favor. But the wonder of God's everlasting goodness and grace is that from before the foundation of the world he appointed unto Zion a mighty captain of salvation who would be able to bear all Zion's sin and to bear it away forever on the accursed tree.

He himself bore our sin in his own body on the tree, that by his stripes we could be healed.

He does not clear the ungodly, but justifies them in the blood of his Son.

Jesus, Immanuel, God with us.

Golgotha, union of everlasting mercy and immutable justice.

Sweet harmony.

❖

The name.

The Lord. The Lord God.

Oh, blessed is the people whose God is the Lord and who trust in his holy name.

For he is God. The mighty one. He is strong to save and to accomplish all his merciful purpose for those who love him. His grace and mercy, his longsuffering and abundant goodness, are not weak and impotent desires of the heart, incapable or even doubtful of realization. He is not a man, that his purposes can be frustrated, that his arm can be shortened, and that his power can fail.

God is he! And if God be for us, who will be against us?

It is God who justifies. Who will lay anything to the charge of his elect?

And he is Jehovah. The Lord. The self-existent. The unchangeable I AM. The wholly independent. He who is of himself, by himself, and for himself. Independent in his mercy and grace, with respect to their origin, with regard to their objects, with regard to their realization. Immutable mercies!

Lord, we pray thee, go among us.

Thou overflowing fount of good.

Hallelujah! Amen!

4

Jehovah Our Sun and Shield

"For the LORD *God is a sun and shield: the* LORD *will give grace and glory: no good thing will he withhold from them that walk uprightly."—Psalm 84:11*

A SUN is Jehovah God!

Wonderfully significant is the sun in nature as an image of the Lord our God.

With relation to our universe, that golden bridegroom of the day, issuing forth from his chambers and going on his way through the firmament rejoicing, is radiating with fullness of life and blessing for every creature.

When in the still and dark hour just before dawn of a day in June you repair to a favorite spot—where gentle zephyrs lisp, the trees murmur mysteriously, and the brook ripples playfully; where the humble wildflower displays the rich beauty of its colored garment for which it did not labor or spin; and where winged beauties sing and call to one another—to wait and to watch for the rising of the sun…

And when, as you watch, a pale glimmer in the eastern sky announces the approach of morning and dispels the darkness of the night, rousing from their slumbers the feathered inhabitants of the woods, who respond to the call of the morning, first cooing sleepily and complainingly, and then, as gradually the pale gray of dawn brightens into the gold of morning, chirruping and singing cheerfully; and when you see how the rising sun, now fast increasing in strength of golden brightness until finally the last streaks of morning cloud have vanished before its splendor, suffuses the entire scene with wondrous glory, pouring life and light over flower and leaf, into brook and meadow, transforming the black robe of night's darkness into a veritable garb of many-colored beauty…

Oh, how wonderful a picture is the sun!

What a fullness of life it pours into the universe.

What a center of blessings it appears.

It draws from sea, ocean, and lake the rain into soft cloud-vessels and pours refreshing showers over field and forest; it nourishes and warms the seeds in the furrows and causes them to sprout; it makes the flowers bloom and reveals their beauty; it spreads life and joy, energy and light, and it calls man and beast to action.

The Lord God is a sun.

A sun not as if there were other suns, for he is God and there is no God besides him, but a sun because he is in himself the fullness of all good. He is light and there is no darkness in him. Such is his being. He does not possess light, but he is light. He does not simply live, but he is life. He does not just contain goodness, but he is goodness. He *is* light and life, brightness and holiness, goodness and grace and mercy, righteousness and justice, joy and peace. He is goodness and perfection, an ever-blessed light. And his perfection is not derived from any other sources. It is absolutely original with him, uncaused, and eternal. As the triune God he lives the life of perfect light by and in himself.

Still more.

The Lord God is a sun also because he radiates his goodness and pours forth his light-life upon all who are in communion with him. He is for them the fount of all good, which spreads grace and glory. Like the rising sun in nature, so he dispels the darkness of the night of sin and death. For he reveals the brightness of his beauty, the glory of his goodness, the perfection of his holiness and righteousness, the blessedness of his grace in Christ Jesus, and through him Jehovah scatters the blessed rays of his own light into the hearts of his children.

For Jehovah God is a sun. The uncaused light in himself, full of grace and glory.

He is also the sole cause of all light and life, radiating his blessed goodness into the hearts of all his children. He makes them partakers of his holiness, love, blessedness, and joy. In their hearts he spreads abroad the riches of his love, makes the night flee away— a night of sin and corruption, of hatred and the lie, of death and hell—and calls forth the dawn of a new day, shining with the light of righteousness and holiness, of love in truth, of heavenly bliss and eternal life.

For the Lord will give grace and glory. He radiates grace and makes his children partakers of it in Christ Jesus. And his grace makes glorious. Even as sin is corruption and makes one inglorious, vile, abject, repulsive, leading to outer darkness in eternal desolation, so grace is goodness and brings glory to those who partake of it, making them full of grace and beauty.

How blessed is Jehovah God!

What a fullness of joy and life is he. Surely he is a sun.

How blessed is his communion! For without him, without the scope of the radiation of his blessed light, there is the darkness of death. In his communion there is grace and glory.

How amiable are his tabernacles, the place beside his altar. How much more blessed to be only a doorkeeper in his house, catching at least some of his blessed light, than to dwell in the tents of wickedness, where all is darkness and death!

O Lord of hosts, light of lights, radiant with eternal perfection, how blessed is the man over whom thou dost spread thy tabernacle and who dwells in thy light!

❖

A sun is Jehovah God. The God of our salvation is also a shield.

At first there seems to be an irreconcilable contrast and antithesis between these two figures. The one lifts us with our thoughts into the lofty and glorious heights of the heavens that declare the glory of God and pour forth knowledge of the Most High; the other drags us down with our imaginations into the mire of the life of this world, of sinful men, corrupt and hating one another. The one causes us to think of life and bliss and the other, of death and darkness. The one witnesses of a fountain of love and blessing; the other brings to our minds the flying darts and poisoned arrows of the enemy, fear, danger, and destruction.

How could the psalmist think of his God under the images of a sun and a shield?

What need has he who walks in the light of the protection of a shield?

Yet how real to experience is the figure.

Scarcely have you begun to meditate upon the rich beauties and blessedness of the Lord God, and to rejoice in the privilege of dwelling in his communion, but you look about for a shield to protect you. For the Lord gives grace and glory. When he does so, he makes you partaker of his light. His light is reflected in your life. With the reflection of his light in your life and walk, you stand for his name and glory in the world. It is true that in the world you are in danger as soon as you bid farewell to the darkness of sin and walk in the light of God, for the world is in darkness and loves the darkness. Because it loves darkness, it hates light, since its works are evil. As it loves darkness and hates light, so it loves and protects its own children and hates and persecutes the children of God's light. The world battles those who dwell in the tabernacle of God's light and reflect his grace and glory. It attacks you. It fights with the deceitful weapons of flattery and vain philosophy, offering you all the glory and riches of the world. It shoots the poisoned arrows of reproach and shame or openly threatens its death-bringing sword.

And all the while it aims at the light in us. All the while its purpose is to extinguish the light poured into our hearts and lives from Jehovah God, who is a sun.

But Jehovah is a shield!

A most perfect shield is he. Imperfect is the best of human shields, never offering perfect safety in battle, never perfectly covering us against the onslaughts of the enemy. But Jehovah's protection is perfect. If he covers us, we are safe. If he watches over us, the enemy cannot reach us. For he is the Almighty, mightier than all the mightiest together, supreme in power. There is no sword that he cannot break; there is no hostile attack that he cannot repel. He never fails to watch, for he neither slumbers nor sleeps. Always his eyes are over the righteous. Constantly he watches to protect the children who dwell in his light and whom he made partakers of his own grace and glory.

He is their shield. He does not hold a shield for them, but offers himself, placing his own power between his children and their enemies in the world.

How safe, then, are they who trust in him!

The enemy is strong, but Jehovah is always stronger. The enemy plots and conspires to destroy the children of light, but all of their plans are vain against the ever-watchful care of Jehovah God. Never can the enemy reach his people to destroy them.

For Jehovah is a sun, and he radiates grace and glory.

And also a shield is the Lord God.

❖

A fountain of good is Jehovah.

He will not withhold any good thing from those who walk uprightly. He will not restrain the ever-flowing fountain of his goodness to pour forth blessings upon those who walk in his way.

Yes, to those who walk uprightly. Not to all is the Lord the fount of everlasting joy and bliss, for he is a sun. The sun blesses those and radiates glory and beauty upon those who stand in the right relation to its light; but it can also scorch and burn and destroy by its unbearable heat. Thus it is with Jehovah our God. Also to the ungodly he is a sun, but a sun that burns, a consuming fire. All good he withholds from them.

To the natural eye this appears different, particularly when we see how the ungodly prosper in the world and how their eyes stand out with fatness. Looking at the appearance of things, it seems as if Jehovah would fill the children of darkness with all good. But in reality this is different, for he does not radiate his grace and glory to the ungodly. And what do all the riches of the world mean, what blessing is there in things, apart from the loving-kindness of Jehovah? If he does not lift his blessed countenance over us in everlasting love, he looks down upon us and upon our ways and walk in constant displeasure and wrath. And if, while objects of his burning wrath, one should possess the whole world, it would only serve to make him ripe for destruction. For the Lord is a sun. All good he withholds from those who do not walk uprightly before him.

Only to the upright he is a fount of joy and bliss.

But where is the man who walks uprightly?

Are not even the holiest of his children characterized by imperfection? Does not even the holiest of them all possess only a small beginning of the new obedience? Do not their feet often slip away from the path of uprightness? Are not their transgressions many? Do not their sins rise up against them day by day?

Yes, but the upright are those whom Jehovah knew in love from everlasting, whom he gave to his beloved Son, whom he regarded in their redeemer, whom he in love ordained to be conformed according to the image of his Son. Those he delivers from the darkness of sin and death by pouring his grace and glory into their hearts. Thus delivered in principle, they surely walk uprightly before him. Perfection may be far away, but a principle of perfection is found with them and dominates their whole lives. Uprightly they walk with a sincere desire to live according to all of his precepts. Often they slip, blunder, and stumble in the way, but even then with their transgressions and infirmities they walk uprightly before their God, as they are heartily sorry for their sins and cannot rest until they have the assurance of forgiveness in Christ Jesus, so that they fear Jehovah.

No good thing will Jehovah withhold from his children.

Oh, even this may seem different.

Often it appears as if Jehovah removes his shield of protection from them and the enemy triumphs over them. Often they complain that they are killed all the day long. Often they lift up their voices to implore Jehovah for what seems to them to be good things, when nevertheless it seems as if the heavens remain shut and they hear no answers to their prayers.

Yet this is only an appearance.

For Jehovah is a sun. Never does he restrain the radiation of his goodness, glory, and grace upon those who walk uprightly.

But sometimes what seems good to us, the Lord knows to be evil. His great and eternal purpose is to make us perfectly conformed to the image of his Son. He will lead us, care for us, and give us things always with a view to his eternal tabernacle, where his beloved will walk forever in his light and behold the beauty of Jehovah God in his eternal temple.

For that end all things must work together. Whatever is conducive to that final glory, to their eternal salvation, is good for the children of light. Even though they may be poverty and want, suffering and affliction, good things they are that form his children for the light eternal.

No good things will he withhold. Grace and glory will he bestow on those who walk uprightly.

And presently he will pour the perfection of his beauty upon them in the eternal day.

How blessed is the man whose God is Jehovah. Now and forever.

O God, our sun and shield.

Hallelujah!

5

A Sure Foundation

"For I am the Lord, *I change not; therefore ye sons of Jacob are not consumed."—Malachi 3:6*

Jehovah, "i am that i am."!

i am is God's name, and he is the only one who can bear the name in truth. Only he can stand in the midst and above the ever-changing flux of all things and say, "I am now. I am yesterday and throughout the far-receding ages of the past even into the unfathomable recesses of eternity. I am tomorrow and in the ages to come. I am forever."

With us and all around us is constant mutation.

Time and change are ever busy.

Once all things were not. They have a beginning and appear on the stage of history for a while to be and to play their part, they grow and develop, they fade and decay, and again they disappear from view and are no more.

The flower of the field springs forth from among the grass and blooms a while in humble loveliness, but with the setting of the evening sun it withers and fades and its place knows it no more. The light of day dawns in the morning, when the king of day issues forth as a bridegroom from his chamber rejoicing; the light shines and increases in strength for a few hours, but it soon dwindles into the gray of evening's twilight and is swallowed up by the black of night. All nature in beautiful springtime bursts forth with fresh life on all sides, displays its hopeful green, and bears it through the summer. But when summer's brightness fades into fall's mists, the leaves drop, the rich variety of colors disappears, and the sting of death soon is manifest everywhere.

As it is in nature, so it is with us.

The babe of today is the young man of tomorrow. For a brief moment he stands in the vigor of youth and in the strength of manhood; but the burden of sixty, seventy, or eighty years soon proves too heavy for him to carry; the strong hand of time bears down upon him and makes him yield to the power of death. Besides, our spiritual nature is subject to the same mutations and fluctuations due to many and various causes. What we love today we frequently despise tomorrow; our strong convictions of the past are uprooted in the future; our hopes of yesterday are our fears today. All of our thoughts, plans, and aspirations are subject to the ever-operative laws of change and decadence.

In every respect it is true of us what the inspired psalmist teaches us to sing.

> The flow'r is withered by the wind
> That smites with blighting breath;
> So man is quickly swept away
> Before the blast of death (Psalter 278:3).

Wherever we turn or to whomever we look, there is among all that is called creature nothing stable, nothing abiding.

There is nothing among created things to which man can cling for refuge; nothing in this ever-changing flux of time in which he can trust and say, "Let me abide." Irresistibly he is carried on and on, ever changing, ever moving, ever decaying, until time's stream bears him into eternity's ocean. The man who clings for abiding refuge to the things that are made is like the desperate wretch, hopelessly struggling against the pitiless current of the Niagara and drifting down into the falls, who clings to a block of wood drifting down with him to the inevitable and rapidly approaching end.

Is there then nothing that abides? Is there nowhere a rock to which our souls can securely cling?

There is. For behind all things fleeting is the one permanent. Above the world of time and change stands he who changes all, yet is himself unchanging. The one point of rest amid universal unrest.

Jehovah, I AM.

❖

I am the Lord.

I change not. I am the absolutely immutable.

How contrary to all we know of the finite and mortal being is this language of the Lord our God! Yet how literally true to our God in application.

He is in and by himself unchangeable, and his being is not subject to the mutations of human nature. He is underived and uncaused, and there never was a moment when he was not. He is not a child of time as we are, and the heavy hand of time does not bear him down. He was never young, and he never grows old. There is neither increase nor diminishing of his power, knowledge, wisdom, glory, light, and life. With himself, as the all-sufficient, self-sufficient, self-dependent triune God, he lives an unchangeable life of perfection. With him is the fountain of unfading light. The eternal present is he, and he lives where it is always day in undiminished splendor, where all things always are, never were or shall be. His mind is an unchanging light; his heart is an ever-flowing and never-exhausted fountain of purest love. There is in him no deliberation or hesitation, no weighing of evidences or consequences; there are in him no spasms of contending volitions and motives. He is the one, continuously living God, never beginning, always being, never ending, always abiding, never bending, always enduring, never changing, ever invariable.

The everlasting God.

The eternal I AM.

Jehovah is his name.

The truth of God's everlasting immutability implies much more. The name Jehovah does not express only that he is the unchangeable God in and by himself, but that he is such also in his relation to his people, so that he becomes the sure foundation upon which the children of Jacob can build, the one rock to which they can cling and upon which they can safely dwell as their everlasting abode.

Jehovah is also God's covenant name.

When he says, "I am Jehovah," he reveals that his relation to the children of Jacob is a covenantal relation, and that this relation is one of deepest, purest, and most fervent love, according to which he is their everlasting friend and savior and they are his friends and servants as beloved children and heirs. He reveals that his covenantal love toward the children of Jacob is not carried on the changing stream of time, and does not arise from nor is borne away by the ever-moving and altering flux of created things, but is as eternal and unchangeable as himself.

The mighty stream of love divine toward the children of Jacob does not have its origin in them but in him, does not spring from time's fountain but from eternity's deep, is in no wise contingent upon anything that belongs to those poor creatures, but rises from the deep fountain of God's heart and flows on and on, a river of God full of water.

He knew the children of Jacob in a love that has its fountain in him alone. In that eternal love he eternally purposed in himself to reveal the greatness and the amazing depth of his love to them, that he would make them like the image of his dear Son, so they could taste the divine sweetness of his love forever.

From that eternal source this river of God's wondrous love flows on and on. We see it when on its stream the Son of God is borne into the world, sent into the flesh for our sins. We behold it, widening and deepening, as the Son walks his way of humiliation, shame, and suffering in the likeness of sinful flesh, until it rushes over Golgotha into the grave of the Lord of glory, and from there lifts him as the head of all the children of Jacob into everlasting exaltation. We feel it when it reaches us in the depths of sin and hell, lifts us aloft, and bears us up into the light of God, where we behold the wonders of his love.

On and on it flows until the purpose of his will is fulfilled. For he is the Lord; he changes not.

Jehovah, I AM.

❖

Jehovah is unchangeable.

Immutable in himself and in all the glorious virtues of his adorable being.

Unchangeable too in his relation of eternal, covenantal love toward the true children of Jacob. This unchangeableness of Jehovah is at the same time the key to the solution of an otherwise insoluble problem and most mysterious phenomenon.

The children of Jacob are not consumed!

All things fade and die and lose their beauty. All that is called creature passes away and is consumed. Even though all things and creatures change, decay, and disappear, the children of Jacob are not consumed. They abide forever.

The wonder of it all is that there are so many causes for their inevitable destruction. We would expect them to be consumed more quickly than anything else.

Thus it was with Israel of old. Did they not pass through the fire of Egypt's oppression and furious hatred? Why is it that when they are swallowed up in a strange land, and the wrath and envy of the king rave against them, the fire of persecution is kindled against them, they groan in bondage and hard labor, and their children are sentenced to death as soon as they see the light of life they are not consumed? How is it that when they pass through the waters of the sea, in which their enemies perish, into that great and terrible wilderness, in which there is neither water nor food and when they are helpless and weak and always surrounded by hateful enemies who plot their destruction, they are not swallowed up in death? And why is it that the children of Jacob, so often rebellious and opposed to Jehovah, turning their backs to the Lord and eagerly following after other gods, incurring Jehovah's wrath and fierce anger, are not utterly destroyed?

Jehovah's anger is a consuming fire. Through that consuming fire the nation passes again and again because of its terrible transgression. But never is it consumed. Always it passes through. A remnant remains and abides, no matter how fiercely the fires of God's wrath burn and consume many of them.

Thus it is with the church of the new dispensation. She is the object of envy and hatred. Scaffolds are built to kill her children. Prisons are erected to swallow them up. Fires are kindled to burn them to death. The devil raves and roars like a fierce lion, and the world rages in fury.

All in vain. The children of Jacob are not consumed!

Or consider the other aspect of the picture. How often does the church assume the aspect of Babylon and apostatize from the living God? She forsakes the truth, follows after the gods of this world, and provokes Jehovah to anger, until God's people complain that the church of Jesus Christ is hopelessly lost.

Yet she is always there. The remnant remains even though the children of Jacob pass through fire and water!

Thus it is also with each one of us individually. When we consider our sins and transgressions, the foul foundation of our heart and mind, our repeated apostasies from Jehovah, our iniquities without number, daily witnessing against us; and when we bring them into the light of God's holiness and righteousness and remember that he is a consuming fire, it is an inscrutable mystery that we were not long ago consumed by the fire of God's wrath.

Until I look at the cross and there contemplate his love, and I remember that the love that erected that cross for his only begotten Son flows from the heart of an unchangeable God.

Then I understand why I have not been swept away and consumed by his wrath.

It is because I have to do with an unchanging love, with a faithfulness that never departs from its promise, with an immutable purpose to bless me that will not be turned aside.

To that cross, and over that cross to God's love, I look backward in grateful adoration. From that cross I look forward, weak and sinful though I am, yet trusting in his unchanging love and believing that I will never be consumed. To that rock I will cling amid the floods of sin that pass over my soul; in the midst of hateful enemies who wish and plot for my destruction; amid a tempting world and through the schemes of a roaring devil. Presently I will pass into the darkness of death and the grave, still clinging to him who is immutable. And in the end when all things pass away and the elements burn and melt, I will be confident that I will not be consumed when he is the rock of my security.

For he, Jehovah, changes not.

Therefore the children of Jacob cannot be consumed.

Jehovah, I AM.

My Lord and my God!

PART II

God's Goodness
in Creation

6

Moonlight Reveries

*"And God made two great lights...the lesser light
to rule the night."*—Genesis 1:16

*"And God said,...and let them be for
signs."*—Genesis 1:14

How marvelous in its beauty is the night!

How full of speech and utterance of knowledge to him who in God's light sees the light.

How comforting and instructing for the pilgrim child of God, passing through a night of sin, suffering, and death to the eternal morning in God's everlasting tabernacle.

I do not mean the dark, wild, and dreadful night, when the furious tempest rages and the wild wind howls and the storm-swept waves roar and the fiercely driven clouds, like panic-stricken demons, chase one another through the dark sky; when the floods rush and the sea groans mournfully and the woods moan and all creation wails.

In such a night I fear. It is the night of terror.

It fills the heart with dreadful apprehension of approaching judgment; it speaks of creation's bondage in corruption, of evil and pain, of suffering and grief, of the creature as it tore itself loose from the heart of its creator and is now restlessly driven about, seeking peace and finding none, terror-stricken and chased as by an overpowering fear; of wrath revealed from heaven and impending destruction.

I mean the still and deep night.

The night of profound peace, when all creation slumbers... When just a mere breath of a breeze floats through the still woods...When only a slightly dimpling ripple runs playfully over the surface of the lake...When high in the deep heavens glides the moon, flooding the landscape with its kindly pale light, daubing the woods with a thousand splotches of twinkling silver, and splashing a sparkling path across the rippled lake...When all is at rest, and the creature just waits for the morning.

How beautiful then is the night!

❖

The queen of the night mingles silent speech with the silvery beams she pours forth into the darkness.

For God said, "Let them be for signs."

Not only to rule the day is the sun set in the heavens, and not only as queen of the night rides the moon along her path in the firmament, and not simply to serve as lights in the darkness do the stars sparkle like angels' jewelry in the darkened sky.

But God said that they should also be for signs.

As signs they speak. "The heavens declare the glory of God; and the firmament sheweth his handiwork. Day unto day uttereth speech, and night unto night sheweth knowledge. There is no speech nor language, where their voice is not heard" (Ps. 19:1–3).

They testify in their own realm of earthly and temporal things and of heavenly and eternal things. For the Lord God, whose counsel will stand and who accomplishes all his good pleasure, who knows and declares all things from the beginning, wrote as with his finger in all this symbol-language of creation not only of the glory of his name, the power of his might, and the unsearchable riches of his wisdom, but also of the wonder of his counsel, the glory of his kingdom, and the beauty of his covenant.

Because of this the earthly is the image of the heavenly; in the temporal there is a picture of the eternal; the natural is a symbol of the spiritual.

True, a silent speech they utter. Their language will never be truly understood by the natural man, whose sphere is the earthly not the heavenly, who loves darkness rather than light, who despises God's word and never understands that also this light, shining from all the works of God's hands, is to be seen only in God's light.

But speech of God it is nevertheless, wonderful to him who has eyes to see and ears to hear.

For signs they are. The greater light by day and the lesser light by night. And every night the queen of the heavens pours her silvery speech into the silent darkness.

Showing knowledge!

❖

A sign in the darkness is the moon in the heavens.

Smiling kindly, she whispers, "Fear not, for the darkness of the night is only a passing shadow!"

For is not her mellow light a reflection of the glory of the sun? What does the moon do except catch some of the sun's golden glory, change it into her own silver beauty, and pour it into the night? Does she not witness that even though the sun sank into oblivion below the western horizon, and although its glad rays do not for the moment brighten my path, yet its glory still exists and its brightness is not diminished?

When the sun does not shine on my earthly habitation and the darkness of night is spread over my dwelling, from the high heavens the queen of the night pours forth the testimony, "The golden ruler of the day still is and shines where I am!"

She thus witnesses that the night is only a shadow.

The night is not like that first horrible darkness, when the earth was still waste and void and darkness was upon the face of the deep. For then there was no light in all the awful void of chaos.

But the night is a mere shadow of turning, a shadow in the midst of a flood of light poured into the wide expanse of the universe.

A beautiful picture this is of the path of God's children in the world. For pilgrims through the night are the children of God, the sojourners to Zion, the seekers of the city of God.

How dark seems the night through which they pass on their way to the light eternal! How dark often is the night of sin, when floods of guilt and iniquity roll over their souls and it seems as if they cannot be delivered from so great a death. What awful night of corruption there still is in the dark recesses of their hearts, whenever new and hitherto unknown darknesses and shadows of death and pollution arise from that hidden source. What night of pain, suffering, and agony of body and soul is the lot of God's pilgrim children when it is with them as with Asaph of old, and their chastisements are there every morning. What darkness of sorrow and grief often overwhelms their souls! What night of reproach and shame, of cruel mockery and enmity they pass through when the enemy raves and furiously attacks for Christ's sake, and persecution is their lot in the world.

And presently...

The night of death yawns threateningly from the dark and dreary prison of the grave.

How dreadful would seem that night. Did the sun of light and life and joy disappear forever when it sank from view in paradise the first? Was its glory extinguished, never to appear again?

God forbid!

The moon in the heavens whispers into the silent night of nature that the sun is still there, though for the moment you see it not.

The earthly is image of the heavenly. The sun of life is still there, even though with sadness of heart you remember its setting in Eden's garden.

Pilgrim, your night of sin and guilt and sorrow and grief, of reproach and shame and tribulation is only for a while.

A passing shadow!

Fear not, O pilgrim of the night, for your light shines. There is a silvery path across your night, reflected from the Sun of Righteousness. It shines still, although you see it not.

Be not afraid!

❖

How beautiful is the moonlit night.

For a sign is the moon, harbinger of the coming morning.

Does not she witness that the sun, though disappeared and hidden from view in the present night, will rise again with new glory and brighter gold and presently break the morning of a new day through the darkness of the eastern sky?

Does not her presence reconcile me with and comfort me in the night, when she assures me of the coming dawn?

Speech from the night for you, pilgrim to Zion!

Oh, surely the night in nature is also the symbol of another night, where the light will shine nevermore and the sun will never rise, the night of everlasting sorrow and pain, darkness, and moaning, wailing, and gnashing of teeth. The fierce night, full of tempest and disturbance, full of moaning and groaning, the night when the sun is darkened and the moon appears as blood and the stars drop out of the seam of heaven—that night is a sign and a symbol of the everlasting night prepared for those who love the darkness rather than the light because their works are evil.

Fierce and full of terror can be the night of nature. Fiercer and more terrible will be that everlasting night of the wrath of God!

But such is not the night of Zion's pilgrim.

His is the moonlit night. That night speaks of the coming morning, for the queen of the night witnesses of the approach of the bridegroom of the morning.

The sun of life, joy, and righteousness set in the garden of Eden. And darkness spread, darkness of sin and guilt, sorrow and grief, and pain and affliction.

For a time we wander through the darkness, longing for the light of day.

But the morning is approaching.

For the Sun of Righteousness is there. He once appeared. He was humiliated. He suffered. He died. He disappeared from view in the awful darkness of his cross. But he appeared again, glorious, full of life and grace; and again he left and disappeared from view. For a while we see him not. But he left us his sure word and promise, his light in the night. It assures us in the midst of night that presently the Sun of Righteousness will rise once more, in unknown glory and beauty, never to set again, to dissipate all the clouds and shadows of suffering and grief, of sin and corruption and death, and to lighten our day with the light of God in his eternal tabernacle.

Fear not, O pilgrim!

Yours is the beauty of the moonlit night.

The night of your affliction is only for a moment, a passing shadow. The morning comes, the day eternal, full of life, light, joy, and covenantal friendship.

For there shall be no night there.

Be of good cheer.

March on!

PART III

God's Goodness in the
Ministry of Jesus

7

The Raging of the Heathen

*"Why do the heathen rage, and the people imagine a vain thing?
The kings of the earth set themselves, and the rulers take counsel
together...saying, Let us break their bands asunder, and cast
away their cords from us."—Psalm 2:1–3*

FOOLISH raging!

The heathen furiously rage.

And will not he who sits in the heavens laugh? For they are raging, they set themselves in battle array and take counsel together, they plot and conspire against the Lord and his anointed.

Their fury is directed against the anointed of Jehovah. Their deepest purpose is to rage against Jehovah, but he is in the heavens. He does whatsoever pleases him. Him their fury cannot reach. So to give vent to their fury against the Lord, they rage against his anointed. Does not the anointed of Jehovah represent him in the earth, in the visible creation, in the world of our experience? Is not an anointed one a servant of the Lord, one who is endowed with power and authority from on high to appear officially as the party of the living but invisible God, to speak for him, to act upon his authority, to rule in his name? Against this anointed of the Lord they rage and plot and prepare the battle because he is the Lord's anointed.

Who is he?

Against whom are all the powers of the world so furious?

He is David.

David is Jesse's son who was called from tending his father's sheep to become the king of Israel. To be sure, the second psalm is strongly prophetic and speaks ultimately of the Messiah and his kingdom. Hardly a psalm is quoted so frequently, comparatively speaking, in the New Testament as this little jewel among the songs of Israel. But a mistake we would make if we would interpret this psalm immediately in the light of its ultimate realization and significance and not consider first that its prophecy has a historical-typical basis. The anointed of the Lord mentioned in this inspired bit of Hebrew poetry is the one who speaks in verse 7: "I will declare the decree: the LORD hath said unto me, Thou art my Son; this day have I begotten thee." The subject of this sentence is the author of the psalm. The author is David, Israel's royal singer. For thus did the church of the new dispensation refer to this prophecy when it broke forth in prayer and praise: "Who by the mouth of thy servant David hast said, Why did the heathen rage, and the people imagine vain things?" (Acts 4:25).

David, the son of Jesse, was the Lord's anointed.

Was not Israel the kingdom of God? And was not David the man after God's own heart, foreordained, called, and empowered to represent Jehovah in this kingdom, and on the basis of the Mosaic legislation, to rule in God's name? Were not many nations made subject unto him? Did they not hate him and hate the law of the Lord, his people, and his cause?

The scriptural term "David" is also David's house, the generations of the son of Jesse.

With David God had established his covenant, and as always, so also this covenant is made with him and his seed in the line of his continued generations. It is of this eternal covenant, of these sure mercies of David, that Psalm 89 sings:

> I will sing of the mercies of the LORD for ever: with my mouth will I make known thy faithfulness to all generations. For I have said, Mercy shall be built up for ever: thy faithfulness shalt thou establish in the very heavens. I have made a covenant with my chosen, I have sworn unto David my servant, Thy seed will I establish for ever, and build up thy throne to all generations…I have laid help upon one that is mighty; I have exalted one chosen out of the people. I have found David my servant; with my holy oil have I anointed him: With whom my hand shall be established: mine arm also shall strengthen him. The enemy

shall not exact upon him; nor the son of wickedness afflict him. And I will beat down his foes before his face, and plague them that hate him. But my faithfulness and my mercy shall be with him: and in my name shall his horn be exalted. I will set his hand also in the sea, and his right hand in the rivers. He shall cry unto me, Thou art my father, my God, and the rock of my salvation. Also I will make him my firstborn, higher than the kings of the earth (vv. 1–4, 19–27).

That Jehovah speaks of the eternal covenant is evident from Psalm 2.

This is plain from all the scriptural passages where this prophetic song is quoted.

Thus the church understood it in Acts 4:25–27: "Why did the heathen rage, and the people imagine vain things? The kings of the earth stood up, and the rulers were gathered together against the Lord, and against his Christ. For of a truth against thy holy child Jesus, whom thou hast anointed, both Herod, and Pontius Pilate, with the Gentiles, and the people of Israel, were gathered together."

He is the Lord's anointed.

It is he who is in David, who is the root of David, and because of whom the heathen rage against the son of Jesse.

He it is who is always in the loins of David's generations, and upon whose destruction the powers of darkness are bent when they are furious against David's house.

It is he who finally appears as the holy child Jesus, against whom all the powers of hell are let loose.

Why?

Does not David rule in righteousness, in the name of the Lord?

Does not Jesus of Nazareth speak the words of eternal life and pass through the land always doing good?

Why then do the heathen rage?

Foolish raging!

❖

Wicked fury.

Oh, how they rage.

How wickedly they set themselves against David, his house, his throne, and his kingdom in the old dispensation. Was ever royal house hated as was the house of David? Was ever kingly dynasty the object of so unreasonable, insane, insatiable hatred as was the line of David's generations? Could not they and the people under their domination with them lament in truth, "Many a time have they afflicted me from my youth...The plowers plowed upon my back: they made long their furrows" (Ps. 129:2–3)?

Why do the heathen rage?

Why are they so furious against the Christ, when in spite of all the attempts of the powers of darkness to prevent his coming, he finally appears?

Is not their fury insane? How they are all gathered against that one man, the holy child Jesus! Big men, men of power and authority, kings and rulers of the earth, men of renown and power in the church, leaders of the people and the people themselves, Jews and Gentiles, Pharisees and Sadducees, Herod and Pilate, Caiaphas and Annas, the Sanhedrin and the Roman soldiers—all are set against him, and their fury seems to be inexhaustible. Does it not appear insane when Herod, plotting to destroy the child Jesus, determines upon the wholesale slaughter of all of Bethlehem's children? Is there not something irrational in the way they are forever watching Jesus, who passes through the land doing good? How they spy upon him! How they attempt to catch him and kill him almost from the very beginning of his public ministry! How they plot and conspire and lay their snares in secret!

When they finally find a traitor to sell his soul for thirty pieces of silver and to take Jesus captive in the dark garden of agony, how they rage! They come against him who was defenseless and never carried a sword, armed to the teeth as against an evildoer. They bring all kinds of insane accusations against him; they beat him and buffet him; they spit upon him and blindfold him; they mock and revile him; they scourge him until the blood runs down his back; they crown him with a crown of thorns and clothe him in the mock-royal robe. They try to satisfy their wrath by inflicting upon him the most cruel and shameful death, the death of the cross. Even then they are not satisfied; still they rave and rage and mock and revile.

Did ever man suffer as he suffered?

Was ever man the object of hatred as he was hated?

Did ever all the world rage as they raged about him?

Why?

An accusation they cannot find. To any evil deed they cannot point. Even when the Roman governor asks them why, they can answer only that they would not have brought him to Pilate if he were not an evildoer. When Pilate in spite of himself must express the verdict that he can find no evil in the man, all they are able to reply is, "Crucify him! Away with him! Give us Barabbas and let him be crucified!"

Why do the heathen rage?

A rational answer there is not. But there is the reply of sin: "Let us break their bands asunder, and cast away their cords from us."

This is their purpose.

The desire to realize that purpose motivates them and their fury.

Wicked rebellion incites them. Insurrection against the Lord and against his anointed.

Their bands, the bands of Jehovah and his anointed, they break; their cords they would cast away from them in their fury.

Bands of righteousness and truth, of holiness and love they are; the cords of the precepts of the Most High they have in mind. For these are the bands of the Lord, and these are maintained by his anointed.

There was a time when man's inner life, his heart and soul, his mind and will and all his inclinations and desires, were harmoniously united by these bands and cords of the Lord. Man was bound by them from within. For in true righteousness, holiness, and truth the creator of heaven and earth had formed him. Then he did not feel them as bands that limited his liberty. Bound from within by the cords of the Lord, he was truly free.

But the arch-liar came.

The deadly poison of the lie was instilled into man's heart, "You shall be like God."

And man felt the bands of Jehovah, of the love of God, of truth, righteousness, and holiness as cords of oppression.

His liberty he felt as bondage.

And ever since he has raised the cry of insurrection, "Let us break their bands asunder, let us cast their yoke away!"

God sent his anointed. The anointed approached man with the cords of the Lord. And they became furious. Away with this man! Crucify him!

Why do the heathen rage?

Wicked rebellion.

❖

Vain imagination.

Why do the people imagine a vain thing?

For a vain thing, an empty thing, a thing that is impossible of accomplishment, that must end in utter and complete failure, do they imagine.

Do they not see? Have they no understanding? Can they not perceive the utter vanity of setting themselves against the Lord and his anointed? Do they not understand that he who sits in the heavens shall laugh at their futile raging? Do they not hear the thunder of the decree, announced by the Lord's anointed, "Hereafter shall ye see the Son of man sitting on the right hand of power, and coming in the clouds of heaven" (Matt. 26:64)?

They hear not, neither do they see, nor do they understand with their heart.

They rage and rave against the Lord and his anointed.

And, behold, they seem to succeed.

The Gentiles in conjunction with carnal Israel set themselves against David and his house. And they appear to have the victory. The house of David appears to be destroyed. The throne of Israel is cast into the dust. First Ephraim breaks his bands asunder and casts his cords away. Judah alone is left. Then the powers from without ally themselves with wicked Israel from within, and David's house is robbed of its glory and power. In captivity the glory of the Lord's anointed is trampled underfoot. A plaything for the nations is the royal dynasty that was to have dominion forever. The tree of David is cut down to the ground.

Yet the root of David remains.

The root of Jesse.

A root in a dry ground, but a root nevertheless. And it lives. It sprouts. It yields a branch. It grows. The heathen recognize him. This is the Lord's anointed indeed. The heir! Again they rage, and again they seem to overcome. They destroy him from the earth.

But he rises from the dead!

He is exalted to glory, high in the heavens, far above all principalities and power.

He comes again, the Lord's anointed.

To establish his kingdom forever.

Hosanna in the highest!

8

The Cross God's Triumph

"And having spoiled principalities and powers, he made a shew of them openly, triumphing over them in it."—Colossians 2:15

ON Golgotha God is the subject supreme.
    The cross is his.
    His self-vindication.
    His theodicy.
    His triumph.
    His glory.

❖

It appears so different.

For is not the world the subject, the cause of the crucifixion?

Are not the principalities and powers in control of things on Golgotha?

Is not God the object when they take the Lord of glory, bind him with fetters, lead him captive triumphantly, accuse him, condemn him, spit upon him and revile him, lead him down to death, nail him to the accursed tree, number him with malefactors, gloat over him, jeer at him, challenge him to escape out of their power and to come down from the cross, and cast him into the pit of death?

Does not Satan vindicate himself and justify his word, "Ye shall not surely die" (Gen. 3:4)? God shall die!

Is not the cross the *krisis* (judgment) with the prince of this world as judge and God as the condemned?

    The devil's justification?
    His triumph?
    His glory?

❖

On Golgotha God is subject supreme.

He is subject, even though he is also object.

He is subject, he is cause, even when the world and the princi-palities and powers are secondary subjects.

Though they know it not, he is the subject supreme even of the act whereby he becomes the object of their evil intentions, their revilings and scorn, their wicked hands with which they nail him to the cross. Voluntarily he came down to us in the likeness of sin-ful flesh; voluntarily he walked among us, condemning the world because its works are evil; voluntarily he delivered himself into the hands of sinners, without sword, without power, helpless, impo-tent, though he might invoke the might of legions of heavenly hosts; voluntarily he submitted himself to their judgment, their condem-nation, their buffetings and their stripes; voluntarily he walked the way of the cross, allowed himself to be nailed to the tree, endured their jibes, and refused to come down; and voluntarily he gave up the ghost and laid down his life.

He was subject in becoming the object.

And they knew it not.

They understood not that the cross they had erected was God's judgment seat and their own condemnation.

They believed not that the subject supreme, in becoming the object, was casting out the prince of this world.

They imagined not that even on Golgotha they would hear the thunder of his wrath and of their own damnation.

The terrible theodicy they failed to see in the blindness of their hardened hearts.

❖

Yet they do see.

And they hear his terrible thunder.

As the hour, God's hour, advances the aspect of the awful cross changes. It becomes manifest to them that this cross, which they had erected, of which they had imagined themselves to be the sole subject, is more than they had intended, passes out of their power, is no longer under their control, has yet another subject. For behold, darkness descends and deepens. God's darkness. And with the darkness comes amazement. Silence. Dreadful silence. The voice of the scoffer is no longer heard. The jeers and jibes have died on the lips of the mockers. Even the crucified one is silent, still hanging on the tree, now almost hid from hostile eyes by the veil of darkness, God's veil. And the silence becomes unbearable. Will, then, not someone speak?

Yes! He, the crucified one, speaks, "Eli, Eli, lama sabachthani." Does he call for Elias? Will someone hasten to his aid? No, for he cries out again, with a voice amazing in its power, and gives up the ghost. The veil of the temple is rent. The rocks split. The graves are opened. Their cross is now God's cross. His judgment. His triumph. And they who had come to scoff return in silence, terrorstruck. "And all the people that came together to that sight, beholding the things which were done, smote their breasts, and returned" (Luke 23:48).

❖

Thus God is the subject of Colossians 2:15.

God raised him from the dead.

God quickened us together with him.

God forgave all our trespasses, blotting out the handwriting of ordinances that was against us.

God took that handwriting, which was contrary to us, out of the way, nailing it to his cross.

God spoiled the principalities and powers, made an open show of them, and triumphed over them.

All through the cross.

His cross.

❖

How well these principalities and powers were represented on Golgotha.

Host of fallen angels.

To them the words "principalities and powers" refer in the text. Always in Scripture these terms point to the angel world. Sometimes they denote the multitude of heavenly hosts that had no part in the rebellion of Satan and his host, as for instance when it is said that Christ is exalted in heavenly places, far above all principality and power and might and dominion (Eph. 1:20–21), or even in Colossians 1:16, where things in heaven are thrones and dominions, principalities and powers. These words picture the angelic multitude as a well-ordered host, with spirits that have authority to rule and spirits that obey, with dominions of larger and smaller scope. But in Colossians 2:15 the terms refer to the wicked multitude of rebellious spirits. Also these are well ordered. Among them are principalities and powers and those in subjection to them. Over them all rules Diabolos, the liar, the murderer from the beginning, the prince of this world.

These principalities and powers stand in a definite relation to this world. This relation is tacitly assumed in the text. For how else could they have been spoiled through the cross? Through that cross God made an open show of them. The cross belongs to our world. It deals with men. These principalities and powers are the rulers of this world not in the sense that they have sovereign rights and power do they exercise dominion, but spiritually and ethically they rule. In the world of man and through it they execute their will and seek to realize their evil purpose. For through his fall man became the ally of the devil. The murderer from the beginning is man's lord; through man the prince of this world seeks to establish and maintain his dominion and to oppose the living God. Neither is the devil alone in his rebellious purpose and opposition to the Most High, for with the devil are a host of principalities, whose chief he is. As a prince of the devils and through them he is also prince of this world who enlists the ungodly in his wicked service, ethically ruling over fallen men.

Through ungodly men as their agents, the devil and his principalities and powers seek to realize their purpose.

In the deeds of wicked men the purpose and character of these principalities and powers become manifest.

At the cross they were well represented. The world was there at its best.

For there was the religious world, the pious, the righteous, the keepers of the law, the leaders of the church, the guardians of holy things, the Sanhedrin, the chief priests and scribes and elders of

the people, under the influence of, in allegiance with, in ethical subjection to the devil and his principalities and powers, ready to do
the will of their spiritual father. There were the multitude of Jews,
whose were the covenants and the promises and the giving of the
law, prepared to follow their wicked leaders. There was Judas, the
disciple of whose heart the prince of this world himself took possession. In these the principalities and powers appeared as angels of
light, in cloaks of righteousness and zeal for the law and the house
of God, watchers over the well-being of the people, whitewashed
sepulchers.

And then there was the world of "common grace," represented
by the Roman governor, occupying the seat of highest worldly justice and righteousness.

And Herod, "that fox" (Luke 13:32).

Worthy representatives of hell!

❖

God spoiled them.

He made a show of them openly.

He stripped them bare.

They stood there in cloaks of religion and piety, of self-righteousness and zeal for the law, of pretended virtue of natural light
and civil righteousness, of goodness and love of justice, so beautiful and apparently real that even people of God were tempted to
mistake them for divinely spun garments of common grace. And
God spoiled them, stripped them naked, tore off all their manmade
cloaks of goodness, and exposed them in their real character of
wickedness and ungodliness and rebellion against the Most High.

For that world and these principalities and powers must be
condemned.

They must be damned.

Into everlasting desolation they must be sent.

But how can they be sent to hell wearing beautiful robes of religion and piety, garments of virtue and common grace, and still
reveal the justice and righteousness of God?

Before they are damned they must be stripped.

Stripped to the skin, these principalities now stand exposed in
their true moral character, to angels and men, to the righteous and

to the wicked alike, of all ages. This open show still stands and will stand forever. Would you know what is the real character of this world, of the angels and principalities, of natural men in their apparent virtue and righteousness, their seeming piety and goodness? Then turn your eyes toward the cross of the Son of God. There you behold them, stripped to their bodies, exposed in all their ungodly rebellion against God and his righteousness.

For that cross is God's cross.

In that hour God sits on the throne to judge the world. And he summons the world, the principalities and powers, before his judgment seat.

When they are all present, he places them all, one by one, before the supreme question: What will you do with me? With my truth? With my righteousness? He comes to them in Jesus, Immanuel, who had revealed the Father in word and work. He comes to them without form or comeliness, without power and majesty, all his divine glory completely hidden behind the form of a weak and helpless man. In Jesus he confronts them, from the throne of his judgment, one and all, with this one question: If I, your God, stand before you without my majesty and power, what will you do with me?

Judas, you who have been in intimate contact with my revelation in the Son, what will you do with me?

Esteemed members of the Sanhedrin, what will you do with the living God?

Scribes, learned in the Scriptures; priests, who serve in my holy place; pious Pharisees; self-righteous Jews; Herod, you fox; and Pilate, representative of worldly justice and virtue and power.

All you principalities and powers.

Answer: What will you do with the living God?

And the answer came in unison: If we can get hold of God without fear of being consumed by his glory, we will kill him!

For we love darkness and hate the light.

We love iniquity and hate righteousness.

We love the lie and hate the truth.

Crucify him! Crucify him!

It was the *krisis*.

❖

God's triumph is the cross.

For in it, by means of the cross, he triumphed over the principalities and powers.

No longer is the devil the prince of the world; no longer do his principalities and powers have dominion over us.

For the strength and basis of their dominion is the guilt of sin, of the sin of the world. The sole sphere of their power and rule is the sphere of death, the corruption of the human nature. Remove the guilt and deliver the human nature from the fetters of corruption and death, and the dominion of the devil and his power are broken forever.

God broke the power of sin through the cross!

"For what the law could not do, in that it was weak through the flesh, God sending his own Son in the likeness of sinful flesh, and for sin, condemned sin in the flesh: That the righteousness of the law might be fulfilled in us, who walk not after the flesh, but after the Spirit" (Rom. 8:3–4). God nailed the handwriting that was against us, the bill of complaint that was contrary to us, to the cross of Jesus, and thus removed it. For Christ fulfilled all its demands, obeying, bearing God's wrath in love, blotting out the handwriting that cursed us.

And we are free. Free from the power of darkness.

Through the cross of Jesus.

God's triumph!

9

Seeking the Father's Glory

"Now is my soul troubled; and what shall I say? Father, save me from this hour: but for this cause came I unto this hour. Father, glorify thy name. Then came there a voice from heaven, saying, I have both glorified it, and will glorify it again."—John 12:27–28

THE hour was approaching.

The hour of hours. The darkest of all hours, yet pregnant with the glorious dawn of eternal day.

The hour of the powers of darkness, which was nevertheless the hour when the arm of the Lord was to be revealed, the mighty arm that would bring salvation to his people, life from death.

The hour of the judgment of this world, when it would seem as if the prince of darkness will sit in judgment over the servant of Jehovah, but when it will be the prince himself who is summoned before the bar of divine justice to be cast out forever.

The hour when the righteous God will pour the vials of his wrath against sin over the head of him in whom he is well-pleased, the Son of his bosom, his only begotten, in order that his love might reach forth in righteousness for those whom he had ordained to eternal glory, and Zion might be redeemed through justice; when Immanuel, God with us, will descend into lowest hell, there to speak the word of perfect obedience, "Even so, O my God, I love Thee!"

The shadows of that hour's darkness were stealing over Jesus' soul.

Now is my soul troubled.

Of the fast approach of the hour, of its close proximity, he had been reminded. He knew it was near. He was fully aware of what the hour would bring. Just a moment ago, when two of his disciples

59

had brought to him the request of the Greeks that they might see him, his mind had been directed to the promise of the Father that in the way of the hour he would see his seed. Beyond, then, across the vale of his suffering, glory beckoned him, the glory of the resurrection, of receiving the promise, of being exalted on high and drawing all unto him. Yet, even so, he must pass through the hour.

Would not the seed remain alone except it fall in the earth and die? And was there for him, the servant of Jehovah, as he stood at the head of all his brethren, another way to reach his mediator's glory than that of the Father's good pleasure?

That was the way of righteousness and justice.

And the way of justice was the way of obedience unto death. He who loves his life will lose it, but he who hates his life in this world will save it unto life eternal.

That was true for the servants.

It was supremely true for their Lord.

Contemplating the glory that lay beyond and longing for it; recoiling as he gazes into the deep vale that must be traversed before the glory can be attained; yet always obedient to the Father who sent him, he cries out, "Now is my soul troubled. What shall I say? Surely it is my earnest prayer that according to his promise the Father will save me from this hour. Yet for this purpose came I unto this hour. Father, glorify thy name."

❖

Amazing prayer!

Did ever prayer have more terrible implications for him who uttered it?

Did ever supplication witness of self-surrender, of perfect submissiveness, of blameless obedience, of being consumed with zeal for the Father's glory, as did this prayer of the Lord?

Father, glorify thy name.

We too take the contents of that prayer on our lips, even as we are taught by the savior. We too say it, and say it repeatedly, "Hallowed be thy name." We too speak of the glory of the Most High as the sole purpose of all things, of our very being and life. But how thoughtless appears our petition and how shallow our hallelujahs in comparison with this prayer that the Father would glorify his name, pressed from the lips and wrung from the troubled soul of the savior! How abstract, how devoid of concrete meaning, how superficial and without realization of the possible implication of that greatest of all prayers our stammering seems, if we think of the awful significance the petition had on the lips of Jehovah's servant, now that the shadows of the darkest of hours are perplexing his soul!

Father, glorify thy name.

God's name. It is himself in his self-manifestation, God as he is revealed, as he is known. Himself as to himself he is manifest from everlasting to everlasting in infinite perfection in his Son; himself as in all the works of his hands he is manifest as God to man, made after his image; himself as he is manifest in Jesus Christ to his own, so that they can know him and have life eternal. That name is glorious, for he is glorious. He is glorious, for he is infinitely good. And the radiation of his infinite goodness, his power and might, his justice and righteousness, his unchangeable truth and spotless holiness, the beauty of his grace and the depth of his love, his unapproachable majesty, is his glory. If he glorifies his name, he reveals, he proclaims, he causes men to know, that he alone is goodness, pure perfection, infinite in all his divine virtues.

Glorify thy name, Father.

Let it be known that thou art mighty and strong, that thy righteousness is from everlasting to everlasting the same, that thou doest all thy good pleasure, that thou art holy and true, the only God who does wondrous things.

Yet such is only the general implication of our savior's prayer in this hour of trouble.

Far more amazing that prayer becomes when we realize that it is not in this abstract and general sense, but with the concrete and specific meaning that in this hour, when his soul is troubled, the Lord utters it before the face of the Father.

Nothing less his supplication signifies at this moment than in me, Father, glorify thy name. In me refers to the hour.

Glorify thy name in me. It can only mean send me for thy name's sake, O Father, in the way of the cross.

Not as an individual, but as the mediator he prayed. From before the foundation of the world was he ordained to be the head of his people, the brethren the Father had given him. These brethren were in themselves hopelessly lost in sin and death. Among them there was no helper, no one to redeem and deliver from the power of darkness. Yet they were ordained to be justified, to be liberated from the shackles of iniquity, and to be made partakers of the highest glory in the eternal tabernacle of God with man. God would redeem them. His own arm would bring him salvation. His name would be known and glorified when he would redeem Zion through justice, for through the dark and deep way of sin he would manifest his mighty power and unchangeable righteousness, his everlasting love and mercy and the beauty of his grace. That arm of the Lord, through whose power he would deliver his people, was revealed in Jesus. God's name was in him.

Alone he was to stand for God's righteousness and glory.

Alone he was to descend into the deepest depth of the vale of death, where God would manifest his divine justice and boundless grace, when he would pour out the vials of his wrath against sin upon him whom he loved.

Alone he was to stand in the midst of the world, defenseless and without an arm of flesh, sole representative of God's light in darkness to condemn that darkness.

Father, glorify thy name.

It meant the way of the cross.

It meant the way through the depth of hell.

The hour. That dreadful hour. The hour, the very nearness of which caused him to cry, "Now is my soul troubled. Father, what shall I say? Oh, save me out of this hour! Yet glorify thy name."

Amazing prayer!

❖

What perfect obedience!

Voluntarily, by an act of his own will, motivated by the love of God and for the glory of the Father, he chooses to descend into the depth of darkness.

Such, indeed, is the mystery of atonement.

Only he who could be active in his passive obedience, who could lay down his life when it was demanded by God's righteousness, who could be priest and sacrifice in one, who could still love God in deepest hell—only he could atone for the sins of the world and reconcile the world unto the Father.

Atonement is satisfaction, and satisfaction is never the mere tasting of the wrath of God. The passive, involuntary, compulsory suffering of the punishment for sin cannot atone. If it could, hell would atone. Forevermore God's unchangeable will for man is that he shall love me with all his heart, mind, soul, and strength, always and everywhere. Me, the living God, the holy and righteous, purest perfection, he shall love. Man's fall into sin and death did not alter the Most High's eternal claim. Though in his sin man is a child of wrath, though in his corruption he can know the living God only as consuming fire, though man must be cast into the pool that burns with fire and sulfur, yet the law pursues him in all his death and misery: Love the Lord your God with all your heart. To atone is to satisfy, and to satisfy is to stand in the depth of hell, to bear all the burden of God's wrath, and in the midst of it to say, "I love thee! Glorify thy name!"

The perfect sacrifice of perfect love. Such was the obedience of Jesus our Lord.

It is this perfect obedience that is voiced in his amazing prayer, "Father, glorify thy name."

Already the hour is come. Even now it begins to cast its shadows upon his soul. No, the deepest stage of the way he must travel has not as yet been reached. The darkness will become more impenetrable, the suffering more intense, the agony more amazing, and the grief more perplexing as he descends into the vale. Yet already he is come unto the hour. To pass through it he is come to Jerusalem. Its terror already takes hold upon him. Full well he knows the awful terror of that hour. He is troubled in soul. All that is human in him dreads the darkness of the way. Yet...

What shall I say?

Father, glorify thy name.

Think not that the servant of the Lord is wavering at this moment. Mistaken are they who would interpret these words as the expression of a first impulse to draw back: "Father, save me from this hour!" Mistaken are even they who would at least read them as a question of perplexity: "What shall I say? Father, save me from this hour?" That moment of wavering, that impulse to return from the way of the cross, would have been disobedience. And the will or the impulse to disobey the Lord never knew.

He could dread the hour, he could shrink from the terror of the darkness of his way, his soul could be troubled, he could be tempted in all things even as we are, but without sin.

He could not wish to disobey.

Knowing that the Father's glory was inseparably connected with the hour, he could not even for a moment desire to sacrifice that glory to his own salvation.

When pressed from his lips is the prayer "Father, save me from this hour," he has his eye on the promise and looks forward to the glory that is promised to him, to the resurrection and exaltation to power. Not by excusing him from passing through the hour, but by glorifying him through it, the Father would save him from its depth and not leave his soul in hell.

Yet even so, he remembers the hour and its purpose.

That purpose was the glory of the Father. Unto the purpose that the Father's name might be glorified he had come to this hour.

Father, glorify thy name. Thy purpose be mine.

The perfect answer.

❖

Hark, a voice!

Distinctly it speaks, "I have both glorified it and will glorify it again."

The heavenly answer—the Father's response to the prayer of his servant: an interpretation and a promise.

For the Father's voice from heaven explains the past and the immediate future, and it contains the promise that the prayer of his servant will be surely answered. Father will glorify his name and save his servant out of the hour.

An interpretation of the past: I have glorified it. Glorified it in the incarnation, in the sending of his Son in the flesh and all that stood connected with it in the public ministry of the Lord; glorified it in the testimony of the Son, revealing the Father, radiating the light in darkness, and condemning the darkness; glorified it in the mighty works of the savior, carrying the testimony that the Father had sent him and foreshadowing still mightier works to come. Indeed, I have glorified it even up to this moment.

And an interpretation of the hour: I will glorify it again. Sorely needed was this divine light from heaven upon that darkest of all scenes, upon the agony of Gethsemane, upon the final battle of Calvary, when it appeared as if the powers of darkness celebrated their triumph, their decisive victory, and that the cause of God's covenant was hopeless, that the light would forever be eclipsed and the Sun of righteousness would set, never to rise again. These darkest moments could be comprehended only in the light of the Father's assurance, "Be not afraid, I am now glorifying my name. I will glorify it again."

Yet the voice came not for the Lord's sake, even in this hour of trouble. Did he not know that for this purpose he had come unto this hour, and that Father would always hear him?

The voice was for those who had ears to hear.

Some did not hear, but thought it thundered. Some always think that it merely thunders when the Father speaks.

Yet some did hear, and some still hear God's interpretation, his word of the cross.

And hearing they are reconciled with God.

And glorify the Father!

10

The Entrance of the King

"Lift up your heads, O ye gates; and be ye lift up, ye everlasting doors; and the King of glory shall come in. Who is this King of glory? The LORD of hosts, he is the King of glory."
—Psalm 24:7, 10

THE Lord of glory, the king, shall come in.

Lift up your heads, O you gates; lift them up, you everlasting doors.

A festive hour of great joy it was for the church of the old dispensation when first these words of the poet were chanted by the joyous procession that had swept up the hillside and, having reached the summit of Mount Zion, had stood before the mighty gates of the old citadel.

The psalm perhaps was sung by a double chorus, one within the fortress, the other advancing, with the ark of the covenant in their midst, up the slopes of Mount Zion. As they reached the summit, the ascending choir chanted the first part of these poetic words, containing a summons to those within to open the gates and to lift up the lintels of those gates so the lofty and exalted king of glory could have entrance into the citadel: "Lift up your heads, O ye gates; and be ye lift up, ye everlasting doors; and the King of glory shall come in"! Then in answer to this peremptory summons sounded the question from within the gates, "Who is this King of glory?" The answer was given somewhat impatiently by the procession waiting outside the gates, "The LORD of hosts, he is the King of glory."

None other than Jehovah—the mighty God of hosts, the immutable, who is of himself and possesses the source of his glorious being in himself; who is from everlasting to everlasting the same, unchangeable in himself and without shadow of turning in his relation to his people whom he has chosen—is the king of glory, whose heralds stood at the gates of the city, demanding that they be lifted for the king to enter. He alone is Israel's king. He had chosen Israel as his people not because of their superiority, but in his sovereign grace and for his name's sake. He had delivered them from all the power of their enemies, for he is mighty in battle, this king of Israel. He had given them his precepts and established with them his covenant, that they would be his people and he their God and king. In the land flowing with milk and honey he had prepared them a place for their habitation, where they could dwell securely under his reign and he could live among them.

The king had chosen Jerusalem as the place of his habitation; more particularly, he had chosen Mount Zion for the establishment of his throne. On Mount Zion he would dwell. There he would show forth his power and majesty. From its summit he would rule over his people, give them his precepts, and bless them.

And now the kingdom was established.

Long the enemy had dwelled among them in the land, even after the people had first been led into their rest. Especially in cities and strongholds the foe had maintained its power. But with the ascent of David, the man after God's heart, to the throne, the Lord had given the people victory over all of their foes. Even the fortress of the Jebusites had been captured. The Lord had manifested himself as the one who is faithful and true and realizes his promises unto his people, as the one mighty in battle and vanquishing every foe of his people. He had revealed himself as the king of glory indeed.

Now he enters into the place of his majesty. He is represented by the ark, the visible representation of his majesty and power. The hoary gates of the ancient citadel must be lifted up!

When the ark enters into the city of God, the Lord of hosts establishes his throne on Mount Zion; the kingdom of God is founded among God's people.

It is the commencement of a blessed commonwealth.

The ark of the covenant that is now brought up to Jerusalem, to Mount Zion, with festive procession, is not only the symbol of God's throne, but is also the heart of the temple. Around it soon would arise the most holy and the holy places, together with the court, with its altars and candlestick and table of showbread. Thus completed, the temple would be the embodiment of the covenant idea: God's dwelling among his people. Not as an oriental despot would this king of glory reign over his people, but as a friend among friends he would dwell among them and lavish upon them all the blessings of his fellowship and love.

Thus Zion rejoices, and rejoicing, God's people sing, "Lift up your heads, O you gates! Lift them up, you everlasting doors! Let the king of glory enter in. Let the throne of our God be founded. Our mighty king-friend stands before the gates. Let his kingdom now be established."

❖

A gladsome day it was for the church.

But even on that day the words of the poet did not enter upon their full and final realization.

Hoary with age though these gates of the Jebusites' stronghold were, it was only with a view to better things to come, as a shadow of other gates far more glorious, that they could be called everlasting.

Surely the joy of the procession that wound its way on the hillside of Zion to its summit was real, for in a real sense God dwelled among his people in the old dispensation. Yet the reality was veiled in shadow, and the shadow pointed to better things to come. The earthly Mount Zion was a shadow of the heavenly, the place at his right hand in the highest; the most holy place was a shadow of the inner sanctuary above, where the Most High dwells in heavenly beauty and glory; the ark was a picture of his throne of glory, the temple was an earthly form of his covenantal fellowship, and David was a figure of him through whom the Lord, mighty in battle, would give his people ultimate victory over all of their foes.

Although these shadows served the old dispensational people of God to live in hope, reality was not yet; although even these shadows were glorious and full of blessed significance, yet all the imperfections that were necessarily peculiar to shadows also characterized them.

To what better things did these shadows point forward?

What other and more glorious everlasting gates were lifted up to let the king of glory in?

The everlasting gates are the doors of heaven. The king of glory is none other than our blessed Lord. The poet's words were fulfilled in a higher and more glorious sense when Christ ascended into the heavens to receive his place of power and his name above all names at the right hand of the Most High.

Christ Jesus is the king of glory, the Lord and David in one, Immanuel, God with us, the central realization of everything that the old temple could express—God of God, yet servant, king under God, yet God himself. He is the king of glory, the glorious king, for he was exalted from the blood and mire of the battlefield through his resurrection and ascension to the place of heavenly majesty and universal power.

Long these gates of the heavenly city had been closed, for by reason of sin our nature could not enter. Between us and the glorious kingdom that was to be established by this mighty king stood the entire, powerful host of the enemy, of guilt and sin, of death and hell. But this king of glory proved himself the Lord, mighty in battle. He met the foe. From his place of glory this Lord had descended upon the battlefield of our nature. Though he deemed it not robbery to be equal with God, he had humbled himself into the form of a servant.

In that form of a servant he met the foes in deadly conflict. They barred the way into the kingdom the Father had ordained for him and his people. These foes of sin and death, of the devil and his hosts, he must vanquish before he could enter into his glory and receive his dominion. What a battle it was, a conflict the likes of which had never before been witnessed, a warfare of righteousness against unrighteousness, a battle of life with death, in which the prince of life, the king of glory, the Lord mighty in battle, left his earthly life on the battlefield, shed his lifeblood in conflict with the foes, and descended into the depth of Hades and hell.

But it was a conflict out of which he issued forth with complete victory on his side.

Guilt was wiped out.

Sin was hopelessly bereft of its power, a vanquished foe.

Death was killed. Prison was captured.

The head of the devil was crushed.

The battle finished, the mighty Lord of glory remained alone on the battlefield, the glorious power of his resurrection radiating from his appearance. About him lay the vanquished powers of darkness. The way into his kingdom was cleared. He gained a right to enter into highest glory as the king of his people, the mighty one of Israel. He ascended from the battlefield into the inner sanctuary, to the highest place of glory and power at the right hand of God.

The king of glory!

The Lord mighty in battle!

From the throne of his father he will reign, and God through him. He will reign in might over the entire world, over all his subjected foes, who even now are loath to admit utter defeat. And he will reign through the blessed power of his grace and Spirit in the hearts of his own.

The kingdom of heaven is come. God dwells with us, through Christ, in the Spirit. The tabernacle of God is with men.

Well may Zion rejoice as he ascends from Mount Olivet, and sing with far more blessed significance than the festive throng that once climbed the slopes of Mount Zion, "Lift up your heads, O you gates! Lift them up, you everlasting doors! So the king of glory can come in."

❖

A festive day it was when the ark was placed within the walls of old Jerusalem.

Far more gladsome was the day when Christ Jesus, having fulfilled all things and conquered every foe, ascended to his place of glory at the right hand of God.

A better day had dawned with this significant event, a day of victory and blessing. The shadows had passed away and reality had come. The lion of Judah's tribe, the root of David, had received the kingdom and entered into his power. He is now in heaven and has all power in heaven and on earth. He rules over all and has a name above every name that is named. He establishes his throne of grace in our hearts. Having overcome the powers of death and hell for us, he also vanquishes the enemy within us and actually delivers us from the power of the devil. Having shed his lifeblood to wash away our guilt forever, he also washes and cleanses our souls from the guilt of sin. Having condemned the power of sin in the flesh, he also overcomes that power in our inmost souls, cuts our bonds in which we are held by nature, and liberates us through the law of the Spirit of life.

Having entered into the sanctuary in heaven, having established his throne, and having received the Spirit, he now enters into the sanctuary of our hearts, breaks down the throne of the devil, and establishes his own rule, the throne of his grace in our inmost beings.

Thus he makes us citizens of his kingdom and subjects us to his rule as friends of God who serve him in willing obedience.

A blessed day has dawned with the ascension of our Lord into the highest.

Yet, ultimate reality has not been reached.

The words of the inspired poet of the old dispensation who composed this precious hymn have not entered upon their final fulfillment.

The king of glory has not yet entered into the last realization of his kingdom, and the tabernacle of God is not yet fully with men. Still things are imperfect in form, though in principle they have attained to perfection. As citizens of his blessed kingdom, we are still imperfect. There is as yet only a small beginning of the new obedience according to which we are wholly subject to Jehovah, our covenant God in Christ, within our hearts. Sin still harasses us from within and from without. Physically we are still in weakness and dishonor, carrying about with us this body of death. Corruptibleness has not yet put on incorruption, and this mortal has not yet put on immortality. Besides, we are still in the world, and in the world we have tribulation. Although in Christ we have the victory, in the flesh we are often defeated; although we are citizens of a glorious and heavenly kingdom, in the flesh we still suffer. The new heavens and the new earth, in which all that is of sin and death will vanish forever, are not yet.

The battle still rages.

Though we live, we still die.

The king of glory, the Lord mighty in battle, must still come. Come into his kingdom. Come to perfect all things.

And he is coming.

Coming all the while and coming quickly.

Coming to complete his glorious kingdom. He is coming in all the events of this present time, in the calling of the elect and the gathering of his church to complete his body, coming in war and peace, in fruitful and barren years, in plenty and famine, in floods and pestilences, in earthquakes and upheavals, in the filling of the measure of iniquity and the preparation of the man of sin, the son of perdition. He is coming to judge the world in righteousness, to save his elect, to establish his kingdom, coming with haste to avenge those who cry unto him day and night.

He will come on the clouds of heaven even as he ascended and all the host of heaven with him. He will come to purge the world, to give his final sentence upon the righteous and the unrighteous, to glorify his people, to make them partake in his victory as they participated in his battle through his grace, and to perfect the tabernacle of God with them.

He will enter into the final and eternal manifestation of his blessed kingdom.

Then who will ascend the hill of the Lord with him? Who will enter with him into the tabernacle of God?

He who has clean hands and a pure heart washed by the king's own blood and cleansed by the power of his grace through faith in him.

Thus the joyous shout of God's people, rejoicing at the entrance of the Lord into his kingdom when he ascends on high, is also still a sigh of hope as they expect his final coming, his entrance into the perfect kingdom: "Lift up your heads, O you gates. Lift them up, you everlasting doors. Let the king of glory, the Lord almighty in battle, enter in. Let him come just once more!"

We are expecting him; we are looking forward to his final coming. Knowing that no iniquity will enter with him into his kingdom, we are keeping our garments pure in the midst of the world.

Come, Lord Jesus, come quickly! Even so, Amen.

11

The Power of Exaltation

*"And set him at his own right hand in the heavenly places, Far
above all principality, and power, and might, and dominion,
and every name that is named, not only in this world, but also
in that which is to come."—Ephesians 1:20–21*

OH, that the apostle's prayer "[I] cease not to give thanks for you,
making mention of you in my prayers; That the God of our Lord
Jesus Christ, the Father of glory, may give unto you the spirit of
wisdom and revelation in the knowledge of him" (vv. 16–17) may
be ours.

And that the God and Father of our Lord Jesus Christ may hear
us.

This prayer of the apostle in behalf of the church at Ephesus is
the prayer that the Spirit of our Lord Jesus Christ wrought in his
heart, in his mind, and through him in the written word, in order
that we too might learn to know what to pray for as we ought.

For of what avail can it be that someone prays in our behalf,
even though he be an apostle, or though he were an angel in heaven,
unless God's answer to that prayer becomes effective and manifest
so that our hearts too yearn and cry out for that blessing from heavenly places that is the contents of the intercessory prayer?

Let then the prayer of the apostle be answered from heaven in
the opening of our hearts and the earnest petition on our part for
the spiritual blessing he invokes upon the church.

That we too may utter this prayer.

This prayer that the God and Father of our Lord Jesus Christ
will give unto us the Spirit of wisdom and revelation in the knowledge of him; that he will so enlighten the eyes of our understanding that we know what is the hope of his calling and the riches of

the glory of his inheritance in the saints; that we know what is the exceeding greatness of the power of God to us, yea, *into* us, of the divine power that operates in the saints and that will not cease to work until it has made them heirs of the eternal glory; that power of God, the standard of which is the mighty power that he wrought in Christ when he raised him from the dead; still more, the power of God that was wrought in Christ when he set him at his right hand in heavenly places, far above all principalities, and power, and might, and dominion, and every name that is named, not only in this world, but also in that of the eternal future.

God and Father of our Lord Jesus Christ! Let this prayer be the constant prayer of the church.

How else will we know and understand and be victorious and rejoice in this world?

The natural man understands not these things. Not only is he carnal and darkened in his understanding, so that he loves and pursues after the lie, but he is also a mere living soul, of the earth earthly, and these things are spiritual, heavenly, eternal. They belong to the category of things that eye has not seen, and ear has not heard, and that have never arisen and can never arise in the heart of man.

Only through the revelation of the Spirit of Christ can they be understood.

That revelation can be apprehended only by him whose eyes of his heart have been enlightened, so he discerns spiritual things spiritually.

And that wonder of enlightenment is wrought only through the grace of prayer.

May that mighty prayer be ours.

❖

Marvelous power in us.

If you would know what is that power of God that is operative in believers even here in this world, that power whereby they were called out of death into life, out of darkness into light, then you must consider the mighty power of God that exalted Jesus Christ.

Jesus is exalted.

He stands at the pinnacle of all created things.

He rules over all in the name of God and has an everlasting dominion in heaven and on earth.

This and nothing less is the significance of the figure that is implied in the words "set him at his own right hand in the heavenly places." Earthly kings would sometimes exalt someone at the right hand of the throne of their earthly power and majesty. This would imply not that the king himself had abdicated, but that he had empowered and authorized the one thus exalted with the actual execution of his rule in the kingdom. The whole kingdom would be subjected unto him as unto the king himself. Thus Christ is exalted at the right hand of the majesty in heaven. The dominion is his under God and in God's name. The power in heaven and earth is given unto him.

All power.

In that he is far exalted even above the first man Adam in his state of integrity in paradise. Adam too had dominion. He was king under God, but he was made a little lower than the angels. His throne was on the earth, and his dominion was limited to the scope of earthly things. But Christ is exalted at the right hand of God in heavenly places. His power and dominion are universal. He stands at the pinnacle of all created things in heaven and on earth.

He rules over all.

He is exalted far above all principality, and power, and might, and dominion. This includes all authority and might, wherever they may be found. Principalities, powers or authorities, and mights and dominions, are the angels who stand before the throne of God and see his face, the heavenly spirits from the viewpoint of their various ranks and orders. Also in the angelic world there is order and degree of power and authority. The reference is primarily to them. But this does not exclude any other principalities and powers. Also the wicked spirits, which once rose in rebellion against him who sits on the throne in heaven, under the leadership and by the instigation of their evil chief, are called principalities and powers (Col. 2:15). Besides, there are mighty powers and rulers in the earth.

Above them all stands Christ, the anointed of God.

Far above them.

Their authority and power cannot be compared with his. They cannot reach up to his exalted position. They are utterly in subjection to him. Under his feet they are. Him they must obey. Against him they can never prevail.

His power is also over every name that is named in all creation. Many are the names that are named in this world. These names denote the creatures in their nature and position, their power and might, their relative significance and purpose in relation to God and to one another and to the whole of created things. They have been determined and fixed by the God and Father of our Lord Jesus Christ, "of whom the whole family in heaven and earth is named" (Eph. 3:15). The creatures, small and great, in all their power and significance, their operation and strife in all the universe, are subjected to the Christ of God.

He has received a name that is above all names.

Forever.

Not only in this world, but also in the world to come, that name remains far above all names. He will never be dethroned. Even though in the world to come he will deliver his kingdom to the Father, that God may be all and in all, he will maintain his position at the head of the kingdom of glory, far above every name that is named in the new heavens and the new earth in which righteousness will dwell forever.

God exalted *him*, the Christ, the anointed, the servant of Jehovah, in his human nature. It is not the Son of God in his divine nature who was so highly exalted. Nor is it divine power with which Christ is invested at his exaltation. The divine nature cannot be exalted, and the divine power cannot be conferred upon any. As the Son of God in his divine nature he is coequal with the Father and the Holy Spirit, almighty, exalted over all, with absolute authority and sovereignty over every name that is named. In that nature he could not be exalted. But this Son of God assumed human flesh and blood, was seen in the form of man, humbled himself into the deepest reproach of shame and suffering of our death and condemnation. That Son of God in that humiliated human nature is now exalted far above all principality and power and might and dominion and every name that is named.

In him the promise is realized.

In his exaltation the Scripture is fulfilled: "What is man, that thou art mindful of him? and the son of man, that thou visitest him? For thou hast made him a little lower than the angels, and hast crowned him with glory and honour. Thou madest him to have dominion over the works of thy hands; thou hast put all things under his feet" (Ps. 8:4–6).

Man in the first Adam goes down in order to crown the second Adam as lord of all.

Now we see not yet all things put under him.

But we see Jesus, who also was made a little lower than the angels...

For the suffering of death crowned with glory and honor.

Glorious exaltation!

❖

Mighty power of God.

Let us not forget that this is the real subject of the revelation of the word of God in this passage.

The text speaks of the amazing and glorious exaltation of Jesus Christ at the right hand of the majesty in the heavens, yet only as a manifestation of a mighty divine power that wrought this exaltation.

It is the working of the mighty power that God wrought in Christ when he raised him from the dead and set him at his own right hand in heavenly places that is the main theme of the divine revelation here. God revealed himself; the mighty God of our salvation is revealed in the resurrection of Jesus Christ from the dead and in his exaltation at the right hand of God. This the church must know.

She must also know the power of God operating in her, in the church, in the hearts of the saints, the mighty power of grace whereby they have been regenerated and called from death into life, from darkness into light.

For knowing that power, they will know the hope of their calling.

To know this power that operated within them, they must know the power of God that wrought in Christ, when he raised him to immortality and exalted him into everlasting and heavenly glory and power, for the power of God that wrought in Christ is the standard of the power that operates in them. According to the power that God revealed in the resurrection and exaltation of the Lord Jesus Christ, he also works in the saints.

Divine power wrought upon Christ to exalt him. And how exceeding great is that power!

It is a power over death and hell and shame and reproach. It is a power that is mightier still than the power whereby all things were called into existence from the beginning; or rather, it is the same divine power of omnipotence, but now revealed in still greater glory than in the work of creation.

For Christ had emptied himself. He had no name left in all the world. He had descended into the deepest darkness of death and of hell. He had removed himself in perfect obedience as far away from this heavenly glory as it is possible to be removed, into that abyss of despair whence there seemed to be no conceivable return. Into that depth reached the power of God. From that depth of nameless despair that exceeding great power of God drew him. That amazing power of God changed death into life, mortality into immortality, reproach and shame into honor and glory, utter powerlessness into highest power, the reproach of hell into the position of glory at the right hand of the majesty in the heavens, the position in which he had a name below all names into that in which he has a name above every name that is named.

Exceeding greatness of the divine power!

This power he wrought not only *upon* Christ, so that he personally is exalted. It also works *within* him.

For in his exaltation Christ received the promise of the Spirit as the head of the church, of all his own whom the Father had given him, so that he became the quickening Spirit.

Through that Spirit the God and Father of our Lord Jesus Christ causes that same exceeding great and mighty energy, the power to quicken, to raise from the dead, to deliver from shame and to exalt to glory, to operate in the exalted Christ.

So that he is able to subdue all things even unto himself.

Impart his own life and glory unto us.

And we will be like unto him.

Amazing power!

❖

Blessed riches of grace.

The contemplation of the mighty working of God's exceeding

great power in the resurrection and exaltation of Jesus Christ from the dead is designed to cause us to know what is the hope of our calling, and what are the riches of the glory of God's inheritance in the saints.

And what is the exceeding greatness of his power unto us who believe.

It is the power that wrought upon Christ to exalt him from the lowest hell to heavenly glory, the power that now operates through the Spirit in Christ, that also works in the church. For he is the head of the church, which is his body. His own are engrafted into him, become one plant with him, and through his Spirit who dwells in the head and in the body they partake of the power of his death, as well as of the mighty power of his resurrection and exaltation into highest glory.

Death is vanquished; eternal life reigns.

Hell is overcome and swallowed up; glory and power and dominion are ours in Christ; with him we are set in heavenly places.

It is true that all of this is ours only in beginning, in principle, as long as we are in the body of this death. But if we know the exceeding greatness of the power of God in us, which he wrought in the resurrection and exaltation of the Lord Jesus Christ from the dead, we will also know the hope of our calling: With him we shall be glorified.

That mighty power cannot rest until by it we will be made like unto him in body and soul.

And reign with him forever.

Blessed hope!

PART IV

❧

God's Goodness to His
Chosen People: Generally

12

God's Great Love

*"For God so loved the world, that he gave his only begotten Son,
that whosoever believeth in him should not perish, but have
everlasting life."—John 3:16*

GOD so loved…

This explains the "must" of verse 14: "As Moses lifted up the serpent in the wilderness, even so must the Son of man be lifted up." Another way than the way of the cross there was not for the Son of man to enter into his glory. He must be exalted, to be sure, but only through deepest humiliation and shame.

For God so loved the world.

All the emphasis falls on the comparison: So he loved…that he gave his only begotten Son.

If you would form some idea of the character, power, depth, height, sovereignty, unquenchableness, and greatness of God's love for the world, you must not look at the world, but at the cross of Jesus.

There the Son of man is being lifted up.

And that Son of man is the only begotten Son of God.

Lifted up is he like Moses' serpent, apparently by men, but in deepest reality by the living God himself. For God gave his only begotten Son.

The revelation of his great love!

❖

God so loved the world.

Hardly necessary it seems, for one who does not intentionally read his own pet theories into the word of God, to explain that "world" in John 3:16 cannot be replaced by "all men."

Is not the "world" of this marvelous passage the object of God's great love? Could ever such love fail to seek and find and save its object? If God so greatly loved the world that he gave his only begotten Son for its salvation, can it be that it or any part of it is lost unto perdition? Yet not all men are saved. Many of the world of men as we know it are never touched by this mighty love. How then could "all men" be the proper explanation of "world" in the text?

Again, does not this word of God emphasize that God gave his only begotten Son? Does not God's giving imply that he gave his Son over to the death of the cross to offer himself as a perfect sacrifice unto God for sin? Was not this gift bestowed on and this sacrifice offered on behalf of "the world"? But could it be that this gift had been wholly or partly in vain, and that even one drop of blood of that precious sacrifice had been shed for one who is lost in everlasting desolation of darkness?

God forbid!

Is it conceivable that so marvelous a love, expressing itself in so amazing a way, would prove itself impotent to save its object and to attain its end? Could it be that God would so humiliate his Son, while the realization of the purpose of that humiliation was not in his power but depended on the evil will of the very men who nailed him to the accursed tree?

To ask the question is to answer it. That God so loved the world that he gave his only begotten Son—what else does it mean than that this world, this object of God's amazing love, was surely saved by his gift and will be saved to the uttermost?

Besides, why should such an arbitrary meaning be given to the term "world"?

It never means "all men" in the Holy Scriptures.

That this term does not always convey the same connotation, a comparison with other passages where the word occurs will readily prove. Did not our Lord, in that rich sacerdotal prayer preserved for us in this same gospel narrative, declare that he prays not for the world (John 17:9)? But surely he prays for the world his Father loved? Are we not earnestly warned in the first epistle by the same apostle who wrote this gospel revelation of Jesus Christ that we must not love the world, neither the things that are in the world, seeing that the love of the Father is directly in conflict with the love of the world (1 John 2:15)? Is it not plain then that the world that God loved is a radically different world from the world that we may not love?

To explain that "world" means all men is individualistic, nominalistic, and Pelagian.

"World" is an organic conception. It denotes beauty, harmony, a living whole, not a number of individual parts.

If you "love" a mechanism and would "save" it, you must be very careful to "save" every individual part, for the whole depends on and consists of the sum total of those parts. When you lose a wheel of your car, the auto is marred and cannot function. When you break a spring of your watch, it becomes useless. But with an organism it is different. When a farmer looks at his golden wheat field and is said to "love" his wheat, does this imply that he "loves" and means to "save" every single part of the wheat as it stands waving in the breeze? Does he not presently cut it, thresh it, pile up the straw, and burn the chaff, while only the wheat proper is put into the barn? Or when the husbandman in early spring trims the vine, so that the largest part is represented by the branches that are cut off and only a few bare stalks are left standing, does he destroy the vine?

God loved the world. But this does not mean that all individual men are the objects of his love and that all are saved. The world as we see it is the wheat as it still stands waving in the field, with straw and chaff. It must still be cut, and the wheat must be separated from the chaff. The world is the vine that must still be trimmed. Yet not those who are lost, but those who are saved constitute the world—God's world, the world of his eternal love. When all the lost are separated from it, it is still the world that is saved.

The world is the organism of God's elect together with the whole creation as it will appear in perfect harmony, heavenly beauty, united in the Son of God.

The world of the eternal, divine conception.

God's own world.

❖

That world God loved.

He so loved it that he gave his only begotten Son.

Oh, profound wonder of wonders! Mystery of mysteries, whose

impenetrable depth ever recedes from our searching gaze, and whose marvel becomes more amazing according as we more earnestly contemplate its divine wonder.

God loved the world.

That means that in his sovereign and eternal conception he beheld that world in its perfect beauty of perfection in Christ, the firstborn of every creature, and that God has united the world with himself, with his own heart, in the bond of perfectness. It means that he is attracted to the world, that his heart goes out to it, even as in time it is lost in sin and misery, lies under the curse and in death; that he longs for it and cannot rest until he has drawn it with cords of love unto himself; that he seeks it until he finds it, and that for it he desires and realizes the highest possible good, eternal life and beauty in the glory of God.

God loved the world.

Make no mistake, as if in the text "God" refers to the Father, to only the first person of the blessed Trinity. One might easily be tempted so to read the text in view of God's giving his only begotten Son. Did not the Father give the Son? Did not the first person of the Trinity give the second person? This would be a serious error. All the outgoing works of God are of the Trinity, of all three persons of the Godhead, each in his position and relation to the others. God, the triune God, loved the world. This love is of the Father, through the Son, and in the Holy Spirit. God, the triune God, gave his Son. This gift is of the Father, through the Son, and in the Holy Spirit. The Father gave his Son in the Spirit; the Son gave himself in the Spirit. The triune God loved the world.

God so loved the world.

How? For the answer you must turn your wondering gaze to Calvary, to the accursed tree that is planted between the crosses of two malefactors. Everywhere else you meet with darkness, wrath, judgment, death, and desolation, for the wrath of God is revealed from heaven over all unrighteousness and ungodliness of men, who hold the truth in unrighteousness. Nowhere is there a streak of light, a way out, a glimmer of hope. Only from Calvary, from the cross of Jesus, the wondrous light of divine love shines into our night and is more wonderful because it penetrates and completely swallows up the darkness of judgment and death.

God so loved the world.

How?

He gave his only begotten Son.

Do you desire to understand a little of the nature of that wondrous love, of its length and breadth and height and depth? Would you measure it? Ah, but it is as great as the gift, and therefore immeasurable. It is as deep as the love of God for his Son, his only begotten, and therefore unfathomable.

How did God love the world?

In order to approximate an answer to this question, consider that God gave his Son, the darling of his bosom, who eternally is in the bosom of the Father, in and upon whom all the infinite love of the Father is concentrated. Consider too that this is his only Son, his all, himself. Consider that he gave him. This means, in the light of all Scripture, that he gave him up, that he gave him as a sacrifice for sin, for all our sins and our transgressions, that he gave him up unto the death of the cross, and that he forsook him into lowest hell, pouring over his head all the vials of his fierce and holy wrath.

How did God love the world?

Consider once more that this giving up of the only begotten of the Father was an act of the triune God. The Father gave him up, the Son gave himself up, the Spirit was active in this giving up of the Son unto the death of the cross.

We know well that it was the person of the Son alone who came into the flesh, who took all our sins upon himself, who suffered and died on Calvary. We understand very well that the divine nature is above every form of suffering, and that all the agonies of death and hell of which Calvary is the scene and spectacle were suffered only in the human nature of the incarnated Son.

But what then?

Does not the fact remain that in that human nature of the incarnated, it was the only begotten Son who suffered? Is it nevertheless not true that in this giving of himself into death you behold and are invited to behold by the text the suffering of the Son of God, and that by this suffering you can measure the height and the depth of the wondrous love of that Son?

Still more.

Even though the person of the Son of God suffered and died on

Golgotha, does not the text stress that even on Calvary you dare not separate the three persons of the Trinity, and that somehow God suffered in the flesh of Christ? Would you not destroy the essence of the text if you would assume that while his only begotten Son writhed in the agonies of death, the Father was unmoved and the Holy Ghost coldly looked on?

How did God love the world?

All human language is incapable of adequately expressing this mystery. But surely we do justice to the text when in our human and imperfect way we paraphrase it thus: God so loved the world, that when he faced the alternative of giving his only begotten Son or letting the world perish, he sent his Son to the death of the cross.

So God loved the world.

Because of this unfathomable love the Son of man must be lifted up, even as Moses lifted up the serpent in the wilderness.

That the world, God's world, might be saved.

Glorious revelation of love!

❖

Eternal life.

Such is the end this love has in view and will surely attain.

That whosoever believes in him should not perish, but have everlasting life.

This world is perishing. It lies in the midst of death because of sin, pines away under the wrath of God, proceeds from sin to sin, from death to death, with no other possible end than eternal desolation in outer darkness. There is no way out as far as the world is concerned.

But God's world must be saved.

It is saved through the death and resurrection of the only begotten Son of God. He is the life and the resurrection. In him is life. All the power of salvation, of wisdom and knowledge, of righteousness and sanctification, of redemption and deliverance, of light and life—it is all in him, and in no one apart from him. Hence the world that is saved must be united with him, must become one plant with him, must partake of his death and resurrection. The bond that so unites that world with him is faith. Hence it is those who believe in him, the "whosoever," who constitute the world that is saved.

They are saved unto eternal life.

The love of God seeks and realizes for its object the highest possible blessedness and glory.

As great as is the love of God, revealed in the gift of his only begotten Son, so glorious is the end attained, the blessing bestowed. Everlasting life is not merely life as we know it without end, nor is it a return to the earthly life of Adam in the state of rectitude. It is the highest realization of the covenant of friendship in God's heavenly tabernacle, where he will take us to his bosom forever, and we will see him face-to-face.

In that glorious liberty of the children of God all creation will participate.

In God's only begotten Son, creation will be united in glory.

Glorious love of God!

13

Sovereign Love

"Herein is love, not that we loved God, but that he loved us, and sent his Son to be the propitiation for our sins."—1 John 4:10

WONDROUS cross of the Son of God!

Gleaming brightly with the light of the love of God in the universal darkness of our night of sin and death.

For this is the meaning of the cross. It is the revelation of the love of God to sinners who are hopelessly lost in death and condemnation, and who could never know that God loved them were it not for the light of love shining from the face of the crucified Christ.

"For God so loved the world, that he gave his only begotten Son, that whosoever believeth in him should not perish, but have everlasting life" (John 3:16). "But God commendeth his love toward us, in that, while we were yet sinners, Christ died for us" (Rom. 5:8). "In this was manifested the love of God toward us, because that God sent his only begotten Son into the world, that we might live through him" (1 John 4:9). Thus, "Herein is love, not that we loved God, but that he loved us, and sent his Son to be the propitiation for our sins."

Nowhere else in this world of sin can this light of divine love be found.

All about us and within us there is darkness of wrath and condemnation. In spite of all that philosophers babble about the love of God, that it is too weak to execute righteousness and judgment upon the workers of iniquity, and in spite of the philosophy of those who think they discover glimmerings of grace in the things of this present time apart from the one revelation of the love of God in the cross of his Son, the truth remains that our present night is a revelation of the wrath of God. In sin bearing more sin, in corruption advancing to deeper corruption, in death giving birth to eternal desolation, in debasement upon debasement, in slippery places on which men hasten to destruction, we behold and are crushed under the burden of God's holy and terrible anger against sin. "For the wrath of God is revealed from heaven against all ungodliness and unrighteousness of men, who hold the truth in unrighteousness" (Rom. 1:18).

In this darkness of wrath and death and desolation there shines the one light of divine love, penetrating the universal gloom, swallowing it up, reaching down into our hearts: the cross of the Son of God.

To be sure, it speaks too of his own love, of the love of Jesus, my savior.

He, the Son of God in the flesh, loved his brethren, and he loved them even unto the end, even to the bitter and shameful death of the accursed tree.

Yet his love is not the last word of the cross.

In and through the love of the dying Christ, shedding his life-blood as a propitiation for our sins, we behold the love of God, for the death of Christ is the death of the Son of God. Deny this, and the cross is made vain, lowered to the level of any other cross.

The death of the Son of God is the realization of a mission.

God sent his Son into the world.

By this mission he commended his love toward us.

Oh, blessed cross of Jesus!

❖

Sovereign love of God.

Precisely that love is revealed in the cross of Christ. That love is sovereign, or free and independent, and has its source in itself.

Herein is love, not that we loved God, but that he loved us.

The word of God here does not simply mean to impress upon us that there was love in the mission of the Son of God to be a propitiation for our sins. It emphasizes a very particular truth. It intends to call our attention to the nature, essence, source, and operation of all true love. True love—wherever you find it, whatever form it assumes, whether you know it as the love of God to you, as your love to God, or as your love to the brethren—always consists in God's love of us not in our love of God. This is clearly and indubitably revealed in the one great act of God's love: the sending of his Son to be a propitiation for our sins. Therein you taste and see not only that God loved us, but that his love is sovereign and free, self-existent and independent.

Love is a bond.

It is the union between persons. Strictly speaking, love does not exist between inanimate creatures or between brute creatures. One abuses this noble word *love* when he speaks of loving his dog, or when she exclaims that she loves your new hat. Love is a bond between person and person. It exists only between rational, moral beings.

Moreover, it is a spiritual bond.

There is a love that operates on a lower level and that is an image of the higher love of which 1 John 4:10 speaks: a bond that is based on and rooted in the natural affinity of our race. A young man loves the maiden of his choice; a mother loves her suckling child. This natural love is found even among animals. Even the robin loves and cares for its young.

Yet all this does not compare with and cannot reach up to the love in the highest sense that Scripture defines as "the bond of perfectness" (Col. 3:14). It is not a mere affinity that has its source in the blood, in physical likeness and adaptation. It is spiritual. It is a bond between soul and soul, between spirit and spirit, between mind and mind, between will and will; it is a spiritual power of attraction that knits being to being in the bond of perfect knowledge.

Love is the bond of perfectness. It is a spiritual bond that is established and functions only in the sphere of moral perfection. Not in darkness, but in the light; not in the sphere of the lie, but in the truth; not in iniquity, but in righteousness; not in corruption, but in holiness—in a word, solely in the sphere of ethical perfection does the fire of love burn, does the light of love shine, does the bond of love knit being to being. The wicked do not love, whatever other bond there is between them. Love is the bond of perfection.

It is the attraction of person to person in the sphere of the light.

It is the longing of spirit for spirit, a seeking and finding of each other, a living into each other's life, a giving wholly of each to the other, a complete passion for the other, a seeking of each other's good, the will to please each other, a perfect delight in each other—all in the sphere of ethical perfection.

Herein is love...

Not that we loved God, but that he loved us.

Impossible it would be to make a statement of this kind to describe and characterize the bond of love between two human beings. Between them, love is and must be bilateral, two-sided, mutual. The love of the one is incapable of kindling love in the other. The bond of love can be established between them only when the love of each meets and mingles with the love of the other, and it can be maintained only as long as each constantly continues to meet the love of the other with his own.

Not so the love of God.

It is strictly unilateral, not only in origin but also in its continued operation. It does not consist in our loving God and in his loving us because we love him. Nor is the nature of love that God and we simultaneously bring our love to each other. It dare not even be said that love is established between God and us by Christ's position between God and us, so that Christ causes God to love us and kindles the flame of the love of God in us. Love is of God. Before we love him, he loved. Before Christ was sent into the world to be a propitiation for our sins, he loved us. To be sure, we love him too; but even then love is of God. His love is the great, the eternal, the unquenchable fire that kindles all our love and that lights all the candles of our love. Even as in the firmament the light is of the sun, and this light of the sun is reflected in the moon, so love is of God, and our love is never more than the reflection of his love.

Herein is love...

He is attracted to us and draws us. He longs for us and makes us long for him; he is delighted in us and causes us to have our delight in him.

He seeks us, and we are found, and we seek him.

He does not rest until he possesses us and gives himself so that we possess him.

Love is the living current that has its source in the triune God, touches us, and takes us up in its stream of delight.

Out of him it runs through our hearts to return to him.

Of him, and through him, and unto him is love.
Sovereign is the love of God.

❖

Oh, blessed cross!
For therein we know that wondrous love of God.

Therein we behold the love as sovereign, free, eternal, absolutely
self-existent, and therefore as a fire that the floods of many waters
are unable to quench.

How otherwise could God have sent his only begotten Son to
be a propitiation for our sins?

Does not this mean that on our part there was no love? Does it
not reveal that both in time and logically, the love of God was prior
to any manifestation of love as far as we were concerned? Does it
not imply that we exerted ourselves with all that is within us to
quench the fire of divine love by the miry, stinky floodwaters of
our iniquities, and that now the flame of his unquenchable love has
penetrated victoriously through those miry waters, licking them up
and consuming them completely?

Propitiation for our sins.

It means that we were enemies of God, dead through trespasses,
standing in proud and wanton rebellion against the living God. It
means that we were guilty, worthy of damnation, objects of the
wrath of God, and that in his justice he could only inflict the punishment of eternal desolation upon us. It means that there was absolutely no way for the love of God to reach us except through the
perfect satisfaction of his justice, that is, through the depth of hell.
It means that we could not nor would ever travel this way of hell in
perfect obedience of love, as we were required to do to make this
satisfaction and become the objects of God's love and favor.

As far as we were concerned, the situation was hopeless.

Propitiation for sins.

It means that there is a covering for all our iniquities. Not a
covering in the sense that our sins are still there but they are hidden
from the face of God, but in the sense of complete coverage of the
damage done by our sins. It is paid for. The justice of God is satisfied. The way through hell has been traveled in perfect obedience of
love for us, in our stead, in our behalf.

But by whom?

God sent his Son!

Oh, mystery of mysteries: God sent his Son to be a propitiation for our sins.

He sent his Son, God of God, light of light, the everlasting darling of his bosom, in whom is the Father and the Spirit.

Himself. He, the triune God, sent him.

The Father, through the Son, in the Spirit, sent the Son.

He sent him in eternity, for in his eternal good pleasure he ordained him to be the head of the church, the firstborn among many brethren. He sent him in the fullness of time, in our flesh and in our blood, in the likeness of sinful flesh, to be like unto his brethren in all things except sin. He sent him all the way of his humiliation and suffering. He sent him, loaded with our iniquities, to the place of judgment and unto the shameful death of the accursed tree. He sent him into the depth of hell to pay the price, to respond with his perfect yes instead of our wicked and wanton no to the unchangeable justice of God.

To be a propitiation for our sins.

What does it all mean?

To be sure, it declares unto us the amazing, unfathomable, and adorable love of God.

The all-important point is that it is the revelation of first—of sovereign, of independent, and of unquenchable—love.

For not the work of Christ evokes and kindles the love of God.

Herein is love, that before Christ died God loved us.

His mission, his cross, is the revelation of love.

Oh, glorious cross of Jesus!

❖

Herein is love.

Glorious revelation of the God of our salvation!

By faith, looking at the wondrous cross of the Son of God, we are confident that all of our sins cannot quench his love. Our sins may be as scarlet, floods of iniquity may rise up against us, and our transgressions may be more than the hairs of our head; our conscience may accuse us that we have sinned and do sin daily, and that we have kept none of his commandments. Yet trusting in God's free and sovereign love revealed in the cross of our Lord Jesus Christ, we know that we may come to him and that if we confess our sins, he will burn them all away in the mighty fire of his love and cleanse us from all unrighteousness.

This is the meaning of the cross.

It is the revelation of a love that sinners need to inspire them with confidence to come to the throne of grace.

Surveying that wondrous cross and its revelation of the sovereign, independent, and never-ceasing love of God, we know that we may, that we can, that we do love him, and that his love will be perfected in us.

The truth that he loved us sovereignly does not make us careless and profane. It does not induce us to say, "Let us sin that his love may abound." On the contrary, the mighty power of God's love draws us, and the unquenchable flame of his love kindles its own response in our hearts and will do so until we dwell with him forever in love.

And nothing can separate us from that love, because love is all of God.

Herein is love…

He loved us.

Blessed revelation!

14

All-Enduring Love

"But God commendeth his love toward us, in that, while we were yet sinners, Christ died for us."—Romans 5:8

HEREIN is love...

Not that we loved God, but that he loved us...

And sent his Son to be a propitiation for our sins (1 John 4:10).

This is the story of the wondrous cross, its meaning, eternal source, and glorious revelation.

God loved us. This is the source of the amazing spectacle on Calvary. God, the creator of the heavens and of the earth, the triune Father, Son, and Holy Ghost, the righteous and holy sovereign of all, who is too pure of eyes to behold sin, loved us, sinners corrupt and damnable in ourselves. This is why that simple yet astonishingly significant sentence could be written in the gospel narrative: "There they crucified him" (Luke 23:33).

God loved us. This incomprehensible, unfathomable truth alone explains the cross of the man of sorrows, the servant of the Lord, the Son of God, Jesus, Jehovah-salvation. The interpretation of the cross is not that God was our enemy, but that Christ loved us and turned God's enmity into love. For God loved us before Calvary. He loved us with an eternal love, before the world was. The cross is the revelation, the deepest, highest, and most amazing revelation of his abiding love.

God loved us. As an interpretation of the accursed tree, this statement must stand alone. Beware lest you add to it!

Say not, "He loved us and we loved him," for this would make Calvary impossible.

Not herein is love: We loved God and therefore he loved us.

Nor herein: Our love met his.

But herein is love: God loved us. Always in this must be found the nature, essence, and constant operation of love.

Of God is love.

Because love has one source not two, and because the one source of love is in God not in us, it could be written, "There they crucified him."

The triune God loved us. The holy three were in that love.

This is the possibility of the cross. The Father loved us, and he sent his Son to be the propitiation for our sins. The Son loved us, and he came to do the Father's will, even unto the death of the cross. The Holy Ghost loved us, and he proceeded from the Father and from the Son, to sanctify the Son of man so he could offer himself without spot a sacrifice for sin acceptable to God.

Of the Father, through the Son, in the Holy Ghost, is also that accursed tree: The triune God is in Christ reconciling us unto himself.

God loved us!

Because love is of God, and of him alone, it is sovereign, eternal, unchangeable, enduring, and victorious.

Many floods cannot quench the fire of his love.

To reveal the glory, the power, the all-enduring strength of God's love, it pleased him to combine in one historical moment our darkest, most evil, and most wanton manifestation of enmity with the most amazing revelation of his love.

Herein is love.

And that "herein is love," and in nothing else, is revealed when God commended his love toward us while we were yet sinners.

Oh, blessed paradox of the cross!

> *Alas! And did my Savior bleed,*
> *And did my Sovereign die?*
> *Would he devote that sacred head*
> *For such a worm as I?*
> *Was it for crimes that I have done*
> *He groaned upon the tree?*
> *Amazing pity! Grace unknown!*
> *And love beyond degree! (Alas! And Did My*
>   *Savior Bleed)*

❖

While...

While we were yet sinners...

God commended his love toward us, in that Christ died for us.

Mistake not the meaning of "while." It does not denote the state and capacity in which God loved us: He did not love us as sinners. This would be impossible. Besides, had that been possible the death of the Son of God would have been unnecessary. Because he could not love us as sinners, because he could not bestow his love upon us in our state of damnableness and corruption, the mighty stream of his love dug its way through the deep and awful canyon of his righteousness and holy wrath to reach us. Nor does that little but profoundly significant conjunction "while" merely indicate when he loved us, although it is certainly true that he loved us when we were yet sinners. But the point is that he commended, set forth, showed, and indubitably proved his love toward us while we were yet sinners.

"While" points to the moment of the cross.

Sinners we were then; more terribly we were sinners at that very moment than at any other moment!

Sinners are those who deliberately miss the mark of the glory of God in their whole life, in all their secret thoughts and desires, and in all their deeds and speech, and who for this reason are guilty and worthy of damnation. They are those who, instead of being motivated by the love of God, stand in enmity against him, hate him, rise in proud rebellion against him; and instead of having their delight in doing his will and in ascribing all glory to his holy name, they wantonly curse him in his face.

Such sinners we were.

Our wanton rebellion and presumptuous pride we manifested in all our walk and conversation.

We began to reveal it in paradise. There we stood endowed with many excellent natural and spiritual gifts, for he had formed us after his own image, and we were gifted with the glory of clear and beautiful light, the light of knowledge, of righteousness, of the love of God in our hearts. There we dwelled, surrounded by the tokens of the blessed favor of the Most High, which with lavish hand he displayed all about us and showered upon us. And we deliberately turned our backs to him, wantonly despised his word, heeded the lie of the devil, and became enemies of the living God!

Ever since, we manifest our enmity.

For we could not escape him. Everywhere we must meet him whom we meant to repudiate and whose name we intended to obliterate from our consciousnesses. The invisible things of him are always clearly seen, being understood by the things that are made, even his eternal power and divinity. God did not leave himself without witness. But the truth we held in unrighteousness. We saw his glory and refused to acknowledge it. We lived in his creation; we ate his bread and drank his water, breathed his air, and received his rain and sunshine. In him we lived and moved and had our being, and we refused to be thankful. We scorned him to his face, changed his glory into the shame of corruptible creatures, and exalted ourselves to the height of divinity in our mad and conceited imaginations.

Such sinners we were.

And while we were yet sinners, he commended his love toward us, although he must have been angry with us and revealed his wrath.

But never did we express this enmity against the living God more furiously than at the moment he poured the vials of his wrath, which would have consumed us forever, over the head of his only begotten Son. For God commended his love toward us in that while we were yet sinners Christ died for us. And this Christ was his Son. He came because he loved us, to deliver us from our sin and death and to bring us back home to the Father.

And how we hated him.

As never before we revealed our pride and corruption. We opposed, contradicted, blasphemed, mocked, and reproached him; spit upon him; accused, buffeted, and scourged him; put him to shame; condemned and crucified him.

Do not say, "We did not know he was God's own Son." For he is the highest revelation of the Father.

The deepest reason we hated him so was our enmity against the living God!

Then, at that very moment, God commended his love toward us.

All our hatred did not change that love.
He took all our abuse of him and bore it in love.
Amazing paradox of the cross.
All-enduring love.

> *Were the whole realm of nature mine,*
> *That were a present far too small;*
> *Love so amazing, so divine,*
> *Demands my soul, my life, my all (When I Survey the*
> *Wondrous Cross).*

❖

God commended his love.
In that Christ died for us.
For that death of Christ was an act of the triune God.
He died, yes; and we killed him, had he not laid down his life voluntarily. Never could we have laid our wicked hands on him, had he not allowed himself to be led as a lamb to the slaughter. Do you not remember how he testified that as the good shepherd, he would lay down his life for his sheep; that no man could take his life from him, but that in obedience from a commandment of the Father, he would lay it down of himself?
He died, yes; and we killed him.
But this monstrous deed would have been impossible if the triune God had not ordained Christ to be the head of his body, the church, and decreed that in the dark hour of wrath and judgment, he would take the place of those whom the Father had given to him. We have taken him and by wicked hands have crucified and slain him, but this was possible only because he was delivered by the determinate counsel and foreknowledge of the triune God.
He died, yes; and we killed him.
Never could we have stretched his already bleeding form upon the tree of shame, never could our wicked hands have hammered the cruel spikes through his hands and feet, never could we have raised him as a spectacle on the hill of the skull between those two malefactors, had not God so loved the world that he gave his only begotten Son, that whosoever believes in him should not perish but have everlasting life.

God commended his love, while we revealed our hatred.

Through the darkest horror of our enmity, God caused the glorious light of his love to shine brilliantly and amazingly.

The triune God.

The Father sent him to Calvary.

The Son in human flesh set his face toward Jerusalem.

The Spirit of God, proceeding from the Father and the Son, led him thither all the way.

Of the Father, through the Son, in the Spirit, Christ died. God commended his love toward us in Christ's death for us.

For he died. All that is in death he tasted. To the bitter dregs he drank the cup the Father gave to him, and he tasted every drop. Death he tasted in such a way as we could never finish tasting it in ages unending. All that is in death of pain and agony, yes; of trouble and amazement, to be sure; of fear and utter desolation, without doubt; but then, as all this pain, fear, trouble, and astonishment are the oppressing hand of the unchangeably righteous God, meeting the sinner in his wrath in the hour of just judgment—all this he tasted.

He died for us.

For his death, as he tasted it in all its bitterness of just wrath, was an act of obedience. Every drop of blood pressed out of him he sprinkled upon God's altar in perfect obedience of love to the Father. Thus his act of dying was the perfect sacrifice for sin, the perfect yes of the Son of God, blotting out the wanton no of our rebellion.

For us he died.

In our stead he suffered the agonies of hell to forgive our sins, to clothe us with everlasting righteousness, and to make us the objects of God's favor.

In our behalf he shed his lifeblood to deliver us from the corruption of sin and the dominion of death and to lead us into the everlasting tabernacle of him who loved us.

God commended his love…

In that Christ died…

Died for us…

And all this while we were yet sinners.

Forbid it, Lord, that I should boast,
Save in the death of Christ, my God!
All the vain things that charm me most,
I sacrifice them to his blood (When I Survey the
   Wondrous Cross).

❖

While we were yet sinners.

Oh, blessed past tense, blessed word of God, which now the believing church can joyfully and triumphantly take upon her lips!

We were sinners, but we are sinners no more.

No longer are we loaded with the burden of the guilt of sin and oppressed by the heavy hand of God's holy wrath. We are redeemed. We are acquitted. There is no condemnation. We have the forgiveness of sins. We are justified, clothed in garments of righteousness in which we enter and forever dwell in heavenly tabernacles of fellowship.

Can you doubt it?

About us and within us the darkness still lingers. A thousand voices from within loudly clamor that we are corrupt, that we cannot stand in judgment, that we sin and increase our guilt daily, that we must be condemned. All about us is darkness, the darkness of death, still revealing the wrath of God from heaven. But God commended his love toward us. In the inky darkness that envelopes us there shines a light that will never be extinguished, we know. It is the light of the all-enduring love of God, shining from the face of the man of sorrows on Calvary.

Sinners we were, but sinners we are no more!

For that love of God has been shed abroad in our hearts, and through the power of his love we have in principle been set free from the dominion of sin.

We love him, because he loved us.

And we know that his love, commended in the death of Christ, will never rest until we have been perfectly delivered.

To be the objects of his love forever!

15

Foreknown in Love

*"For whom he did foreknow, he also did predestinate to be
conformed to the image of his Son, that he might be the firstborn
among many brethren. Moreover whom he did predestinate,
them he also called: and whom he called, them he also justified:
and whom he justified, them he also glorified."*
—Romans 8:29–30

OH, depth of riches!

And blessedness of assurance: "Whom he did foreknow…them he also glorified."

Do not ignore in the text a reason and a firm ground for what was expressed in the preceding: "We know that all things work together for good to those who love God, whom he called according to his purpose."

Such is the assurance of those who love God.

The indubitable ground, or reason, of this unspeakably blessed assurance is "for whom he did foreknow…them he also glorified." The end is certain. And the end is a great good—glory everlasting. Because the end is firmly determined, all things that intervene between those who love God and that glorious end must work together for good, that is, for the realization of the ultimate glory God has prepared for those who love him.

The end is sure because the beginning is unchangeably certain. The final glory and all that must lead to it were determined by the eternal predestinating purposes of the triune Jehovah. These predestinating purposes have their deepest source in his eternal foreknowledge. Whom he did foreknow, he also did predestinate.

Farther back you cannot go; more deeply you cannot penetrate into the divine mystery of salvation; for a more profound source you may not search. The eternal foreknowledge of the Most High is the fountain of your salvation.

You must not misinterpret this divine foreknowledge.

Never identify the knowledge of the eternal God with the reflected knowledge of mere man. Attempt not vainly to deprive this foreknowledge of the Most High of the glory of its divine character. Read not, as many despoilers of Scripture would, that God predestinated those whom he knew before would be willing to believe in Jesus Christ, be willing to accept him, be willing to walk in his ways, and be willing to fight the good fight to the end. Then you dethrone the Most High and enthrone mere, sinful man; then, even though you still retain the term *predestination*, you make it void of any real significance; then God predestinated, but his predestinating purpose is predetermined by man's will. Then you put God in subjection to man. Then all certainty and assurance that all things will work together for good to those who love God, to you and to me, is deprived of its firm foundation, for all things are contingent upon the changeable will of man.

The foreknowledge of God is eternally first.

It is before all things and causative of all things. We know things after they exist; God knows all things before they have being. We know things because they are; God knows things that will be. Our knowledge is determined by the things we perceive; God's knowledge determines that things will be and how they will be. The foreknowledge of God is in the most absolute sense independent and sovereign; it is all original conception, not perception. As the conception of the artist is before the work of art and determines it, so the foreknowledge of God is causally before all things that are and become. The Most High is self-existent and independent in all the works of his hand, and sovereignly independent also in his divine foreknowledge. It is determined by nothing outside of himself, but it determines all. Thus God foreknew his people, those who love him, those whom he predestinated to be made like unto the image of his Son. He did not perceive them before they were, but he conceived them so they would be.

But there is more.

This eternal, divine, causative foreknowledge of God is also the knowledge of love.

It is not simply a cold conception of his divine mind, but it is a knowledge that is suffused with the warmth of eternal love. It is not a mere eternal thought of the divine mind; it is the full, infinitely profound throb of the divine heart. It is the knowledge of fellowship, of most intimate communion, of covenantal friendship.

Thus God foreknew his people.

Sovereignly he conceived them and engraved them in the palms of his hands.

That sovereignly conceived people he loved. Loved for his name's sake. Loved because they were a revelation of his own glories, and they eternally proclaimed his own virtues.

He foreknew them with an eternal and unchangeable knowledge of love.

This foreknowledge is the deepest source of all that they are.

Of the certainty of their salvation.

Blessed assurance!

❖

Whom he did foreknow...

No, he did not merely know something about them; he knew them.

This knowledge of them, this eternal knowledge of love in the Most High, was in him the deep motive for the predestinating purpose to which he ordained them.

For whom he did foreknow them he also did predestinate to be conformed according to the image of his Son. He did not simply choose them, distinguish them, set them apart, and call them by name, but he ordained them to become partakers of a very definite and exalted glory.

Surely election is also the particular and individual calling by name in the eternal counsel of the Almighty of every one of his children. It is the writing down in the book of life of the names of all his people, with sovereign determination, as citizens of the kingdom of heaven. But in Romans 8:29–30 attention is called not to the persons who are chosen, but to the glory unto which they are elected; not to the blessed objects and participants in this gracious distinction, but to the end unto which the Most High chose them. He preordained them, and the end unto which they were ordained is nothing less than conformity to the image of God's Son, that he might be the firstborn among many brethren.

The purpose of this glorious and blessed predestination is not in the many children and must not be sought in them, but is in the eternal Son of God, the only begotten of the Father, and through him in the eternal glorification of the triune God, of the Father himself. For the Son is the only begotten of the Father, the effulgence of his glory, the express image of his being, his face, the eternal, infinite Word. All the fullness of the divine glory dwells in him, is revealed in him, beams forth through him. In him the Father beholds his own infinite glory with eternal love.

It was the Father's purpose to reveal that glory of his Son, his own glory, outside of his own infinite being. He purposed to glorify himself by revealing his Son. It was his will to reveal his Son by making him from eternity to eternity the only begotten and the firstborn among many brethren. The glory of the only begotten must be reflected in the glory of the firstborn, Immanuel, the Lord Jesus Christ. And the glory of the firstborn must be reflected and multiplied in the glory of thousands and millions of brethren who are born after him and through him. Thus the glory of the triune Jehovah is mirrored in the firstborn and in the innumerable faces of the brethren God has given to him.

The glory of Jehovah revealed in the faces of the firstborn and of his glorified throng of brethren. This is the purpose.

The Son must be the firstborn; he must come in the flesh, unite himself with the brethren, become one with them in nature, pave the way for them into eternal glory, break through the womb of things earthly and sinful and corrupt, be exalted into heavenly perfection, and become the first heir of all things, partaker also in his adopted human nature of the glory of the divine nature. When his brethren are like unto him, he must eternally be the chief among them, ruling among them as firstborn, robed in royal majesty and clothed with power, and blessing them as their everlasting high priest with blessings of God's covenant and friendship.

They, the predestinated brethren whom the Father gave to Christ, must be conformed according to the image of the Son.

Such is the end of God's predestinating purpose concerning them.

Made like unto the Son of God.

God's purpose was not that they should become divine in essence and nature. This is forever impossible, for God is one and there is no God beside him. He cannot give his glory to another. He cannot impart his being to the creature. Even when all the brethren will be perfectly conformed according to the image of his Son, there will still be an infinite chasm between the being of the Infinite and the finite beings of the brethren of the firstborn Son of God. Their glory will never be original. All their beauty will never be independent. Eternally it will be a reflection of the glory of God through the glory of the firstborn Son, whose brethren they are.

Yet though there will never be identity in essence, there will be affinity of life and likeness of form.

Even as in the glorified human nature of the firstborn there is the highest possible likeness with God, the most intimate relation and fellowship between that nature and the divine, so that the person of the eternal Son of God lives, thinks, wills, and feels also in human nature and causes the divine life to vibrate in that glorified human nature; so that likeness, relation, and fellowship with the Son of God will also be imparted to the brethren and the eternal covenantal life of the Most High will vibrate in the hearts of the children God has given to the firstborn Son.

Such is the glory unto which they are preordained by the Father.

To be conformed according to the image of his Son.

That end is certain. It is fixed by the predestinating purpose of him who never changes, with whom there is no variableness nor shadow of turning.

For whom he did foreknow, he also did predestinate.

Glorious mystery of salvation!

❖

Oh, blessed counsel of the Most High! Its fountain in the eternal and sovereign foreknowledge of infinite love. Its end in the glory of many brethren, whose blessed distinction is to be conformed to the image of the Son of God.

All the way provided for and divinely determined in infinite wisdom. For whom he did foreknow and predestinate unto that glorious end, them he also called, justified, and glorified.

The apostle is not speaking of what is realized in time, although his words might leave this impression, for he writes in the past. God has called them, has justified them, and has glorified them. It appears all accomplished, finished, and perfected.

Yet the apostle is speaking of eternity and not of time, of the counsel of God and not of its realization in us. Well may he speak thus, not only because the counsel of God is certain of fulfillment, so that when the Almighty determines anything it is the same as if it were all accomplished, but also because the thoughts of God's heart and mind are the ultimate reality of all things. With God the calling, justification, and glorification of the brethren of the first-born are accomplished facts, real in his unchangeable and eternal counsel. With him, in his divine mind, there is from all eternity a beloved, predestinated, called, justified, and glorified people.

He has engraved them in the palms of his hands.

What is eternally real in the perfect counsel of the Most High becomes real for us in time and in the experience of a succession of moments, of days, weeks, years, and centuries—the history of the church and covenant of God in the world as the unveiling of the eternal thoughts of the eternal God.

We are called in time not by the word of man and the willing consent of our own choice, but by the irresistible power of the grace of him who calls the things that are not as if they were; called out of the darkness in which we are born by nature into his marvelous light; called out of the bondage of sin and death into the glorious liberty of the children of God; called into the blessed fellowship of God's covenant. He who is so called will know by experience the blessed operation of the calling grace that flows from the eternal foreknowledge of the triune Jehovah.

We are justified in time. We are born in sin and guilt, are by nature the children of wrath, and have no right to be called the children of God and no right to the inheritance of glory with the firstborn Son of God. But he justifies us. He makes us heirs and partakers of the adoption unto children and of the forgiveness of sins and causes us by the testimony of the indwelling Spirit to cry out, "Abba, Father." He justifies us by implanting us in the Lord Jesus Christ, causing us to be one plant with him, by faith working through love.

He also glorifies us in the end. He never leaves nor forsakes his people. He sanctifies and preserves them in the midst of the world and through the battle of life, guarding them against the power of the devil, of sin, and of death. He will raise their mortal bodies, take them into the house of many mansions, and make them like the glorified body of the firstborn Son. He will receive his people into his eternal, heavenly kingdom, where death and corruption will have fled away and the tabernacle of God will be with them forever.

Surely all these blessings of the wondrous grace of our covenant God become ours and are bestowed upon the church of God's elect in and through the process of time. Successively they are made our possession until all things are accomplished.

But with the unchangeable God it is different. All these things are real in his counsel. There, in God's firm decree, we are called, are justified, and are glorified. What takes place in time is the unveiling of his eternal purpose.

Thus all things are certain. And all things must work together for those who love God. For all his counsel must be realized in them.

Oh, the depth of riches!

16

Singular Love

"Behold, what manner of love the Father hath bestowed upon us, that we should be called the sons of God."—1 John 3:1

BEHOLD!

What marvelous love was bestowed upon us!

No cold, matter-of-fact statement the apostle makes before the church of all ages. Rather it must be seen as a shout of ecstasy pressed from the author's heart under the influence of an over-mastering emotion. Rapt out of himself and elevated above the reach of ordinary, natural perception, caught up in the sphere of heavenly and spiritual mysteries, he beckons the church to come with him and to contemplate these heavenly joys, "Behold, what manner of love the Father has bestowed upon us! Sons of God we are called."

The full implication of this marvelous truth has not yet been revealed. The term "sons of God" is still pregnant with possibilities that will not be fully realized until the day when we will see God as he is. But potentially, in spiritual principle, and in Jesus Christ we are all we ever will be. For now we are sons of God.

What unspeakable glory!

There is in the divine family of the ever-blessed Trinity one Son. In him dwells all the fullness of the Godhead perfectly, infinitely, unfathomed, and inexhaustible. Father's life is his life, Father's power is his power, Father's glory is his glory, Father's mind is his mind, Father's will is his will. He knows the Father as he is known by him; he loves the Father as he is loved by him. He is the perfect effulgence of Father's glory, the express image of his person, and he lives with Father, in his bosom, in everlasting, infinite, perfectly intimate, and confidentially friendly communion of unblemished love.

To be called sons of God is to be called after him.

Not as if we should be or aspire to be God, as the Son of God is. The essential difference between God and us, between creator and creatures, between the infinite and the finite, between the Son and the brethren of Jesus Christ will never be removed. Even so and barring all pantheism, which is of the evil one, and strictly maintaining the eternal distinction between the ever-blessed God and his creaturely children, we do not overestimate the glory and the marvel of love the apostle has in mind if we state that to be called sons of God is to be called after the only begotten of the Father.

To be sons of God implies that also we in creaturely measure partake of Father's life, Father's glory, and Father's love. It signifies that we are his and that he manifests the glory of his image through us. It means that God's mind, heart, will, and all that is within him are motivated by the living power of a Father's love toward us, so that his thoughts over us are always paternal thoughts, the counsel of his will is dominated by fatherly love, and the desires of his heart are paternal longings to bless and to glorify us, to have us with him in everlasting light of bliss and to press us in heavenly glory at his bosom. It means that our minds, wills, and hearts are dominated by this overpowering influence of a son's love toward him, so that we think as sons, will as sons, love as sons, and long to walk as sons in Father's light, to know him as we are known, to see him face-to-face, and to rejoice forever in the secret communion of his covenantal friendship.

To be called sons of God means that God calls us such, that he operates within our hearts until we call ourselves such and cry, "Abba, Father," and that he will so fill us with his life and so impress upon us the glorious image of his Son that presently the whole world will be compelled to call us children of the Most High.

To be called sons of God. Singular blessing. Marvel of love.

Behold! What manner of love!

Bestowed upon us.

As by faith with the apostle, we rise to the elevated plane of vision to behold the wonder of blessings bestowed upon us, and to contemplate with the apostle the marvel of divine love that becomes manifest in this unspeakable glory, let us not fail to emphasize this little but so significant "us."

Upon us this love was bestowed!

Upon whom?

Were we perhaps worthy of such love? When this love found you and me, where were we? What was our state before him who revealed such marvelous love toward us? What was our name? What were our rights? What was the condition of our hearts and minds before him who loved us? Could we claim any right to such love? Was there perchance within us some smoldering fires of love to which his love responded, or some lingering remnants of beauty that kindled the fire of so great a love in his divine heart?

We know better.

Search as we may, never will we find within ourselves an inkling of anything that might explain the mystery of this great love. Rather, the longer and more deeply we search in our hearts and lives, the greater the mystery of this love looms before our wondering eyes.

Rights we had none, unless condemnation can be called a right. For we were guilty, sins innumerable as the hairs of our heads testifying against us. Daily we were adding to these condemning sins and thus gathering veritable treasures of wrath for the day of righteous judgment. Our name was children of our father the devil. For true though it is that Father originally formed us after his image and that our features still bespeak that noble origin, even this remembrance of a former glory only witnesses against us. The fact is that by nature we are children of the devil. Our minds, so evidently adapted to the light of God, wantonly chose the darkness in preference to that light; our wills, so plainly formed to will Father's will, foolishly submitted themselves to the slavery of Satan; our hearts, so manifestly fitted to throb with the love of God, we sinfully filled with enmity against him. Children of wrath we were, hating God and one another, our backs toward Father, our faces toward hell.

Thus we were and there he found us, neither longing for him nor seeking him, wallowing in sin, groping in darkness, defiled in our blood.

And upon us, so guilty, so miserable, so abominable, he bestowed such manner of love.

Oh, what impenetrable mysteries!

What marvel of love!

❖

Behold!

Neither fail, as you contemplate in rapt adoration the wondrous blessing of sonship bestowed upon such abominable objects, to consider also the manner in which the Father bestowed it upon us.

For to contemplate the manner of the bestowal of God's love upon us is to gaze in mute adoration into the unfathomable depth of divine love.

Father's way to our sonship lay through the awful death of his only begotten!

It could not be otherwise.

Given the love of Father, whereby he was impelled to call us his sons, the death of his only Son must follow as a divine necessity. Indeed, as long as you view the cross as the mere *cause* of God's love, you cannot feel the thrill of John's ecstasy. God's love must be viewed as first with respect to our love and first with regard to the death of his only begotten Son. The awful cross followed with absolute necessity from the greatness of God's love.

There was no other way.

For we were not sons.

Neither could we be called sons of God as we were. An awful spectacle it would have been had God merely called us his children, who were full of sin and iniquity and had abomination written in all of our features. If he would call us children, the glory of his name demanded that he make us worthy of the name.

To be made worthy of that calling, we must be washed—washed not outwardly but inwardly, not naturally but spiritually—from all our guilty stains.

To wash us from these guilty stains no solution was sufficiently powerful except the blood of the Son of God.

That blood God provided. He sent his Son in the likeness of sinful flesh to provide the blood to wash away the sins of those whom in love he would call the sons of God. It was his Son, the child of his bosom, whom he loved with infinite love. It was his only begotten Son, his dearest, his all, upon whom he lavished from eternity the streams of his infinite love. He was God himself, the brightness of Father's glory. Father sent his Son as the gift of his love. And he sent him into all the depth of darkness, suffering, humiliation, death, and hell of which the cross remains forever the silent symbol. For God so loved the world that he gave his only begotten Son, that whosoever believes in him should not perish but have everlasting life!

Thus John's "Behold, what manner of love" takes us to the foot of the cross on Golgotha's mount. There on Calvary's hill I see the love of the Father bestowed on us. There I behold a love that stops at nothing to gain and embrace its object. There I see the love that shrinks from no sacrifice, not even from what is dearest, but gives him up even unto the death of the cross. There I behold the love that can stand alone because it is first and that is not evoked by any beauty or loveableness on the part of its object, but arises from the depth of God's infinite being.

Love stronger than death, deeper than the deepest sea, measureless in its wide embrace, higher than the heavens, transcending the understanding of the boldest human mind.

The love of God in Christ my Jesus.

What manner of love!

Behold!

❖

Marvel of the love of God.

For he not only exhibits his love to us, but he also bestows it upon us.

A mere exhibition of his love would avail little. Some would have it so. God merely shows the love he manifested in the gift of his Son in order that by the wonderful sight of his beautiful love men will open their hearts to him and thus become sons of God.

Contrary to Scripture and to the experience of every child of God is such a presentation.

Would we not shut our hearts more tightly and seal them against God's marvelous love, were the cross nothing but a sign for recognition and response of men, an expression of the longing to see its own likeness in them and nothing more? Would not our eyes refuse to see, our ears refuse to hear, and our hearts refuse to be filled with the fire of that love, if after the Father had exhibited his love, it remained up to the wills of men to respond or not to respond?

But God bestows his love upon us. For he sent forth the Spirit of his Son into our hearts, and that Spirit is a Spirit of sonship.

The Spirit of sonship carries the fire of the love of God, according to which he called us sons of God, into the depths of our hearts, by it melts them into contrition and repentance because of sin, and creates the Spirit of sonship within us so that we cry, "Abba, Father!"

Behold, then, what manner of love was lavished upon us; a love first in its eternal origin, boundless in measure, unfathomable in depth, shrinking from no sacrifice in search of its object, faithful and persevering until it has found its way into our hearts.

Behold and believe. Believe and confide. Confide and respond, so that his "my children" evokes our "my Father." And responding, walk worthy of the calling of so great a love.

As sons of God and children of light.

And in thankful worship adore the marvel of this love of the Father.

Soli Deo Gloria!

17

Divinely Distinguished

"But we are bound to give thanks alway to God for you,
brethren beloved of the Lord, because God hath from the
beginning chosen you to salvation through sanctification of the
Spirit and belief of the truth: Whereunto he called you by our
gospel, to the obtaining of the glory of our Lord Jesus Christ."
—2 Thessalonians 2:13–14

BUT...

Amazing contrast!

Similar to that found in 1 Peter 2, where the apostle writes about those who are appointed to stumble over the stone and then addresses the church, "But ye are a chosen generation..."

Both the context and the text of 2 Thessalonians 2 speak of a work of God. What else can create sharp and amazing antitheses? God is light, and there is no darkness in him. This is why he creates the light and forms the darkness.

In the preceding verses the apostle wrote about the work of God with respect to the antichrist and God's world. In verses 13–14 he speaks of the work of God in his own, the elect, the beloved of the Lord. In the context he spoke of a work of God that resulted in a strong delusion, so that men believed a lie; here he speaks of his sanctifying Spirit and his efficacious calling unto the belief of the truth. There the delusion and belief of the lie must end in the damnation of all who had pleasure in unrighteousness; here the calling unto the belief of the truth has its purpose in the obtaining of salvation, the glory of the Lord Jesus Christ.

How beautifully the church is distinguished when contrasted with the antichristian world.

Distinguished by grace!

Chosen, called, sanctified, glorified by grace.
Divinely distinguished.

❖

Unto salvation.

More specifically: to the obtaining of the glory of our Lord Jesus Christ, for salvation and the obtaining of the glory of the Lord Jesus Christ are very closely related and refer to the same thing. However, they can be distinguished. Salvation is the general, more comprehensive term; the glory of our Lord Jesus Christ is the more specific term, which looks at salvation from the perspective of its final realization and perfection. But the two can never be separated. Salvation is the obtaining of the glory of our Lord Jesus Christ. And the obtaining of the glory of our Lord Jesus Christ is salvation.

Glorious distinction!

Chosen unto salvation. Chosen, sanctified, called unto the obtaining of the glory of our Lord Jesus Christ.

Salvation comprehends the whole of the work of God in Christ by which the sinner, the whole church, the whole creation in the organic sense, is lifted from the depth and darkness of guilt and sin and condemnation, of corruption and death and the slavery of sin, of the curse and vanity, into the glory of the heavenly kingdom, the glorious liberty of the children of God, eternal life, perfect knowledge of God, perfect righteousness, perfect holiness, participation in the divine nature, friendship and fellowship on the heavenly plane with the living God in the new heavens and the new earth. It is the divine work that was promised from the beginning of the world; that was centrally realized in the cross and resurrection and exaltation of Jesus Christ and is perfect in him; that is wrought in its firstfruits in the hearts of the believers, when they are regenerated and sanctified and called out of darkness into his marvelous light; but that will not be finished and manifested in all its beauty and perfection until they are glorified body and soul, the whole church is gathered in, and the new heavens and earth are formed, in which righteousness will dwell.

Until Christ will appear.

For then we will obtain his glory. And in the obtaining of the glory of the Lord Jesus Christ, salvation will have reached its end, its final perfection.

The glory of our Lord!

All glory is of God. Apart from his glory there is no glory. It is as the Lord taught us to say in the doxology of the perfect prayer, "Thine is the glory."

Glory is the radiation of infinite goodness and perfection. And there is none who is good, who is infinitely perfect, save God himself. He is the perfect one. In him are all the perfections that are. And in him they are infinite. There is no end to his perfections. He is a light and there is no darkness in him at all. He is knowledge and wisdom, he is righteousness and holiness, he is truth and justice, he is love and grace and mercy. Therefore he is glorious, for glory is the shining forth, in himself or outside of himself, of his infinite virtues.

This glory is also Christ's.

There are not two glories, the glory of God and the glory of Jesus Christ. On the contrary, these two are one. The glory of God is given to Jesus Christ, so that it radiates from and through his human nature. In him dwells all the fullness of the Godhead bodily. All the fullness. Not merely a part of it. You cannot separate the divine virtues into two or more groups and say that one group of these divine perfections is imparted to the Lord, while the other is withheld from him. All the fullness of the Godhead dwells in him bodily. The perfect revelation of God is he. In the highest possible, though still creaturely measure, the divine virtues are imparted to and shine forth in and through the human nature of the Lord. God's knowledge and wisdom, God's righteousness and holiness, God's beauty and grace and mercy, God's power and authority—all are imparted to the Lord. He is clothed with them. That is the glory of the Lord.

It is in a very particular sense his glory, for it shines forth through him from within.

He is the eternal Son, God of God, in human nature. And the beauties of the Most High are in a creaturely yet in the highest possible degree imparted to that human nature.

In his humiliated condition this glory was hidden. Occasionally it would flash forth in his word of power and eternal life and in his marvelous works, so that even sinful men would fall down in worship and implore him to depart from them. Yet in his state of humiliation his human nature could not be bearer of this glory.

Prophetically it shone forth when his body was transfigured on the mount. There the disciples beheld his glory, a glory as of the only begotten Son of God.

When he is risen from the dead and received into heaven, and all power in heaven and in earth is given unto him, that glory is fully realized.

The obtaining of that glory is the perfection of salvation.

For we will share it.

Always it will be the glory of Jesus Christ, never ours. He merited it through his suffering and death and resurrection, and he possesses it in himself as the eternal Son of the Highest. Yet also to his people he will impart it. To each redeemed saint according to the measure of his capacity and according to his position and name in the eternal kingdom will be given perfect righteousness, holiness, wisdom and knowledge, power and authority, and heavenly beauty.

The fullness of the glory of Christ will be reflected in all the thousands upon thousands of the glorified saints.

It will be the glory of God in the Lord Jesus Christ, shining forth from the whole church.

That will be glory indeed!

Blessed distinction.

❖

Divinely distinguished.

Even as there is nothing of us in that glorious end, so the way in which that distinction is realized is wholly God's.

He sanctified us through his Spirit, and he called us into belief of the truth. He chose us unto salvation through sanctification of the Spirit and belief of the truth, whereunto he called us.

Sanctification and belief of the truth.

By the one we possess salvation, the glory of our Lord Jesus Christ, *in principle*; by the other we possess it all by faith and hope.

Sanctification is the divine work of the Holy Spirit whereby we are delivered from the power and pollution and dominion of sin and receive the beginning of a new life, the firstfruits of all the spiritual blessings in Christ, a new light, a new knowledge, a new righteousness and holiness, new power to fight the good fight even unto the end. This sanctification reveals itself in us as the beginning of perfection. Sanctification is perfection in principle. It is perfection in the midst of imperfection. It is the spirit surrounded by the flesh. It is holiness in the midst of corruption. Therefore it reveals itself as fighting, always fighting to have dominion in our whole life. It expresses itself in sorrow over sin and hatred of all corruption, and in a new delight after God.

It is the beginning of the obtaining of the glory of our Lord Jesus Christ.

Yet even now we possess final salvation, for we have been called unto the belief of the truth. The truth is the gospel, the word of God concerning his Son, which sets forth the fullness of the salvation we have in Christ and assures us of the divine purpose to realize that glorious salvation unto us. Belief of that truth is the activity of saving faith in the Lord Jesus Christ as it embraces that gospel, appropriates all its promises, and relies upon it in life and death, so that the believer is saved by hope.

Unto that belief of the truth we are called.

Called by the gospel.

Called by God.

For he called us through the gospel.

The gospel is more than a mere presentation. It is more than a mere setting forth of the salvation in Christ. It is not an offer. It is a calling. It addresses itself to you. It calls you to believe the truth. It does not merely say that there is perfect righteousness, but it calls you into the state of that righteousness. It not only explains to you the glory of the resurrection, but it also calls you into that glory. It calls, "Come unto me and I will give you rest! Come to the waters and drink! Forsake your way and taste that the Lord is merciful and that he abundantly pardons!"

The gospel is his word.

No, more. He calls us through the gospel. Otherwise we would not hear, believe, and embrace the promise and have eternal life and the glory of the Lord Jesus Christ—so foolish are we, so darkened in our understanding, so perverse of will that we refuse to heed that blessed call of the gospel.

But he calls!

When he calls, we hear and believe the truth and are saved.

Glorious, divine distinction.

❖

Adorable source.

For why, oh why, should he thus sanctify us and call us to believe the truth unto the glory of the Lord Jesus Christ?

Does he not give unto others a strong delusion so that they believe a lie and are damned?

Why then should he call me and you to believe the truth unto the obtaining of salvation, the glory of the Lord? You say, "We are beloved of the Lord." Truly, thus the text instructs us. And because we are beloved of him, he sanctifies and calls us unto the belief of the truth, so that we obtain that unspeakable glory. But does not the question return with double emphasis: Why? Why should we be loved of him, while others are not?

What is your answer?

Will you have the courage to stand before his face and reply, Because I made myself more worthy of that love, and therefore of that divine distinction, than others? Will you pretend to search for the answer to this question in yourself?

God forbid!

There is only one answer: The divine distinction is and remains divine, purely divine even to its very beginning, to its eternal source. He has chosen us.

More cannot be said.

Some read the words of Philippians 2:13 differently. They say that the Greek word translated as "hath chosen" does not signify election at all but means "hath taken." So they would translate the text as "He hath taken you from the very beginning of my preaching of the gospel to you." However, the translators did not err when they rendered "hath…chosen." The form of the word denotes a taking for oneself, for one's own possession, and therefore a preference, a choosing. Besides, when the Scriptures speak of "the beginning" without any further modification, it must be taken as referring to the beginning of all things.

This then is the answer.

From the very beginning God took you unto himself, made you his portion, his peculiar possession, preferred you.

When he created the world he had his mind on you, that you would be his own and obtain the glory of Jesus Christ. With a view to you he created all things. With a view to your glory in Christ he has ruled all things ever since.

What shall we say then?

We can only say, "Thanks be to God! Of him, through him, and to him are all things. Glory to him forever!"

18

A Heritage in Him

*"In whom also we have obtained an inheritance, being
predestinated according to the purpose of him who worketh all
things after the counsel of his own will: That we should be to the
praise of his glory, who first trusted in Christ."*
—Ephesians 1:11–12

WE!

Notice the use of the first person throughout.

> *Blessed be the God and Father of our Lord Jesus Christ,
> who hath blessed us with all spiritual blessings in heavenly
> places in Christ: According as he hath chosen us in him
> before the foundation of the world, that we should be holy
> and without blame before him in love: Having predesti-
> nated us unto the adoption of children by Jesus Christ to
> himself, according to the good pleasure of his will, To the
> praise of the glory of his grace, wherein he hath made us
> accepted in the beloved. In whom we have redemption
> through his blood, the forgiveness of sins, according to the
> riches of his grace; Wherein he hath abounded toward
> us in all wisdom and prudence…In whom also we have
> obtained an inheritance [In whom also we were made a
> heritage] (vv. 3–8, 11).*

We, us, and *our* throughout.

Beware that you do not change these pronouns into *they* and
them and *their*!

Although by making this alteration you would not change the
objective sense of the passage, you would fail to consider the riches
of which it is speaking in the right light and from the intended
viewpoint. Of the glorious riches of grace in Christ Jesus the apostle is writing here. But he displays and enumerates and evaluates

these glorious riches not merely in order that you should admire them as you would a beautiful estate of some millionaire in which you have no part and that you pass by on the road, but that you should rejoice in them as being your own!

It is the language of personal possession, of appropriating faith, that Scripture here places on the lips of the whole church.

Yes, indeed, of the whole church.

Some apply these words only to the Jews and make "also we" refer to the Jewish Christians in distinction from the converts out of the Gentiles.

It can be granted, especially in the light of the last part of verse 12, that this distinction is before the mind of the apostle. The words "we...who first trusted in Christ," or "We who had before hoped in Christ," no doubt refer to the church of the old dispensation.

Even so the words do not apply to the Jews as such, but to the Old Testament church, whose old hope was now realized in a far more glorious way than they had ever been able to conceive. In the old dispensation Israel was the church, the peculiar possession of Jehovah, the only heritage of God and the whole church. Now they had become part of a more glorious and far richer whole: "We who first hoped in Christ have now become a part of God's heritage, being predestinated according to the purpose of him who works all things according to the counsel of his own will." All things he works.

This implies, according to the tenth verse, that he will gather all things again in Christ as their everlasting head, and thus make unto himself a glorious heritage.

Of that glorious heritage we also have become a part.

To the praise of his glory.

We also.

❖

Made into a heritage.

Thus the text should be read.

Not as if it made an essential difference whether we read "have obtained an inheritance" or "have been made a heritage." The two do not exclude each other, but rather are supplementary to each other. For the truth is that when we are made into a heritage of

God, we also obtain the inheritance. The wonder is that the inheritance we obtain is exactly that we become the heritage of God. The fact is that the only inheritance one can ever obtain is the joy and glory and riches of being a heritage of the ever-blessed God.

Consciously to be God's eternal heritage, his peculiar possession in which he has his delight, upon which he looks with loving favor—that is the inheritance we obtain.

But the fact is that in the text the viewpoint is not that of our obtaining an inheritance, but of our being the heritage of God, more specifically, of our being a part of God's peculiar possession. For not the active form "we have obtained," but the passive "we have been made" a heritage is used in the original.

A figure is used here.

What was done with the land of Canaan, when the children of Israel took possession of it, is the basis of the figure. The land of Canaan was apportioned by lot to each of the tribes of Israel, except the tribes of Reuben, Gad, and half of Manasseh, so that each tribe obtained its own portion in the land of Canaan. Thus they all obtained their own part of the heritage that was promised them, and the particular part of the land that was assigned to each tribe by lot was its peculiar possession. All of Israel inherited the whole land, and the whole of Israel in the whole land was the peculiar possession, the heritage of Jehovah, but each tribe occupied its own peculiar place in that possession.

Such is the figure implied in our passage.

A figure it is, not in the sense that anything serves as an illustration of a subject that is being discussed, but because the figure in this case was designed to be the prototype of the reality that was to come. Israel in the land of Canaan was very really the heritage of God, his peculiar possession, Jehovah's portion, but it was at the same time the shadow of things to come, the picture of a better hope, the type of the ultimate and eternal realization of the "purpose of him who worketh all things after the counsel of his own will." For he has purposed in himself to gather together in one all things in Christ, the things in heaven and the things on earth, and to make the church in Christ heir of that glorious inheritance. Of this, Israel in Canaan is the beginning, but also the figure and type.

Even as Israel in the old dispensation in the earthly land of

Canaan was the peculiar possession of God, so Christ and his glorious and perfected church in the new heavens and earth is the ultimate realization of Jehovah's heritage.

Beautiful heritage!

Peculiar that heritage will be, no longer in the sense that it will be a small portion of God's handiwork that will be the object of his delight, in distinction from the rest of the world that lies in darkness and serves dead idols instead of the living God, as was Israel in the midst of the nations around them; but only in the positive sense that it is the object of God's everlasting love and favor, and that it will be solely to the praise of the glory of his grace in the beloved. For God's peculiar heritage will then embrace all things in heaven and on earth.

That heritage will be one, a glorious, harmonious whole, in which each part will serve in its own peculiar place and position to enhance the beauty of the whole.

In the whole of all things as God's heritage, the church of Christ will occupy the chief place.

That church will not consist of a multitude of individual saints but will be a well-ordered whole, in which each part, each group, each individual will occupy the particular place assigned to him by the grand builder and artificer.

For that place each church in every period in time and each individual believer are foreordained and prepared in time.

Thus it could be said to those whom the apostle had in mind in our passage, and to the church of every age: We also have been made a heritage, a peculiar portion in the great heritage of God.

Marvelous work of God!

Blessed heritage!

❖

We also became a portion.

Wonderful wisdom of God, and marvelous providence of him who works all things after the counsel of his own will.

No doubt the passage refers to the church of the old dispensation, which for years constituted the entire heritage of God, but now became a part of the larger and all-comprehensive possession of Jehovah. This is evident from the text, which qualifies this portion of God's heritage as those "who first trusted in Christ." This is shown too by the words "ye also" of the next verse, referring to the church gathered out of the Gentiles.

We also...and you also.

We who before hoped in Christ, and you who are now sealed, became a portion of the great, harmonious heritage of God.

All became one in Christ, yet each in his own place.

Amazing revelation of God's wisdom! Israel had before hoped in Christ. Yes, they were the whole of God, even then. Theirs were the covenants and the promises. In the land of Canaan they possessed a partial realization of the promise. But in Christ, the one who was to come, they had their hope. Reality was not yet. They lived under the law, and under the law they could only take hold of shadows. Hence they looked forward in hope. In the promised seed they trusted. On him they fixed their hope. For him they looked. When he would come, they would become the glorious and everlasting heritage of Jehovah in eternal reality.

They first hoped in Christ; no one else.

They were the heritage of God, not the other nations. When they looked for the realization of the promise and fixed their longing eyes on the future, they still envisaged that glorious future only as an elevation and perfection and extension of their own national existence. Though their prophets sometimes spoke of larger things, who understood the glorious purpose of God? Who of those who before hoped in Christ could possibly apprehend the larger purpose of God's good pleasure?

Now the wider purpose of the God of their salvation had been revealed.

It had been known that it was the good pleasure of God's will that in the dispensation of the fullness of time God would gather together in one all things in Christ, things in heaven and things on earth, and that they, who had before hoped in Christ as a single and isolated nation, would merge into the larger whole of God's heritage and become a portion of a universal church and a universal inheritance. The smaller heritage had widened into a universal possession, and what was formerly the whole now had become a part of a far more glorious whole; and in becoming a part, it had entered into the possession of a more glorious inheritance.

The whole had changed into a portion, and the portion it had become was more glorious than the whole it had once been.

Marvelous mind of God!

His adorable wisdom and purpose it was that had become manifest in it all.

Had they not been predestined unto this, according to the divine purpose?

How else could this marvelous history be explained? No blind fate could possibly work out such a glorious purpose. There is manifest wisdom in it all. This wisdom has its source in the counsel of God's own will motivated by infinite intelligence and perfect though incomprehensible wisdom. It has a purpose, an ultimate aim, an omega, to be attained, with a view to which all designs in that same counsel serve as means to an end. That purpose is that in the highest possible way we and all things should be to the praise of his glory. And this highest possible revelation of his glory and praise is to be attained by gathering together in one all things in Christ, things in heaven and things on earth.

Such is the purpose of him who works all things after the counsel of his own will.

According to that purpose, in harmony with it, they who had before hoped in Christ were predestinated. Hence they could not possibly remain the whole of God's heritage.

Because of that divine predestination according to that purpose, they could not remain isolated; they must merge into the greater and more glorious whole.

A portion they became.

And richer than the former whole is now the portion.

Amazing purpose of God!

❖

Soli Deo Gloria!

Yes, emphatically and exclusively: to God alone the praise!

That we should be to the praise of his glory. We who before hoped in Christ and have now become a portion of God's glorious heritage; we who after we heard the word of truth, the gospel of our salvation, were sealed into that glorious heritage of God by the Holy Spirit of promise.

Let us say without qualification, "To God alone be the praise! Blessed be the God and Father of our Lord Jesus Christ, who has so blessed us with all spiritual blessings in heavenly places in Christ."

Do not attribute to man any praise that belongs to him alone.

For he not only purposes all things, but he also works all things after the counsel of his own will. His counsel is not a dead design, the blueprint of an architect to be worked out by others under his direction. It is the living, almighty, eternal decree of the living God. The counsel of God is the counseling God. He alone works out his own counsel. He perfects his own work. He attains his own aim. He realizes his own purpose. He works all things according to that purpose. All things have their own place in that marvelous counsel of God. All creatures have been predestinated to their own place and to serve their own purpose in his eternal good pleasure. Rational and nonrational creatures, men and angels, good and evil, things in heaven and things in earth and things under the earth— all things literally are comprehended in that living counsel of the Most High.

According to that purpose he himself works all things. Therefore they cannot fail.

Because of this, the praise will forever be his alone.

The praise of his glory.

19

By Grace

*"For by grace are ye saved through faith; and that not of
yourselves: it is the gift of God."—Ephesians 2:8*

For!

Let us not overlook this little but significant word.

For by grace are ye saved. The conjunction presents the truth
expressed as a reason for something else, an explanation of something that has been mentioned in the context. It informs us that
this statement does not stand alone, that it is not an isolated truth
that one can accept or not accept without much effect for the rest of
the content of his faith, a truth that one can either deny or confess
as of little or no practical significance and importance.

For by grace are ye saved.

It means that salvation by grace and by grace only is an indispensable condition for something else, a ground, a foundation,
without which that something else cannot stand. Denying it is like
destroying the foundation of an edifice: you pull down the whole
structure. It is like cutting away at the root of a tree: you kill the
tree.

That for which this statement is the reason can be read in the
immediately preceding verse: "That in the ages to come he might
shew the exceeding riches of his grace in his kindness toward us
through Christ Jesus."

God is rich in mercy.

And he saved us. Even when we were dead in sins, he quickened
us together with Christ, and raised us up together with him, and
made us sit together in heavenly places.

All this in order to show the exceeding riches of his grace.
Through our salvation the riches of his grace must be displayed.

But how is this possible unless salvation is by grace?

By grace only.

❖

In grace your salvation has its source.

For the eternal fountainhead whence the whole blessed stream of your salvation gushes forth is sovereign election.

Chosen you are unto salvation before the foundation of the world. And the motive of God's election of his people is grace—sovereign, absolutely free grace.

Pure grace.

Nothing else determined God in predestinating you unto conformity to the image of his Son. There are those who find in man the reason and the determining factor of God's election. They too would emphasize that salvation is all of grace, not of works. It is grace that God sent his only begotten Son into the world, and grace that you may become partaker of the blessings of salvation in him. They speak too of election unto glory. Only the elect actually become heirs of eternal salvation. But election? According to them, is it also of mere and pure and sovereign grace? Ah, no! It is not of grace, say they, but of works. Yes, of works, though they themselves would use other terms to describe their view of election. Is it not an election of works that teaches that God found or foresaw in the elect a willingness to accept Christ and the terms of his salvation, in distinction from others whom he foreknew as stubborn and unwilling to come to Christ?

Then it is not of grace. Then it was man, his goodness, the foreseen choice of his will to receive Christ that determined God's choice. Then it is not grace that makes the elect acceptable to and beloved by God in his eternal counsel, but it is some element of goodness in man that induced the Most High to prefer him above others. When God shows forth the riches of his grace in the salvation of the elect, they will always be mixed with this excellence of man.

But God forbid!

For you are saved by grace.

This implies that your salvation is of God from beginning to end, from its eternal source in the counsel of God to its final manifestation in glory in the day of Christ.

Grace ordained you unto salvation. This signifies not that God's election is arbitrary, but that it has its reason and motive in God alone. Of him are all things. God is gracious. Full of grace is he in himself, apart from any relationship with or attitude toward the creature, for he is good, the sole good, the implication of all infinite perfections. As the supreme and only and infinitely good, he is the perfection of all beauty. He is pleasant and altogether lovely, and there are pleasures at his right hand forevermore. Eternally he is attracted by his own beauty, for he is God triune, Father, Son, and Holy Ghost. Of the Father, through the Son, in the Spirit, God knows himself, beholds himself, his grace and beauty, and inclines unto himself in eternal and infinite divine favor.

This infinite loveliness and divine pleasure in his own beauty is God's grace.

By grace you are chosen.

By the knowledge of and attraction to the loveliness of his own perfection, God was divinely urged to ordain his people—a people who would be perfect as he is perfect, lovely as he is lovely, for whom he has foreknown, them he also did predestinate to be conformed according to the image of his Son—a people upon whom he looked with eternal good pleasure, a people in whom he would show forth the infinite riches of his grace, a people who would taste that the Lord is good.

For by grace are you saved.

❖

Blessed grace.

For by grace are we reconciled unto God.

The same grace that motivated the Most High to ordain us unto salvation, according to which it was his purpose to make us lovely even as he is lovely, explains why he reconciled us unto himself through the death of his Son.

Saved we are by grace.

This means that we were lifted from the deepest depth of sin and shame, of guilt and condemnation, of corruption and death, to the highest possible bliss of eternal righteousness and life and glory.

Saved we are.

Created we were with all the elect in the first man Adam, who was made a living soul; who had life, but not in himself; who lived without being the lord of life; whose glory was corruptible, whose righteousness could be lost, whose life was mortal, and who was of the earth earthly. In him we violated God's covenant and became guilty, liable to death and damnation, subject to corruption, children of wrath. Our condition was hopeless as far as we were concerned. For in Adam we could sin, but we could never pay a ransom for our sin; we could die in him, but we had no power to regain life in God's favor; we could turn away from the Fount of life, but never could we return to him. We could only increase the guilt of our sin every day, through every word we spoke, by every deed we performed, with every breath we took. Enemies of God we were, hating him and hating one another.

Saved we are.

Saved by grace, by free and sovereign grace.

For even then, when we were dead in sin, objects of God's righteous wrath, who could never be restored to the favor of God unless we would willingly take the way through the depths of hell, he loved us and reconciled us unto himself.

Us he reconciled. Do not express this differently. Do not say that he reconciled himself to us, for to reconcile is to restore a relation of love and faith and friendship that has been violated and broken, the relation of the covenant. On his part that relation was never violated. He is the eternal I AM, who changes not. With an eternal, immutable, sovereign love he loved his own, even when they were rebels. Us he reconciled. Us he restored to that state in which we were the proper objects of his favor and blessing, the state of eternal righteousness.

For such is reconciliation: restoration to favor in the way of perfect justice.

Justice required satisfaction, and satisfaction of the justice of God with respect to our sin could be accomplished only by a voluntary act of perfect obedience even unto death. Not merely to suffer the punishment for sin is satisfaction. Even the damned in hell suffer the agonies of death, yet they do not atone for their sins. God demands that we love him. This means that the sinner who violated God's law and trampled underfoot his covenant must love God in his righteous wrath, love him in death and hell, if ever the sinner is to atone.

This act of perfect obedience we could never perform.

Reconciled we are by grace.

For when in sovereign grace he chose us and ordained us to be conformed according to the image of his Son, he chose us in him. By grace he ordained his Son to be the head of the church, to become flesh, to assume the burden of our sin and guilt, to enter into our deepest woe, to become sin for us, so that we could become the righteousness of God in him.

By grace he was sent into the world.

By grace he chose the way of suffering and death, the way through the depth of hell, there to lay upon God's altar the sacrifice that would be sufficient to satisfy the justice of God.

God was in Christ reconciling the world unto himself.

That he could show forth the riches of his grace.

For by grace we are saved.

By grace only.

❖

Mighty grace.

For grace is also the power of God by which we are delivered from the dominion of sin and death.

Reconciliation alone is no salvation, nor could it possibly lead to salvation if the operation of grace ceased at the cross. It must be applied, so that from darkness we are translated into life, from sin into righteousness, and with cords of love we are united again with the heart of God.

How could this be accomplished?

Will we say that from the cross onward salvation is the work of man? That God has done his part, and now man must realize what God has accomplished? Or will we allow the grace of God and the will of man to mix, harmoniously and sweetly to work together to perfect the salvation manifested on the cross of Christ? Will we say that on God's part he is willing to save all men, that he offers the reconciliation accomplished on the cross to everyone with the intention to save everyone, and that for the rest it depends upon the choice of man's will?

God forbid!

The riches of his grace must be revealed.

By grace are we saved.

Through faith we are saved. It is not *on condition* of faith, a condition that man must fulfill if God is to bestow the blessings of salvation on him. There are no conditions unto salvation at all. It is not because of faith, as if faith were the new work required to obtain salvation. There is no work unto salvation—not even faith or the work of faith.

For by grace are we saved, through faith.

Faith is the means unto salvation.

It is the spiritual tie that unites us with Christ, the spiritual faculty whereby we know him, taste him, long for him, trust in him, rely on him, appropriate him, live out of him as the young tree draws its life-giving sap out of the ground through its roots.

Through faith.

It is God's means, a means of grace, a power that is wrought in our inmost hearts by the mighty grace of God. By grace you are saved, through faith; and that not of yourselves, it is the gift of God.

By grace he unites us with Christ.

By the power of grace he quickens us together with him, making us new creatures. By grace he calls us, powerfully, irresistibly, sweetly, out of darkness into the light of the gospel. By grace he implants the faith in us whereby we embrace the Christ of God and all his benefits.

It is not of ourselves; it is God's gift.

Salvation is of the Lord.

Wonderful grace.

❖

Abiding grace.

For we are saved.

Because it is by pure and sovereign grace that we are saved, we will surely be saved even unto the end of eternal glory.

Always salvation is of the Lord; never does it become of us.

Always it is by grace; never does it become of works. Even as it is in free, divine, absolutely sovereign grace that he chose us and ordained us to become conformed according to the image of his Son; and even as it was by that same grace that he reconciled us unto himself through the death of his Son; and even as it was pure grace that wrought the faith within us whereby we lay hold on the Christ of God; even so it is by grace that we are preserved unto the final salvation that will be revealed in the last time.

By grace we are preserved.

Through the power of that gracious preservation we persevere.

For on the one hand, even our perseverance is not by works, nor on account of works, nor by virtue of our cooperation with the grace of God. It is of pure grace. Yet on the other hand, this preserving grace of God is not a power that remains external to us, so that we are passively, unconsciously perhaps, carried into glory. It is a power within us that causes us to hold on to the God of our salvation.

Grace preserves, and we persevere.

Who shall separate us?

Unchangeable grace!

20

Riches of Grace

"And of his fulness have all we received, and grace for grace."
—*John 1:16*

MARVELOUS confession! Let us not overlook the personal confession concerning Christ in these words from John's gospel.

Out of his fullness have all we received.

This is not a mere dogmatic statement by a theologian. It is not even a mere objective testimony of the fullness and glory of the Son of God. But it is an expression of experience, of the experience of faith with respect to Christ as the ever-flowing, ever-abundant, ever-satisfying fountain of grace.

John the Baptist witnessed of him. He spoke of Christ as the one who came after him but was preferred before him, and was before him. He confessed that he was not the Christ and pointed away from himself to the Lamb of God who takes away the sin of the world, bearing record of him that he is the Son of God.

This testimony of John was amply corroborated by the experience of those who had sought Christ and found him, who had been implanted into him by a living bond of faith. For to as many as received him, who were born not of blood, nor of the will of the flesh, nor of the will of man, but of God, to them he gave power to become the sons of God. Having spiritual contact and fellowship with him, they learned to know him as the superabundant fountain of grace: "Of his fulness have all we received, and grace for grace."

Blessed Christ.

Amazing source of spiritual abundance.

All we—apostles, their converts, the whole church, the believers of every age—have received out of him. He alone is the fullness from whom all receive and are satisfied.

Even grace for grace, a never-ending stream.
Wonderful testimony!

❖

Grace for grace.

Grace is the glorious beauty, the blessed pleasantness, the sweet attractiveness of God's eternal and infinite goodness. For God is the implication of all infinite perfections. As the only good, he is supremely fair, beautiful, and pleasant. He is such in himself, apart from any relation to the creature, for all God's perfections are eternal, and he is the I AM also in his grace. As the infinitely good God, he is beautiful; and as the triune, he eternally beholds the beauty of his perfections and is attracted to himself.

Such is God's grace absolutely, eternally, in God.

Grace is the attitude of sovereign favor the eternal God is pleased to assume with relation to the people of his choice in his eternal counsel of election. Eternally he has them with him and before him, not as they are in history, in their sin and corruption, but as he sovereignly conceived of them in his good pleasure in Christ, the firstborn of every creature and the first begotten of the dead. He beholds no sin in Jacob, no iniquity in Israel. Nothing but beauty and perfection and glory he beholds in them. For whom he has foreknown, them he also did predestinate to be conformed to the image of his Son; and them he also called, justified, and glorified. He engraved them in the palms of his hands. They are continually before him. Always he is inclined toward them in eternal loving-kindness and regards them in favor.

Such is God's grace eternally, in his counsel, toward his people.

Grace is the revelation of this eternal good pleasure of favor and loving-kindness to the people of his love, as they come into the world as sinners, guilty and damnable, corrupt and defiled, children of wrath; as they walk in darkness and increase their guilt daily; as they lie in the midst of death and there is no way out. Even to them, who have forfeited every token of favor and have made themselves worthy of eternal damnation, God reveals himself as gracious, justifying the ungodly, forgiving their iniquities, adopting them unto his children, and making them worthy of eternal life and glory.

Such is God's grace, revealed in time as an attitude of unchange-able favor to his people in their sin and death.

Grace is the wonderful, amazing, exceedingly mighty power of God, operating through Christ in his Spirit, whereby he changes the sinner from a cursing rebel into a praying child, from a blas-pheming fool into a praising saint, calling him out of darkness into his marvelous light, instilling into his deepest heart the new life of the risen Lord, cleansing and sanctifying him by his Spirit through the word of God, preserving him in the midst of a world of dark-ness and corruption, and preparing him for the inheritance incor-ruptible and undefiled that never fades away.

Such is the grace of him who quickens the dead, as a power operating in the elect unto salvation.

By grace are you saved.

Grace is the implication of all spiritual riches and gifts and blessings with which the God and Father of our Lord Jesus Christ fills us from above. Indeed, grace is one; but it is amazingly rich in a diversity of blessings, of new life, of faith, of hope, of righteousness, of the forgiveness of sins, of the adoption unto children, of the love of God, of the peace that passes all understanding, of patience, of strength to fight the battle, of comfort and consolation, of light and joy, of knowledge and wisdom, of the resurrection from the dead and eternal glory.

Such is the grace of him who has blessed us with all spiritual blessings in heavenly places in Christ.

Grace is the effect and reflection of all these riches and favors of the God of salvation in the sinner who is so favored. By the power of God's beautiful grace, the sinner also becomes good and beauti-ful before God and men, and this spiritual beauty is supremely ex-pressed when in humble adoration he prostrates himself before the Most High and exclaims, "O, my God! Grace, thanks, be to thee!"

Such is the grace of God perfected in us.

Grace for grace or, according to the original, grace instead of grace. The phrase is somewhat difficult to translate. Yet, as fre-quently is the case with the wonderful language of Holy Writ, the general meaning is clear.

Grace instead of grace means that one gift of grace follows upon another, so that we are overwhelmed by its riches. Hardly have we had time to receive and appreciate and give thanks for one blessing, when another is bestowed upon us. Grace upon grace.

Grace upon grace means too that the stream of grace is continuous. It never ends. It never ceases. We could never live or stand or persevere except for that constant stream of grace.

Grace upon grace surely means that it is always and ever grace. Never does one gift of grace put us in a position to merit the next. Grace is always the last word.

Grace for grace signifies that the stream of grace is inexhaustible. Out of Jehovah's fullness we all receive constantly and abundantly, yet he is always full!

We all received, and do receive, and will receive to ages unending, grace for grace.

Amazing mystery of salvation!

❖

Out of his fullness.

He, the Christ, is the fullness of our emptiness.

Full of grace and glory is he in himself.

For he is the Son of God, God of God, Light of Light, the Word who was in the beginning with God and who was God, the only begotten Son who is in the bosom of the Father, the image of the invisible God, the express image of his substance, and the effulgence of his glory. In him are light and life and glory and eternal joy.

The inexhaustible fullness of divine grace is he.

He is also the fountain of abundant grace for us, for God ordained this Son from before the foundation of the world to be the revelation of all the fullness of grace. "It pleased the Father that in him should all fulness dwell" (Col. 1:19). He, the eternal Son, was ordained to be the firstborn of every creature and the firstborn of the dead, in order that in all things he might have the preeminence. He was ordained to be the head of his church, all whom the Father gave him, that he might be the captain of their salvation and through him God would lead all his children to glory. He, the Son, was ordained to be God's mediator for his people, the strong arm of the Lord, to take their sins upon his mighty shoulders, to represent them in the hour of judgment, to blot out the guilt of their iniquities, and to prepare for them garments of righteousness, clothed in which they can walk before the face of God and dwell in his house forever. He was ordained to be the living head of his church, which is his body, the fullness of him who fills all in all, in order that in him the wondrous stream of divine grace could break through unto us and its fountain would be opened unto everyone the Father gave to him.

His fullness.

In the fullness of grace he was revealed in the fullness of time. For he, the glorious and eternal Son of God, became flesh and dwelled among us, and we beheld his glory, the glory as of the only begotten of the Father, full of grace and truth. He came in the flesh and blood of the children, his brethren. He was sent in the likeness of sinful flesh and for sin. He, the Lord, was seen in the form of a servant and came in the likeness of man. He united himself with us in an everlasting union, and became our Immanuel, God with us.

The Son in the form of a servant.

God in human flesh.

The eternal fullness in the form of our emptiness.

Thus, and only thus, could the eternal fullness become the fountain of grace upon grace for us. For in that form of a servant, standing at the head of all his own, he could and did bear the iniquity of our sins. With the load of our transgressions upon him, he took our place before the face of God in the dark hour of wrath and judgment and obediently descended into the depth of death and desolation. He completely emptied himself to become our fullness. Down into hell he went, freely, obediently, from love of the Father and of his own, in order there in the depth of hell to sprinkle his lifeblood upon God's altar, to atone for all our transgressions, and to obtain from God the right to fill us forever with the fullness of his grace.

There on Calvary the divine fullness, the Son of God in the flesh, emptied himself.

There he labored and toiled, with bloody sweat upon his brow, in agony of soul and body, to break through the floods of our iniquity.

And he had the victory!

In Joseph's garden on the third day, the fountain of life and grace broke through the darkness of our death, for God raised him from the dead and gave him testimony that he had finished the work, that he had blotted out the sins of all his brethren, and that he had merited the right to clothe them with garments of eternal righteousness and to fill them with his blessings.

Light broke through the darkness.

Sin in the flesh was condemned forever.

Death was swallowed up of life.

And he ascended into the highest heavens, was clothed with all power in heaven and on earth, and received the promise of the Spirit, in order by that Spirit and through his word to cause the fountain of his fullness to flow into our emptiness forever.

O blessed Lord! Light that dispels our darkness, righteousness that overcomes our unrighteousness, fire of love that consumes our enmity, our resurrection and life.

Fullness of our emptiness.

Fountain of grace.

❖

Out of his fullness…

We have received, we all, even grace for grace.

Even this that we received of him is not of ourselves; it is all of him.

In us there is no power of receptivity for him. In us is the darkness, and never will we turn to the light unless his light first penetrates into our night. In us is the power of corruption, and never will we seek to be clothed with the garments of righteousness he prepared for us unless he first breaks the shackles of iniquity that hold us in bondage. We lie in the midst of death, and before we can even drink from the fountain of life and grace that is Christ, the power of his resurrection must break the bonds of our death.

We received and do receive of him even grace for grace.

It is true, there is in this reception of grace out of his fullness also activity on our part, the activity of faith, whereby we become deeply conscious of our own emptiness, of our darkness and death, of our sin and iniquity, of the hopelessness of our state; whereby we apprehend him in the fullness of his light and love and righteousness and complete redemption; whereby we long for him, to drink from the fountain of his grace and to taste that the Lord is good; whereby we know him, seek refuge in him, cast ourselves upon him, and appropriate him and all the riches of salvation in him.

But never is this act on our part first. Nor could it be.

Nor is it thus, that his act whereby he imparts of his fullness to us and our act whereby we receive of his fullness meet in cooperation to accomplish our salvation. On the contrary, he is always first. He imparts of his fullness to us, and we receive. He gives us the faith, and we believe. He draws us, and we come.

He draws us to the fountain, and we drink.

Grace for grace. Always grace.

Thanks be to God!

22

Thy Mercy, O Lord

"Let thy mercy, O LORD, be upon us,
according as we hope in thee."
—Psalm 33:22

NEW YEAR'S morning.

Yet there is nothing new under the sun.

Old things have not passed away; all things have not become new.

Still we move about and whirl around, with all men and all things, within the vicious circle of vanity, hemmed in on all sides by impenetrable darkness, limited everywhere by things earthly and temporal, and there appears to be no way out.

Vanity of vanities!

It is still true also on New Year's morning that our eyes open upon a scene of labor and toil that yields no profit. Generations come and go, children are brought forth with travail, men pass away in sorrow, and there is no progress from one generation to another. The sun rises and sets, and in its course through the heavens it witnesses the same scenes of fruitless activity and toil every day. All things earthly are like the wind, which "goeth toward the south, and turneth about unto the north; it whirleth about continually, and the wind returneth again according to his circuits" (Eccl. 1:6); or like the rivers that run into the sea without ever filling it.

New year?

Many there are on the first morning of another year who would fain see something new, who express the hope for something new, who bless their fellow men as if there were a basis for the expectation of something new. Men also continue to boast that their houses will stand forever.

Yet there is no new thing under the sun.

All things are so full of labor that man cannot utter it.

As far as eye can see the new year bears the same aspect as the old. It invites us to meet the same problems, to pass through the same labor and sorrow, the same sufferings and death. Man's days are still like the grass. Still his life flourishes as the flower of the field, with precarious tenderness, and still the winds blow and pass over it to snatch it away. And still its very place forgets that it ever was.

New year?

Ah, but how old, how frightfully old do all things appear, when especially on this first morning of the year nineteen hundred forty we look about us in the world! Even as of old, men reveal that the picture Scripture draws of them is true and that they are filled with all unrighteousness, fornication, wickedness, covetousness, maliciousness; full of envy, murder, debate, deceit, malignity; that they are whisperers, backbiters, haters of God, despiteful, proud, boasters, inventors of evil things, disobedient to parents, without understanding, covenant breakers, without natural affection, implacable, unmerciful; that there is none who seeks after God, none who does good. That their throat is an open sepulcher, that with their tongue they use deceit, that the poison of asps is under their lips, that their mouth is full of cursing and bitterness, that their feet are swift to shed blood, that destruction and misery are in their ways, that there is no fear of God before their eyes, that they know not the way of peace, that...

But why say more?

With the memory of the horrible world war still fresh in their minds, while the wounds inflicted in that terrible conflict are still bleeding, and while the ruins caused by shells and bombs are still testifying of the destruction war brings to the world, the nations are at one another's throats again, armed to the teeth, hatred in their hearts, murder in their eyes!

Germany-Poland; France-England-Germany; Russia-Finland.

Covenants are made and violated as if they never existed.

The mighty trample underfoot the weak and boast of it.

The way of peace they have not known, though all profess to seek it.

New year? Ah, but how old, how hopelessly old is the world and are all things that present themselves to our eyes!

Progress? Culture? Ah, but how wearily and despairingly we move and whirl about in the vicious circle.

No, indeed, there is no new thing under the sun.

Vanity of vanities!

❖

What shall we say then?

What shall be our attitude on this first morning of the year of our Lord nineteen hundred forty?

Shall we just deliberately close our eyes to reality, to the woe and misery of the world, to the fact that there is indeed nothing new, and vainly meet one another with the blessing of a "Happy New Year" in the earthly sense? Shall we just pull our wishbones and speak of wealth and prosperity, of life and health, of houses that stand for aye, of the coming glorious day of man?

Then on New Year's morning we join the company of the blind who lead the blind.

Shall we put our trust in the basic goodness of man, or perhaps in the superficial goodness of a common grace, and join our voices to theirs who boast of the progress of culture and civilization, of science and art, of the power and ingenuity of man, and who, in spite of the glaring fact that such horribly old things happen all about us, persist in their promise of a new day of peace and prosperity, because man's efforts will ultimately be crowned with success?

Then on New Year's morning our number is the number of mere man: six hundred sixty-six! Toil without rest. Efforts without success. The week without the Sabbath.

Shall we sit down in dumb despair, confessing that there is no hope, no light anywhere in the darkness, no life in the midst of this death, no way out of our misery and woe, no victory, no peace?

Then on New Year's morning we are one of those who seek death and cannot find it.

But God forbid that we should either boast in man or despair because of him.

Rather let the dawn of the first day of the year of our Lord nineteen hundred forty find us on our knees, humbly seeking the face of him who revealed himself in Jesus Christ.

Not to ask him for things he will never give. Not to seek earthly things, but to leave all things to him, if only we can be assured of his everlasting mercy.

Then all will be well.

Our days may be like the grass, our life like the flower of the field. All things may be vanity in this present world of sin.

But from everlasting to everlasting is the mercy of the Lord toward those who fear him.

Let, O Lord, thy mercy be upon us.

According as we hope in thee.

❖

Thy mercy, Lord.

We hope in thee only.

There is in this prayer the expression of an attitude of humble dependence.

We feel helplessly lost in sin ourselves and realize deeply that we can do nothing apart from him. We are conscious of our ignorance and darkness, and we acknowledge that we do not know the way. We are like a man who travels in an utterly strange, mountainous country, intersected by hidden ravines and dangerous precipices. We cannot find our way. We are surrounded by dangers. All our self-confidence is gone. A guide we need. Someone we look for who knows the way out, upon whom we can depend, in whom we can trust. We do not care to control things ourselves, but we are wholly willing to leave all things to God, to follow where he leads, to depend solely on him.

We hope in thee.

And we are conscious of misery. We are in trouble, in darkness and death, in the power of sin and corruption. What is more, we humbly acknowledge that we are wholly unworthy of God's favor and have nothing on which to plead for deliverance from our wretchedness. All our pride is humbled in the dust.

In the world there is such a thing as proud dependence. When we are conscious of our worthiness, of our riches; when we can afford to reward our guide royally; when we feel that we can order him about and that we really do him a great favor by trusting in him and permitting him to lead the way then we are dependent, but pride is the chief characteristic of our attitude of dependence. Not so in this prayer. We hope in God; and we implore his mercy.

Humble dependence.

Dependence upon God who is God.

On him of whose praise this psalm is full.

He it is who made the heavens by his word and all the host of them by the breath of his mouth; who gathers the waters of the sea together in a heap and lays up the depth in storehouses; who spoke and it was done, who commanded and it stood fast. He brings the counsel of the heathen to nothing and makes the devices of the people of no effect. His counsel shall stand forever, and the thoughts of his heart to all generations.

With whom shall he be compared?

He even fashions the hearts of men alike and considers all their works. But for his power all things are vain. There is no safety in the multitude of a host, in the power and invention, in the ingenuity and wisdom of man. A horse is a vain thing, and he shall not deliver anyone by his great strength.

But blessed is the nation whose God is Jehovah.

Blessed is he who in humble dependence looks away from the creature, in order to confide solely in the Lord his God.

O Lord, we hope in thee.

Thy mercy be upon us.

❖

Thy mercy.

Thy everlasting mercy, which is from everlasting to everlasting upon those who fear thee, be upon us.

For if that mercy is upon us, we need nothing more; we will ask for nothing else.

There is in this prayer the expression of an attitude of childlike trust, of a confidence that commits the way wholly to him.

Blessed trust!

How often we are lacking in that quiet trust that is confidence in God. We would trust him then in part only. Oh, we do seek his face, and we do implore his help, and we desire to be the objects of his mercy. But at the same time there are a thousand other things, vain things, things of mere man, of the creature, conditions, circumstances, on which we rely, in which we seek rest, or of which we are afraid. The assurance that he guides and cares is really not sufficient. His word of promise alone cannot satisfy our soul. We want to see. We desire to understand. Besides, we would like to explain to the Most High just how our way should be, to dictate to our guide in just what direction he ought to lead. When there is sickness we would have health; when there is sorrow we desire joy; when adversity meets us in the way we cry for prosperity; when there is war we pray for peace; and when presently the dark shadows of death grow longer and steal over our soul, we want to live.

The result is that we do not taste the joy of wholly trusting in the name of our God and of resting assured in the will of him who assures us that all things work together for good to those who love him, whom he has called according to his purpose.

The peace that passes all understanding and that is the sure fruit of committing the way to him alone does not set our soul at rest.

Thy mercy, O Lord.

Let it be upon us, and it suffices.

For according to that mercy he loved us with an everlasting love. In his abundant mercy he predestinated us to be made like unto the image of his Son, the firstborn among many brethren, and purposes to deliver us from all our misery and to make us heirs of the glory of his heavenly and eternal tabernacle, where there will be no night, where the former things will be forgotten, and where he will wipe away all tears from our eyes. In that abundant mercy he gave his only begotten Son and sent him into our death and darkness, so that we live in the everlasting light of his countenance.

In that same eternal mercy he determined your and my way, which must lead all of us and each of us individually to the glory and to our particular place in the glory that he would have us inherit.

That may be a way of adversity, of suffering and sorrow, the way of death. But in his mercy it is the way to eternal life and glory.

Let that mercy, then, be upon us, Lord.

And it will quite suffice.

Childlike trust.

❖

For we hope in thee.

According as we hope in thee, let thy mercy be upon us.

There is in this prayer the expression of an attitude of calm assurance. Of the assurance that our prayer is answered, that our petition is heard of God much more certainly than I even feel in my heart that I desire it of him. Many things we ask that we will never receive, because we do not seek the things above, but the things below, even in our prayers. But the prayer for his mercy, the prayer that he will forgive our sins, that he will deliver us from all our woe, that he will lead us to his eternal glory, and that he will cause all things to work together for our salvation—that prayer cannot fail.

For we hope in him. And this hope is also the work of his grace. Never does he forsake the work of his own hands.

Blessed assurance. According as we hope in thee, O Lord.

So let thy mercy be upon us.

Now and forevermore!

23

Everlasting Mercy

*"But the mercy of the LORD is from
everlasting to everlasting upon them that fear him."*
—Psalm 103:17

Man...but...God.

How wholly different!

Our little, fleeting breath of life...but...God's abiding eternity, never begun, never ending, always perfect.

As for man, his days are like the grass. As a flower of the field so he flourishes, precariously because of its tenderness and the fiercely blowing winds...but...the mercy of Jehovah is from everlasting to everlasting.

As for man, he is like the tender flower, dangerously flourishing in the open field, exposed to the rough wind that blows regardless of the flower's delicateness. The flower is soon gone, and the place of it knows it no more. Man and the flower are forgotten when they are gone. Although man appears to occupy a large place in the midst of the transient things of time, the gap that was expected when the cruel wind of death removed him is astonishingly small, and it is soon filled.

But the mercy of the Lord is from everlasting to everlasting.

Marvelous!

The one is a matter of everyone's everyday experiences, for we all fly away and are soon cut off. People rejoice over us, because man is born into the world. Hardly are the birth pangs forgotten when they mourn because the grave yawns to swallow us up, and all that lies between the pangs of birth and the sorrow of death is one hopeless struggle of the tender flower against the fierce winds. Our lives are nothing but a continual death. The best of them is labor and sorrow. There is nothing abiding.

Nothing?

But...

Oh, what a *but*. The mercy of the Lord is everlasting!

The eternity of God's mercy is not a matter of experience, for how can our fleeting existence comprehend the eternal God? Yet it is experienced, although it is not perceived by the natural eye or tasted by the natural heart. It is apprehended by faith.

For his mercy is not far above us, outside of us, beyond our reach, but is with us, upon us, right in the midst of our fleeting world.

The one abiding reality in the midst of all things transient.

The mercy of the Lord upon those who fear him.

From everlasting to everlasting.

❖

Wondrous, mysterious mercy.

Upon us it was from everlasting.

Mercy reaches out for us, children of time. Mercy touches us as we are in the midst of the ever-changing, yet never-changing scenes of time. Mercy takes hold of our fleeting existence, permeates it, determines it, and controls it.

But mercy is not of this world; its spring is not among us.

Mercy is from everlasting. It constantly casts its blessed shadows over us, yet far transcends our keenest perception and recedes into eternity. Beginning it never had, for it does not belong to the created things, but to the creator.

Mercy is of God. It is in him the eternal will to bless its object, to remove from the good, the righteous, the perfect, all misery and to fill him with good; to wipe away from his eyes all tears and to cause him to sing and to shout with joy; to give unto him heavenly beauty for the ashes of sorrow, the oil of joy for mourning, the garment of praise for the spirit of heaviness, and to make him taste forever that it is blessed to be righteous and holy and to say that God is good, to be like him.

As such mercy is, it must be eternal, even as God is eternal.

From everlasting.

Ultimately and absolutely, mercy is the will of God to bless himself, a will that is eternally perfect in its realization, for he is the ever- and infinitely blessed God. He is good. He is a light and there is no darkness in him. Perfect righteousness and spotless holiness is he. With him there are pleasures forevermore. He wills eternally to be blessed and rejoices in the eternal realization of his infinite blessedness. As the living God—the triune, Father, Son, and Holy Ghost in the one being of infinite perfection—he lives a divine life of perfect bliss and infinite joy in himself. From everlasting is the will of God to bless its eternal object: himself.

Upon us, upon those who fear him, is his mercy from everlasting.

For he willed to have a people who would in the highest possible sense be like himself as the reflection is like what it reflects—in righteousness and holiness and truth, in knowledge and love and life—a people who would know him as they are known, who would dwell in his tabernacle, who would taste that the Lord is good and eternally acknowledge his goodness, who would experience his blessedness and rejoice with a joy unspeakable and full of glory; a people whom he ordained to be made like unto his Son. That people he willed to bless from everlasting, and from everlasting his will to bless them is also realized in his eternal counsel. For whom he did predestinate, them he also glorified.

From everlasting is his mercy upon us.

Upon us, who are in the midst of suffering, whose lives are nothing but a continual death, who are in darkness because of the present night, sojourners in a strange land; whose days are like the grass, which today is and tomorrow is cast into the oven; whose corruptible lives are like that of the tender flower dangerously flourishing where the fierce winds blow; who cry and lament in their present misery; who groan and moan and wail because of anguish of soul and body; who worry and are anxious because of want and poverty; who are afraid of all things, of things above and things below, of heights and depths, of things present and things to come; who are always overcome with death, oppressed with fear, overwhelmed with sorrow—upon us, reaching out for us, is his mercy—his will to bless, to change our moaning into rejoicing, to wipe away our tears, to deliver us from all our woes, to make us partakers of the highest conceivable bliss in eternal glory.

From everlasting.

His mercy is not an afterthought. It did not begin after we were plunged into the misery of our present death. It was before our death. It is not evoked by our moaning and groaning. It anticipates our tears. It is not determined by the things of this present time. It determines them from everlasting.

It is sovereign, rooted only in God.

It is not conditional, not contingent upon anything we might be or not be, do or not do; it is before all our doing and not doing.

It is unchangeable because it is from everlasting, the sole unchangeable reality in the midst of all the changing vicissitudes of our transient existences, the abiding thing.

It is the motive that determined all things that are and will be, the history of this present time.

The axis around which all things revolve.

As for man...

His days are as grass; as the flower of the field so he flourishes.

For the wind passes over it, and it is gone, and the place thereof will know it no more.

But...

Oh, blessed but!

The mercy of the Lord is not from among these fleeting things.

It is from everlasting.

Amazing mercy!

❖

Constant mercy.

From everlasting to everlasting.

Surely, in its profoundest sense this means that God's mercy is eternal, from eternity to eternity.

But eternity we do not know and cannot comprehend. It is not time. It is related to time only as what is wholly different from time, from all we know, see, hear, taste, touch, and experience, as different from time as God is absolutely different from not-God, the creator from the creature. Strictly speaking, we do not understand, we only repeat a mystery when we say, "From eternity to eternity." Eternity we do not experience in time.

And yet we do.

Not as eternity, but as that which constantly abides as the immovable rock in the midst of the swiftly flowing stream. A literal translation of the Hebrew is, "But the mercy of the LORD is from age to age upon them that fear him."

By faith only we experience eternal mercy as the only abiding reality in the midst of all that passes away, from age to age the same. Mercy expresses the unchangeable attitude of God toward those who fear him. It is the blessed word that denotes the motive of everything he does in time for them, to them, and in them. His mercy is upon them; his will to bless them with heavenly bliss and unthinkable joy constantly reaches out for them and holds them. Mercy is upon them when he sends his only begotten Son into the world in the likeness of sinful flesh; when he sends him into our deepest woe; when he causes him to bear our sins on the accursed tree and makes him taste our death for us all; when he raises him from the dead and gives him a name that is above all names; when he sends his Spirit into our hearts; when he has his eternal mercy preached among us, that we might believe, that in the darkness of this present time our hope and expectation might be in him; when he calls us out of darkness into his marvelous light, that we might show forth his praises and declare that the Lord is good.

Constant mercy.

Always upon us.

Constantly the motive of all he sends us. The guiding power in our earthly way.

Yes, his mercy is upon those who fear him, from age to age, from day to day, from hour to hour, from moment to moment. It never leaves us. It never relinquishes its hold upon us. Even when the way is dark and steep and rugged, his mercy leads us in the way. Even when poverty and want cause us to be filled with anxiety with regard to the things of this present time; even when the pain of death causes us to writhe in agony and when sorrow upon sorrow overwhelms our soul; when our punishment is there every morning…

Oh! Then it may seem, indeed, as if his mercy withdrew itself into the mysterious everlasting whence it is.

But the mercy of the Lord is from age to age upon those who fear him!

The sole abiding reality.

Your sorrow will pass away.

His mercy never.

❖

Never-perishing mercy!

For even as it is from everlasting and because of this truth, the mercy of the Lord is also to everlasting.

We look backward, contemplating that mysterious eternal reality, mercy, and not being able to express its eternity, we say, "From everlasting it is; never a beginning it had; in the past it always was." Looking forward in the future, contemplating the transient things of time and, in the midst of them, the one abiding reality, mercy, and still not knowing how to denote adequately its eternal nature, we say, God says, and we repeat it by faith: It is never-ending; in the future it always will be.

Will be upon us.

Upon those who fear him.

We then will always be never-perishing objects of his never-ending mercy.

With his mercy we will abide forever. The world passes away and the lust thereof, the lust of the eyes and the lust of the flesh and the pride of life, for these are not the objects of the Father's mercy. How could anything abide that he does not will to bless? Love not the world, neither the things in the world, for if you love the world, the love of the Father is not in you, neither is his mercy upon you. But he who does the will of the Father, he who fears God, abides forever, for the mercy of the Lord is upon those who fear him, and how could any perish whom he wills to bless?

We shall not die, but live.

We will abide as the objects of his everlasting mercy, which is from everlasting and out of the mysterious everlasting will reach out for those who fear him and be upon them to everlasting.

Abundant mercy!

So abundant that the suffering of this present time is not worthy to be compared with the glory that his mercy will reveal in them.

Joy unspeakable and full of glory.

The inheritance incorruptible and undefilable and that never fades.

Never-ending mercy!

❖

To those who fear him.

The fear of the Lord is the sole thing that counts.

For his mercy is not upon all. The mercy of the Lord is not general. It is very particular. It is upon those only who fear his name.

Not as if his mercy is upon them because they fear him, for quite the contrary is true. It is not our fear of his name that evokes his mercy, but his everlasting mercy is first and is the everlasting cause for our fearing him.

Yet the truth remains. His mercy is not upon the ungodly; it is confined to those who fear him. The way is narrow. It is very narrow. It becomes narrower as you go on. Not one step to the right or to the left can you make without forfeiting the taste and the blessed assurance of his mercy. It is for those who hate sin and eschew it, who love righteousness and pursue it, that God purposes his everlasting mercy. For those who are still beset with sin and often stumble, but who have a strong and heartfelt desire to be delivered from all iniquity and to be pleasing to him, the light of his mercy shines.

The end of the matter is clear—the only end.

Fear the Lord, all you people!

And taste his mercy forever!

24

Far Off...Brought Nigh

*"Wherefore remember, that ye being in times past
Gentiles in the flesh, who are called Uncircumcision by that
which is called the Circumcision in the flesh made by hands;
That at that time ye were without Christ, being aliens from the
commonwealth of Israel, and strangers from the covenants of
promise, having no hope, and without God in the world: But
now in Christ Jesus ye who sometimes were far off are made
nigh by the blood of Christ."—Ephesians 2:11–13*

WHEREFORE remember!

Because you are saved by pure grace...

Because salvation is not of works, lest any man should boast...

Because you were dead through trespasses and sins, wherein
you walked according to the course of this world, according to the
prince of the power of the air, the spirit that now works in the children of disobedience...

Because there was nothing on your part that made you worthy
before God of anything but damnation, while you walked in the
lusts of the flesh and fulfilled the desires of the flesh and of the
mind, so that by nature you were mere children of wrath even as
all men...

Because it was the revelation of the rich mercy of God and of
his great love wherewith he loved us then, when we were dead in
sins, that we were quickened together with Christ, and raised up
together, and placed together with him in heavenly places; and
because the revelation of this exceeding great kindness and grace
toward us in Christ Jesus is the purpose of it all, in order that he
alone is glorified...

Therefore remember.

Never forget your past!

Bear constantly in mind from what depth of darkness and hopelessness you have been saved and delivered into your present state of liberty and hope and joy.

Let nothing of yourselves ever enter into the work that was purely a revelation of God's mercy.

Let it be perfectly clear before your consciousness that when God saved you, your salvation was impossible as far as you were concerned.

And never forget the deep misery of your condition in that former state.

In order that the glorious grace of God is extolled.

For by grace are you saved.

Wherefore remember!

❖

Far off you were.

Oh, how far? Absolutely separated!

Even your flesh witnessed that you were far off, for in the flesh you were uncircumcised Gentiles. Even that which is called the Circumcision and which is made by hands, which therefore was also in the flesh, despised you and expressed your despicable state by calling you the Uncircumcision.

Far off you were from the commonwealth of Israel and from the covenants of promise, aliens and strangers to that commonwealth and to those covenants, having no part in them whatever.

Such was your legal state, for God had established his covenant with Israel exclusively.

The *covenants*, the apostle writes. Not as if there were many covenants, for the covenant is one. There is one God, one Christ, and one covenant of God with his people. This is the everlasting covenant of friendship of God in Christ Jesus. But this one covenant is revealed repeatedly and in different forms throughout the old dispensation. It is revealed as a covenant of friendship in paradise, when God promises to put enmity between the seed of the serpent and the seed of the woman. It is revealed to Noah, who found grace in the eyes of the Lord and who walked with God, as a covenant that will be made with all creation, will embrace every creature, and will continue in the line of Noah's seed. It is revealed to Abraham as the covenant that will continue in the line of and that will be definitely fulfilled in his seed, so that in him all the nations of the earth will be blessed. It is revealed to Isaac and Jacob, to Israel at Sinai, where the seed of Abraham is constituted into the commonwealth of Israel. It is revealed to the king after God's heart as "the sure mercies of David" (Isa. 55:3).

It is finally realized in Christ.

One covenant frequently covenanted.

They are the covenants of promise. The covenant is called a covenant of promise not because the essence of the covenant is the promise, the realization of which would be contingent on our acceptance of it. The essence of the covenant of God is the fellowship of friendship that is a reflection of his own glorious triune life of perfect communion. But the apostle is writing about the dispensation of the Old Testament, when reality had not yet come, when all the blessings of salvation and the covenant itself still existed in the form of shadows, and the people of God looked forward in hope to the realization of all things. The covenant was a matter of promise. Even though God's covenant is centrally realized in the new dispensation through the blood and in the Spirit of Jesus Christ and with a view to the final revelation of the blessedness and glory of that covenant, it still remains a promise, and it will remain such until the heavenly commonwealth will be realized and the tabernacle of God will be with men.

That covenant had been established with and limited to the generations of Abraham.

It had been very definitely circumscribed and exclusively defined by the law. Of that definite limitation circumcision had been the sign.

Not as if all who were children of Abraham according to the flesh were also children of the promise. Such was never and such will never be the case. There were those who were Israelites in the flesh only, even as by the absence of circumcision the heathen were Gentiles in the flesh. Many there were who boasted of this circumcision made by hands, as if their carnal relation to the commonwealth of Israel had any saving significance. It was this so-called circumcision, that which is called circumcision made by hands, that looked with disdain upon the uncircumcision. But even in the old dispensation no flesh had any reason to glory in the presence of God. The children of the promise only were counted for the seed. Yet the law of circumcision was exclusive. All who belonged to the commonwealth of Israel received the sign of circumcision in the flesh, and all who lived outside of the scope of circumcision were aliens from the commonwealth of Israel.

This then was the state of the Gentiles before they were brought nigh by the blood of Christ.

No right had they to the circumcision.

No part did they have with the blessings of the constituted theocracy.

The covenants of promise did not concern them.

Absolutely separated from it all were they.

Far off, indeed!

❖

Far off.

And oh, the misery of it!

The Ephesian Christians knew historically what it meant to be aliens from the commonwealth of Israel, strangers from the covenants of promise, for they had been Gentiles in the flesh.

In this historical sense, we who are born in the line of the covenant of God, and thus from our infancy by God's grace are brought nigh through the blood of Christ, cannot remember this state of alienation. But we too can remember, for we know what we are by nature: dead through trespasses and sins. We know the spiritual misery and hopelessness of it all.

Without Christ, having no hope, and without God in the world. In these phrases the apostle sums up the elements of the miserable, inexpressibly sad and desperate condition of those who are aliens from the commonwealth of Israel.

Without Christ, separated from him, having no connection with him, no claim on him. This is mentioned first because it is basic. Christ, the Messiah, is the promise *par excellence* of the covenant of God with his people. If the covenant is limited by the law of circumcision, Gentiles in the flesh have no part with this covenant of promise. If they are strangers to this covenant, they are strangers to the promise: They are separate from Christ. They cannot reach him, embrace him, believe on him, hope in him. To be without Christ means to be outside of the sphere in which the blood of atonement and reconciliation is valid, outside of the sphere of the Spirit of Christ, the sphere of life, the sphere of redemption and of resurrection.

Without Christ.

Therefore without hope.

Oh, the unspeakable misery expressed in that brief phrase: without hope. Notice that the apostle does not specify the expression. He does not say, without the hope of eternal life, or simply: without *the* hope. No, he leaves the matter unlimited: without hope. He who was an alien from the commonwealth of Israel, a stranger to the covenant of promise, and who was therefore separated from Christ, what hope had he? He had no hope at all. There is no hope, no ground of hope, no possibility of hope, no room for hope in this world without Christ.

It may seem different. The ungodly, he who is without Christ, may simulate hope, may act as if he too is full of hope: "Hope springs eternal in the human breast." We are children of time. Always we move onward. In the present we cannot rest. Because of that fact, and because death is in every moment of our life and is always in the present moment, the present never satisfies. So man always looks forward in time. He stretches himself to some future moment. And always, whenever that future moment has become present, it disappoints: In it too is death. Again he looks toward the future to bring him the desired rest and satisfaction. He hopes and always lives in expectation.

But in vain.

For that death, which is present in every moment of his existence, compasses him about on every side. There is no way out.

The only way out is the resurrection of Jesus Christ from the dead. But he is without Christ.

His expectation always perishes when it seems to be realized and perishes finally in death, eternal desolation.

Without Christ.

Without hope in the world.

Without God.

No, not without a god the Gentiles were in the world. They were not atheists in the strict sense of the term. Many were the gods they invented and in whom they attempted to put their trust. But without God, without the living God, were they in the world. Not that anyone will ever be able to rid himself of God, for he is everywhere. He encompasses us. He meets us. He demands that he be acknowledged as God, glorified and feared with thanksgiving. He surrounds us in his wrath. He is our terror. A consuming fire is he.

But the Gentiles were without the God of salvation, separated from his favor in which there is life. Without his saving help in this world, full of sin and death.

Oh, the misery!

❖

But now.

You who were so far off are made nigh.

You, who were aliens from the commonwealth of Israel in the past, now have been received as citizens of the kingdom of heaven.

You, who were strangers to the covenants of promise, now have been included in the number of those with whom God establishes his everlasting covenant of friendship. The promises that in times past were limited to those who were comprised within the law of the circumcision now have been extended to you.

You, who were without God in the world, now may call him your God, and he will not be ashamed. He is for you. His friendship embraces you. His saving love encompasses you. He is the God of your salvation in the midst of this world of darkness, sin, and death. And you seek him and thirst after him as a hart pants after water brooks.

You, who were without hope, now have become heirs of the incorruptible, undefiled inheritance that never fades away, through the resurrection of Jesus Christ from the dead. The darkness is past and the light of hope that makes not ashamed now shines.

From afar you were brought nigh; from strangers you were made citizens; from children of wrath you were transformed into dear children of God's marvelous love; from death you were called into everlasting life; from darkness you were translated into light;

from the despair of hell you were lifted to the heights of the hope of eternal glory.

All in Christ.

He is Abraham's seed, the seed of the promise, the head of the commonwealth of Israel, the central realization of the covenant of promise. In him all the promises of God are yea and amen. To be in him means to be reckoned in him and to have a right to all the blessings of the covenant. To be in him signifies also to become one plant with him, to be engrafted into him, to live out of him, to become partakers of all his benefits. In him we are brought nigh to the covenant that was established with Abraham and his seed, for in him we are indeed the seed of Abraham and children of the promise.

Through his blood.

For in that blood there is the end of the law of circumcision and the reconciliation of all whom the Father gave him from before the foundation of the world, not only of the Jews, but also of the Gentiles.

Wherefore remember!

Lest flesh should glory in his presence.

By grace are you saved.

Soli Deo Gloria!

25

His Workmanship

*"For we are his workmanship, created in Christ Jesus
unto good works, which God hath before ordained that we
should walk in them."—Ephesians 2:10*

LEST any man should boast.

God alone is God. As such he must be acknowledged by every creature.

Of him, and through him, and unto him are all things. Never is anything of us and through us. Nor is anything partly of us and through us. Hence his alone is the glory for ever and ever. And this glory must be attributed to him. He will give it to no other.

Therefore salvation is of the Lord.

It is by grace, from beginning to end by grace only; not of works, lest any man should boast.

To boast, to claim part of the glory that belongs to God only, and therefore to claim all the glory that is his alone, is the tendency of sin, the inclination of the sinful heart. "Ye shall be as gods" (Gen. 3:5) is the slogan that expresses the deepest motive of the natural man. He refuses to glorify God as God and to be thankful.

So he is always inclined to deprive God of his glory, to say that salvation is of his own works. It is hard for him to confess that sovereign grace alone is the source and ground and power of salvation. Somehow he always attempts to introduce his work into the work of God, to share in the glory of the divine work that delivers him from guilt and clothes him with an eternal righteousness, that cleanses him from the pollution of sin and sanctifies him unto the service of the living God, that lifts him out of the depth of the misery of death and hell into the glory of eternal life and heavenly bliss.

In various ways he seeks to escape the consequences of salvation by grace and to maintain that he is saved by works. Sometimes he attempts to work out his own righteousness and to make this righteousness of works the basis of his salvation. Sometimes he apparently is willing to confess that he is saved by grace, but he contends that it is works that make him worthy of this grace. But in the measure that he introduces his own works into the wonder of salvation, he deprives the God of salvation of his glory.

Man boasts.

Yet no man may boast in the presence of the Most High.

His alone is all the glory. He alone calls the things that are not as if they were, and he alone quickens the dead. He alone is Lord, the creator and the redeemer. Jehovah of hosts is his name.

Therefore all works as a cause, a ground, a reason, a means of salvation, or as contributing anything whatsoever to this divine wonder, must be excluded.

By grace are you saved.

Not of works, lest any man should boast.

He who glories, let him glory in the Lord.

❖

Created unto good works.

This must have all the emphasis.

It is not *of* works, or *by* works, or *because of* works that we are saved, but *unto* works. Our works are never first, but always last; they are never the cause, but always the result. God is first, and our work cannot begin except where God's work is finished. We work out our own salvation, but only because God is working within us to do and to will of his own good pleasure (Phil. 2:13).

Created unto good works.

So it was in the beginning: Man was created unto, with a view to, with his purpose in the performance of good works.

He was made a working being. By this he was adapted to reflect the likeness of his creator, to bear the image of his God. He was so created that even as God works, so he might also work. In this he was distinguished from and stood exalted above all the rest of the earthly creation. All the works of God's hand function, operate, move, each in their own place and with their own purpose. The sun, moon, and stars move in their orbs and fill the universe with their light and energy and glory; the clouds gather and empty themselves upon the thirsty land; the lightning flashes and the thunder roars, the tempest rages and mighty waves of the ocean rise mountain high, rivers flow and brooks murmur; the beasts of the field rejoice and the birds of the air sing their songs of gladness and cheer; the earth yields its increase and the trees bear their fruit. All things move and operate and function in their place and according to their purpose.

But man works.

He was made a rational, living soul, a being capable of reflecting the virtues of God, with mind and will and heart. Consciously and willingly he performs his deeds. He labors and toils and exercises dominion over the various aspects of the earthly creation, subjecting them unto himself and employing them as his servants; he beholds all the works of God in the light of his rational eye; he ponders them and interprets them and reads the word of God in them; he loves and hates, he rejoices and grieves, he sings and prays as a rational and moral being that is related to the world and to God.

He works.

A working being he was created in the beginning. And he was made capable of performing good works.

Good works are those, and those only, that serve their proper purpose, God's purpose: the glory of his name. For that glory man had to work. From a heart moved by the love of God he was to reach out for that glory of his creator, to behold it with his eye, to perceive it with his ear, to know it with his mind, to desire it with his will, to speak of it with his mouth, to work for it with his hands, to devote himself unto that sole purpose, to consecrate all things unto it, and thus to declare the praises of the Most High before all creation and before his face—such was man's purpose, the purpose of creation. Only those works that are performed with that purpose in view are good.

But man fell.

He became evil, dead through trespasses and sins, darkened in his understanding, perverse of will and heart, impure in all his desires and longings and aspirations. An enemy of God he became, motivated by hatred against the Lord of heaven and earth, incapable of doing anything that is pleasing to God, seeking to destroy the glory of God and to exalt himself as the god of the universe.

His nature is corrupt, wholly in the power of sin and death.

His works are evil.

For still he works. Work he must inevitably. Work he does with all his soul and mind and power. But the works he performs are evil, always evil, ever coming short of the glory of God.

But God!

God, who is rich in mercy, according to the great love wherewith he loved us, freely, divinely, sovereignly...God, who calls the things that are not as if they were, and who quickens the dead...God, who creates, always creates; who creates when he calls out of nothing, and who creates when he calls out of death...God created us, his people, his church, once again.

For we are his workmanship, created unto good works.

❖

Adorable wisdom of God.

For his workmanship we are, created unto good works that he before ordained. The works of the church as a whole and of believers individually are ordained for them, predestinated in infinite wisdom from before the foundation of the world.

But of course.

Does not even man ordain beforehand the work that a certain mechanism that he constructs is to perform for him? Does he not adapt each part of the mechanism to the function of the whole?

Does not a great composer, creating a grand oratorio, ordain beforehand the parts that the various voices of a mighty choir are to sing, in order to attain the beautiful harmony he has in mind?

Would not God, then, who is infinite in wisdom and might, when he chose unto himself a church that would be to the praise of the glory of his grace in the beloved and that would forever declare his glorious virtues, ordain the good works that church would perform before his face and before all the world? Would he not ordain in minutest detail each part of the grand oratorio that is to sing his praises and assign to each voice its own place in the mighty chorus that will forever cause the new creation to rebound with glad hallelujahs? If the church is to reflect the fullness of his own glory in Christ, then must not God ordain just how the whole and each member are to serve that purpose?

But of course.

We are created unto good works, but lest any man should boast at all, even these works are not of our creation, of our conception, of our determination, but of God's ordination and predestination. We do not invent them, but he ordained them. We do not bring them to him, but he brings them to us. He does not become obliged to us when we perform them, but we owe him our everlasting gratitude for the part we perform.

He ordained it all.

All the good works the church performs in this world, as she is redeemed from sin and guilt by the blood of Christ, as she is raised from death to life and called from darkness into his marvelous light, as she becomes his workmanship, created in Christ Jesus, are ordained by him. All the praises her members sing, all the prayers they utter, all the glories of God they confess, all the suffering and death they endure, all their patience and tribulations, all their expressions of faith and trust and love of God in this world—these are all ordained of God from before the foundation of the world. There is a fullness of good works the church must perform even in this present time and in this present evil world, a fullness of testimony that she must bear, a fullness of suffering she must endure, according to God's eternal counsel. So the part each individual believer is to perform in the realization of this fullness of good works is ordained by infinite wisdom.

Which he before ordained.

Yes, even the good works that the glorified church must perform in the new heavens and the new earth unto the everlasting ages have been ordained by the all-wise artificer and builder of the new Jerusalem.

He designed it all.

He chose his church and predestinated her to be conformed according to the image of his Son.

He ordained before the good works by means of which that church should show forth the praises of her God.

Oh, depth of wisdom!

❖

His workmanship.

Created in Christ Jesus.

For he not only predestinated his church and ordained her good works, but he also forms his people and enables them for the good works he ordained for them.

In the good works he ordained they must walk. He did not ordain a mechanism that would function according to his design and purpose, but a church of living believers, a living organism of rational and moral beings who would willingly perform the good works he ordained for them, sing his praises, and show forth the glory of his infinite virtues from the love of their hearts.

That is to walk in good works.

To be busy in the works God prepared for his people, ordained for them from eternity, each in his own place, willingly, consciously, motivated by the love of God in the heart, and with the avowed purpose to glorify the God of his salvation—that is to walk in his good works.

Unto this end he created us in Christ Jesus.

It is evident that the term "created" does not refer to our original creation in the beginning. Originally we were not created in Christ Jesus, but in the first man Adam. The apostle is not speaking of the human race, but of the church, saved by grace. Nor is this term "created" to be considered as a hyperbole, exaggerating what actually is accomplished when God forms his people unto the good works he ordained for them. Rather is this work of God to be considered a creation that is more wonderful still, a more marvelous revelation of his divine power than that whereby he called into existence the first world. Then he called the things that were not as if they were; but in the work of salvation he calls life out of death, light out of darkness, righteousness out of corruption, heavenly glory out of the depth of hell. Those who are capable of bringing forth only fruit unto death he forms into willing agents of the good works he ordained for them.

Yes, his workmanship we are, created, re-created out of death into life.

Created in Christ Jesus.

Christ he ordained to be the firstborn of every creature and the first begotten of the dead, the head of the church. In Christ he chose us, making us one with him forever. One we are with Christ, by his eternal election, both juridically and organically. In Christ, and in him only, he gives us all the blessings of salvation and makes us a new creation, fit unto all the good works he ordained for us.

In Christ he gives us the right to become new creatures, for by our sin we forfeited the right of the unspeakable blessing to walk in his good works. But through the blood of Christ he cleanses us from the guilt of sin and clothes us with an eternal righteousness.

In Christ he makes us partakers of all the wonders of his grace and makes us new creatures. In Christ he gives us new life, the eternal life of his resurrection; in Christ he calls us out of darkness into his marvelous light; in Christ he gives us living faith, so that we may be rooted in him and draw our all from him; in Christ he justifies and sanctifies us and makes us willing to walk in his good works.

Presently he will give us the eternal glory of his heavenly covenant in Christ.

His workmanship.

Created in Christ Jesus.

Glorious work of God!

26

The Light of God's Countenance

*"Offer the sacrifices of righteousness, and put your trust
in the LORD. There be many that say, Who will shew us any
good? LORD, lift thou up the light of thy countenance upon us.
Thou hast put gladness in my heart, more than in the time
that their corn and their wine increased." —Psalm 4:5–7*

BLESSED joy.

A gladness in the heart that surpasses the rejoicings of those
who bathe in the luxuries of ever-increasing wine and oil.

A joy that is caused by the blessed light of God's countenance
lifted up over us. A gladness that flows from the sole fount of all
real joy, our gracious covenant Jehovah.

He who knows the covenantal fellowship of Jehovah, who has
once tasted the all-surpassing joy, the riches of grace, the peace-affording trust there is in the assurance that the lighted countenance
of the Lord is shining upon us from above, cannot but repeat the
prayer of the poet: "Lord, lift thou up the light of thy countenance
upon us." Then all is well. For then I know that there will be gladness in my heart more than all the joy of those whose treasure is in
the world.

"Lord, lift thou up the light of thy countenance upon us."

It is a prayer. Yet let it not escape our attention that it is a confession, an answer to the many who ask the question of doubt and
despair, "Who will show us any good?" Rather than ask this question, rather than look about to expect help and salvation from men,
the child of God professes his childlike, absolute trust in the Lord.
Rather than grumble in unbelief and lack of confidence, he would
directly appeal to the God of his salvation, praying, yet confessing
the name of his God in prayer, "Lord, only lift up the light of thy

countenance, and I will be satisfied, yea, filled with gladness, with a joy of heart the world knows not."

Many say, "Who?"

I say, "Lord, thou; the light of thy face is sufficient."

God's countenance is his personal presence with his people. It is his personal self-revelation, the revealed reflection of what lives in God's heart concerning his people. Even as the face of man, who is made after God's image, reflects the life of his inmost soul, mirrors his love and his hatred, his joy and his sorrow, his pleasure and his displeasure, the secret stirrings of his heart, so God's countenance is the perfect revelation to us of his divine attitude and disposition with relation to his people. Such is the meaning of the poet's prayer. To be sure, God's face also reflects his inmost thoughts concerning the wicked. His face is against them; he frowns upon them in his holy wrath. There is terrible darkness in his face when he looks down on them, even as the pillar of cloud was darkness to the pursuing Egyptians as they assayed to follow God's people through the sea. But here the psalmist speaks of the light of God's countenance, of the revelation of what lives in the divine heart forever concerning the people of his sovereign love.

Nor are we left to conjecture what the light of God's face expresses.

It is the reflection of eternal goodwill.

Was not the priest of old enjoined to pronounce the blessing of Jehovah upon the people of his choice, redeemed by him and delivered from the house of bondage: "The LORD make his face shine upon thee, and be gracious unto thee" (Num. 6:25)? God's shining face is the revelation of his everlasting grace. The light of his countenance is the reflection of the eternal loving-kindness that has its source in him alone, in his sovereign good pleasure, that is independent of the works of men, that is not of him who wills nor of him who runs, that is, for this very reason, unchangeable as Jehovah himself, that can stand alone more firmly than the lonely rock in the midst of the raging sea and the beating waves, that is faithful, though we are unfaithful, that reveals itself while we are yet sinners, that justifies the ungodly. That light is the reflection of the everlasting mercy, rich and abundant as the divine heart and love itself, in which he sovereignly determined to save his people, to redeem them, to cleanse them from sin, to clothe them with righteousness, to deliver them from the death and darkness of this world, to cause all things to work together for their good and to be conducive to their eternal glory, to receive them in his covenant of friendship, transforming them according to the image of his Son, finally to spread his eternal tabernacle over them and wipe away all tears from their eyes.

That is the light of God's countenance.

Lord, lift it up.

Let it shine upon me from above, in the darkness of this desert night, as I am traveling as a sojourner and stranger in the world. Lift it up, as in the terrible desert of thy people's wanderings the pillar of fire was lifted up above their camp.

But it was lifted up, once for all.

God's shining countenance in the face of Jesus Christ. The light of God's eternal grace reflected in the face of Jesus Christ; in his sufferings and death, in his resurrection and glory, and in his wonderful exaltation at the right hand of the Most High. God's face, shining with unfathomable mercy upon his people, lifted up for all to behold.

Lord, let it shine upon me, so that I may behold and believe, and believing may trust, and trusting may have peace...

The peace that passes all understanding.

Gladness in my heart.

Blessed joy.

❖

Joy in the light of God's countenance. An all-surpassing, permanent gladness of heart that is independent and raises itself above the changing vicissitudes of this world. A joy and gladness that is not caused by things, that do not have their reason in an abundance of possessions, but solely in the assurance, in the knowledge, and in the experience of God's shining face lifted up over us.

"Lord, lift thou up the light of thy countenance...Thou hast put gladness in my heart, more than in the time that their corn and wine increased."

It is the prayer and its answer.

It is the yearning of the heart and its fulfillment.

It is the hope and its realization.

It is cause and effect.

The lifting up of the shining countenance of Jehovah over his people is the cause; exuberant, all-surpassing, permanent joy and gladness of the heart is the effect.

It is gladness in the heart, not a superficial passion, not a ripple on the surface of the emotions that causes merriment for a moment, but the force of which is spent with the night of drunken revelry by which it is caused. It is gladness indeed, a happy state of the soul, of the mind, and of the will, caused by the consciousness of a great good and by the possession of real blessings. For in misery and desolation the soul cannot rejoice. Though it is true that the child of God can rejoice in tribulation, in suffering and pain, in persecutions and reproach, it is only possible because he is conscious of an all-surpassing good in the midst of surrounding dangers and present afflictions. It is a gladness that is not caused by external circumstances and therefore is not dependent on them. It is a joy of the heart—the center of our spiritual life, whence are all the issues of life—a profound joy, a spiritual joy, a gladness that raises itself above the changing experiences of the present time because it has its source in the love of him who never changes, in the light of the countenance of Jehovah, the only good and the overflowing fountain of all good.

The shining face of God lifted up over us is the highest good, filling the heart with purest joy, lasting gladness, truest delight. And the light of that countenance of our God, shining upon us in Jesus Christ our Lord, is the implication of all conceivable good. For shall not he, who gave us his only begotten Son and delivered him for us all, with him freely give us all things? Does not the blessed light of God's shining face, beaming forth assurances of everlasting mercies, carry with it the joyous certainty that all things work together for good to those who love God?

Incomparably greater, richer, and deeper, because essentially different this gladness is than the joy of those who are exultant over ever-increasing luxuries of corn, wine, and oil. Surely the men of this world appear joyous. Their state would seem enviable and is often considered such even by the children of God in moments when their feet nearly slip. Worldly men appear to have more than heart could wish. They prosper in the world. They need not ask from morning until night whether there will be labor for their hands, bread to supply their families, homes to shelter them, garments to cover their nakedness. Without the worries of the poor, free from the cares of the indigent, independent from men, they walk day by day, boasting in their strength, proud in their prosperity, wanton in their abundance of goods. They say to their soul, "You have many goods, laid up for years to come; eat, drink, and be merry!" They are envied by God's people (as long as they do not enter the sanctuary), when waters of a full cup are wrung out to them, when their punishment is there every morning, or even when they must wait for their appointed portion every day and can buy only their measure of wheat for a penny.

Envying the wicked in their apparent prosperity, God's people are inclined to complain, "Is there no knowledge in the Most High?"

When the days come wherein even the measure of wheat for a penny and the three measures of barley for a penny fail them, when day by day they walk the streets in vain, wanting employment and finding none, they are in danger of wailing with the children of the world, "Who shall show us any good?"

So foolish are they and ignorant.

For as they ask this question of fear and doubt, of anxiety and worry about the morrow, their eyes are turned away from the light of God's countenance over them and are fixed expectantly but in vain upon man and the things that perish. They become oblivious of their joy and gladness, which is greater, richer, and deeper than all the gladness that is dependent upon ever-increasing wine and oil.

Will not the gladness of the world perish with their corn and wine?

Does not the joy that fills the heart in the assurance that the light of God's face is lifted up over us endure as long as the everlasting faithfulness of Jehovah?

Is not the gladness that has its reason in abundance of material things superficial, limited, carnal, a mere semblance of joy, the dance of death in the darkness of this world, the revelry of those who make it their foolish slogan, "Let us eat and drink for tomorrow we die"? And is not the joy that is put into our hearts by the light of God's countenance a joy of the heart, spiritual, all-comprehensive, the assurance of present guidance and the hope of eternal life through him who loved us even unto death?

O, we of little faith!

The psalmist knew of distress, of want and suffering, of enemies who troubled him, who loved vanity, who sought after leasing, who would always turn his glory into shame.

He knew of those who rejoiced because their oil and wine increased. And he heard the complaint of others who asked in the despair of unbelief, "Who shall show us any good?"

In the midst of it all he prays and confesses, "Lord, lift thou up the light of thy countenance upon us."

Then all is well!

Then there will be gladness in our hearts, which the world knows not, but which is truer, richer, greater than the joy of those whose corn and wine increase.

Joy that never fails.

❖

Peace-affording gladness. A joy that is rooted in tranquil reliance and childlike trust in the Lord, and in which we can offer unto him the sacrifice of righteousness.

To offer sacrifices of righteousness does not mean that we bring something to him, enrich him with our goods. The very thought would be an abomination to the Most High. Is not all the gold and silver, are not the cattle on a thousand hills the Lord's and his alone? Is not he the absolutely self-sufficient one, who only gives and never receives, who only fills but never is filled, the overflowing fountain?

What then shall we render unto him?

With what shall we meet him?

Only with those sacrifices in which we acknowledge that he is God. The offerings of broken and contrite spirits, of humiliation before his face in the consciousness of our own nothingness and his all-ness, our own sins and undoneness and his righteousness and holiness, offered in the assurance of the light of his countenance and his great goodness, his unfathomable loving-kindness and mercy revealed unto us in the light of his countenance shining in the face of Christ Jesus our Lord. The sacrifices of a righteousness that is not our own but his are pleasing and acceptable in his sight.

Yet how shall we bring them?

How, if we walk not in the light of his countenance?

How, if we are envious of the wicked and lust after their prosperity? How, if we wail with the world that the ways of the Lord are not equal? How, if we cry out in unbelief, "Who shall show us any good?"

Impossible!

Offer sacrifices of righteousness and trust in the Lord. These are inseparably connected. To trust in the Lord implies that we walk in the knowledge of his shining countenance lifted up over us, in the assurance of his great love wherewith he loved us, in the confidence that in his eternal mercy he ordered all things to work for our salvation and that he will surely bring it to pass, and in the confidence of faith to cast our way upon him.

Though the fig tree does not blossom and all things fail, yet in the light of God's countenance we can trust and rejoice.

The joy of everlasting peace!

PART IV

❧

God's Goodness to His Chosen People: Specifically

27

The Righteousness of God Manifested

*"But now the righteousness of God without the law is
manifested, being witnessed by the law and the prophets; Even
the righteousness of God which is by faith of Jesus Christ unto
all and upon all them that believe: for there is no difference."*
—Romans 3:21–22

But now!

By the deeds of the law no flesh shall be justified in his sight.

That was impossible even in the old dispensation, even under
the law. It is impossible now. It will forever be impossible.

There was a time when the child, still a minor and not having
attained to the freedom of the age of majority, was placed under the
tutorship and government of the law. "Law" means the entire code
of precepts given to the people of Israel at Mount Sinai through
Moses, the mediator of the old covenant. It was headed by the moral law of the ten commandments, as the foundation of the entire
law, but it included the law of the shadows to regulate Israel's worship and religious life and the precepts for their civil life as a nation
in the earthly land of the promise. Always its deepest principle was
expressed in the maxim, "Love the Lord thy God."

The works of the law were prescribed therein.

But justification through these works of the law was not at-
tainable. No flesh could possibly be justified in the sight of God
through these works.

To be sure, the law held out the promise of righteousness and
life. But it was only for him who continued perfectly in all that was
written in the law. Whoever slipped, even once, even with regard
to its smallest detail, it anathematized: "Cursed is everyone who

continues not in all that is written in me." How then could mere sinful man, who enters into the world as a violator of the law, under the curse because of sin, and who can only increase his guilt daily, meet the demands of the law and be justified?

The law always left him with a guilty conscience, with the consciousness that God must condemn him.

Through the law is the knowledge of sin.

But now!

The works of the law are not God's ordained way into righteousness, and never were.

Even the law and the prophets testified to the children of promise, who were under the law, of a different righteousness, a righteousness without the law, which is valid even after the law has served its purpose and disappears.

Then it was not yet manifested.

But now it is.

The righteousness of God.

By faith of Jesus.

❖

Amazing wonder of grace!

Righteousness of God, without the law.

Righteousness before God as a free gift, without works.

Does it not sound paradoxical that righteousness is given to us of God?

Righteousness is a legal status, the status of one who measures up to a certain standard according to the verdict of a competent judge. In this case the standard is the law of God, the expression of God's will concerning us. Just as a wall is perfectly perpendicular when it is in accord with the plumb line, so a man is righteous when in his inmost nature and in all his works he is in harmony with the standard of the will of God concerning him. He is a righteous man who is what he ought to be in his deepest soul and being, in his thinking and willing and in all his desires, as well as in all his outward life and walk, according to the sentence of the Most High who judges righteously.

How then can this righteousness, this legal status, be given to anyone? How can it be bestowed as a gift?

Such is the meaning of the phrase "righteousness of God" in Romans 3:21–22.

It does not refer to the divine virtue of righteousness. That the righteousness of God is manifested does not mean that God has revealed himself as righteous. To be sure, righteousness is a virtue of God. God is absolutely good in himself. He is a light and there is no darkness in him at all. Pure goodness is he, the implication of all infinite perfection. He is therefore his own standard. In all his willing, knowing, and acting he is always in harmony with the perfection of his own glorious being. This is God's righteousness.

But to this the text does not refer. This is plain from the whole context, which centers on the question of how a man is justified before God. How can he be declared righteous when the Most High judges him and pronounces the verdict? This is also evident from the text itself. It is a righteousness that is manifested entirely apart from the law and that has nothing to do with keeping or not keeping the law.

The righteousness of God is by faith of Christ Jesus, that is, unto those and upon those who believe.

It is therefore a righteousness that concerns us.

It is our righteousness.

But it is not of us. It is of God.

It is God's answer to the question, how can we be righteous in his sight? How can we be justified when he judges us? The answer is, never by a righteousness of our own. Never by the works of the law. We can only sin and increase our guilt daily. But a righteousness was manifested of God, of which he is the author and he alone; which he conceived, which he realized in our behalf, which he also bestows on us, who are in ourselves sinners and worthy of damnation; a righteousness that is not of us but of God from beginning to end, and which we receive of mere grace, as a gift of God to us.

What a gift it is!

It includes not only the forgiveness of sin, so that God's judgment over us is that we are so perfectly righteous that it is as if we had never had or committed any sin whatever, but it also is the divine declaration that we are worthy of being called his children and heirs.

The inheritance is eternal life. We, who are condemned on every side, our own consciences even bearing us witness that we are worthy of wrath and damnation, are judged worthy of eternal life and glory.

Such are the implications of this righteousness.

And it is freely bestowed.

Without the law.

Without works.

Of God.

❖

Now it is manifested.

The righteousness of God without the law.

It was not manifested before. In the old dispensation, when the children of the promise were placed under the law, it was still hidden.

But now it is made plain, clearly shown before the eyes of all.

Not as if there were no knowledge at all of this righteousness of God by faith in the days of the old dispensation. The difference between the two dispensations certainly cannot be that in the old the saints were justified and saved on the basis of works, while in the new they are justified without works by faith. In that case, how would the saints under the law have been saved at all? It holds for the old dispensation as well as for the new that no flesh will be justified in the sight of God by the works of the law.

Then, however, this righteousness was witnessed by the law and the prophets as something that was not yet, that was still to be realized, that was not yet manifest.

The law and the prophets, that is, the entire Old Testament Scriptures, bore testimony to this righteousness that was to come. They brought the shadow of it to the minds of the believing saints. They foreshadowed it in all the ceremonies of the law, in circumcision and the Passover, in tabernacle and temple, in altar and sacrifice, in Sabbaths and holy days. Christ was the end of the law, the end that the law had in view, to whom it pointed, to whose righteousness it would direct the faith of the worshiping Israelite under the law. Never was the law intended to impress the people of God of the old dispensation with the hopeless demand that they must be justified by its works. The law itself witnessed of another righteousness, without works, in him who was to come. And so did the prophets. All delivered the good tidings, the gospel of peace, that Zion was to be redeemed through justice and that God would save his people.

But this righteousness was not yet manifested.

Beyond the shadows faith could only anxiously look in hope.

But now!

It is come. That which was hidden in God, that of which the saints of old saw only the figures and shadows, the promise that they saw afar off, has now been manifested.

For the righteousness of God, that marvelous gift of his grace, was realized in the death and resurrection of Jesus Christ. He is the revelation of the God of our salvation. He it is who was ordained of God from before the foundation of the world to realize the righteousness of God. He is the anointed head of his church, of all the saints who are chosen in him and given him as his own, that he might bear their iniquities and, in the hour of judgment over Zion, carry them to the place of execution and die in their stead and in their behalf, bearing the wrath of God for them, redeeming them from all the guilt of sin, and meriting by his perfect obedience eternal life and glory for his own. "God was in Christ, reconciling the world unto himself, not imputing their trespasses unto them" (2 Cor. 5:19).

The righteousness of God was realized.

And it was manifested.

For God raised Jesus Christ from the dead, and in that resurrection he rendered the verdict that Christ is righteous. Righteous as the head of all his people, for he had taken their place in judgment, assumed the burden of their sins, and obeyed in the hour of wrath.

He was delivered for our transgressions.

He was raised for our justification.

In the glorious and blessed resurrection of our Lord the righteousness of God is clearly come to light.

It is declared by God himself in the gospel concerning his Son. Even as the shadows of this righteousness of God were witnessed by the law and the prophets, so the fully realized and manifested righteousness in Christ Jesus is revealed in and proclaimed by the gospel.

But now...

No flesh can possibly be justified by the works of the law. Through the law there can only be the knowledge of sin.

But there is a righteousness without the law.

A righteousness of God, freely given.

Blessed gift!

❖

By faith of Jesus Christ.

Not to all, not over all is this righteousness of God.

For not as in Adam all men die, are all men saved in Christ. Nor can this righteousness be apprehended in any other way, by any other power, than by faith of Jesus Christ.

The faith of Jesus is the faith of which Jesus, the revelation of the God of salvation, is the object, the ground, the content, the all. It is not of man—not of him who wills, neither of him who runs—but of God who shows mercy. It is the righteousness of God that is manifested, and it remains God's righteousness to the last. He conceived of it in his eternal counsel; he realized it in the death of Jesus Christ and in his resurrection from the dead; he declares it in the gospel; and he bestows this marvelous gift of grace on whomever he wills, giving them the power whereby they receive it—the faith of Jesus Christ.

It is the bond of union with the Lord.

Faith is to our souls what the roots are to the young tree planted in the ground. It is the spiritual power, the gift of God's grace, whereby our souls cling to Christ as the ground of our righteousness, as the one in whom is all our salvation. It is the power to know him in all the fullness of his grace; to rely on him with all our hearts, in time and in eternity, as the sole basis of our righteousness; to draw out of him and appropriate unto ourselves all the spiritual blessings in heavenly places.

The faith of Jesus Christ.

Therefore this righteousness of God is unto those and over all those who believe. It is unto them, intended for them, even entering into them, into their deepest hearts and minds, causing them to know that this righteousness is over them, that God's verdict is upon them, redeeming them from all their sin, declaring them worthy of eternal life, and causing them to rejoice in peace with God forever. By the testimony of this righteousness of God in their inmost hearts, they joyfully confess, "We, therefore, being justified out of faith, have peace with God through our Lord Jesus Christ."

Unto all and over all.

There is no difference. Righteousness of God by the faith of Jesus Christ does not have regard to your social standings, makes no distinction between rich and poor, does not ask whether or not you are Jew or Greek, whether you know the law, whether you are circumcised or uncircumcised. It has no regard for your works or lack of works. It is without distinction unto all and over all who believe.

All who believe.

They all.

No one else.

For all have sinned, under the law or without the law; and all who believe are righteous before God forever. Not because your faith of Jesus Christ is another good work by which you are accounted righteous before God. Faith does not work into righteousness, it only receives it. Neither because faith is the power whereby you perform good works. The believer is righteous before all works.

But faith connects you forever with Christ, your righteousness.

The righteousness of God.

Glory to him!

28

Longsuffering over Us

"The Lord is not slack concerning his promise, as some men count slackness; but is longsuffering to us-ward, not willing that any should perish, but that all should come to repentance."
—2 Peter 3:9

WHERE is the promise of his coming?

Scoffers, walking after their own lusts, mockingly cast the question into the teeth of God's people.

They look not for the promise.

Loving the present world, walking after the lusts of the flesh in the darkness of covetousness, their hope is not and cannot be fixed with longing upon the moment of final deliverance, when the Lord will come to avenge his people and to justify his cause in the sight of the whole world.

Not longing for the hope of his coming, they cannot tolerate the testimony of the church, witnessing of the hope that is in them as they look for the final salvation and for the grace that is to be revealed unto them in the appearing of the Lord Jesus Christ in glory. They wickedly contradict the testimony of believers, trying to deprive them of the joy of their hope and to silence its voice forever.

Where is the promise of his coming? Is not that promise as old as the ages of history? Have not the saints from the beginning witnessed of that hope? Did they not, for the hope that was in them, forsake the world and count the reproach of Christ greater riches than all the pleasures and treasures and favors and glories of Egypt? Did they not, with their eye on that hope, prefer to suffer with the people who were partakers of the same hope with them? Did they not suffer shame and mockery; were they not deprived of all their earthly goods; were they not chased over the earth, cast into prisons and dungeons, put to death with cruel tortures, because they tenaciously clung to the hope of his promise? Where, then, these mockers tantalize, where is the promise of his coming? Is there even a sign that the promise will ever be realized? Do not all things remain as they were from the beginning? Have not all things remained unchanged? Vain hope!

Thus they mock. And God's people often take it to heart.

Not as if they will fail to put their trust in God's promise. The Lord is true and faithful. The promise is not the word of man, whose breath is in his nostrils, but the sure word of Jehovah concerning the glory he has in store, according to his everlasting counsel, for those who love him. He is the amen. And as he is, so also is his promise: faithful and without repentance.

But is not the Lord slack concerning his promise?

Does he not give the enemy reason to mock and to cast the slander of their wicked unbelief into the teeth of the people of God?

Does he not delay the final realization of his kingdom?

God's people long for the coming of the Lord. It is their final, their only hope. True, there are periods in the history of the church when even in her the light of that hope appears to be dying out. The things of this world then have a mighty hold on God's people. Their spiritual life is waning and pining. Their faith is not strong; their life is no testimony of the love of Christ or of their distinctive character as a peculiar people of God, a chosen generation, a royal priesthood. A people that is called out of darkness into God's marvelous light to show forth his praises disappears; the spirit of this world dominates in the church, and the children of light appear to have made common cause with the children of darkness. As God's people learn to love the things of this world, their hope of things to come appears to be a lifeless thing, a dead dogma, a creed without faith.

Yet this cannot last.

For a time they seem to be overcome by the spirit of this world, but they have been begotten again through the resurrection of the Lord from the dead. The life they have received must assert itself anew, until their longings and aspirations have once more become divorced from the things of the world, and against the world they profess in word and deed that they are strangers in the earth and seekers of the city that has foundations, whose builder and artificer is God. So they live in hope. The promise of his coming is the joy of their life. Here they must suffer. In the world they must have tribulation, for striving for the faith of the gospel, they must provoke the fury of the adversary. But when the promise of Christ's coming will be realized, they will have the victory. No more battle, no more suffering, but the full glory of God's eternal kingdom and covenant, the inheritance incorruptible, undefiled, and that never fades away.

The promise of his coming.

But is not the Lord slack concerning that promise?

Is it not true, as the mocking enemy emphasizes, that this promise was given from the beginning of history? Was it not given in paradise? Did not all the saints of the old dispensation possess it? Was it not renewed when the Lord first came, suffered, died, arose, entered into glory, and shed forth his Spirit upon the church? Has not the church ever since looked for that blessed promise?

Can it be denied that for the hope of that promise the people of God have suffered innumerable reproaches?

How can it be denied that things remain as they were from the creation of the world?

Is the Lord slack concerning his promise?

Where, oh, where is the promise of his coming?

❖

Behold, I come quickly!

Over against the anxious query of his people, counting it slackness when the promise is not yet realized, the Lord assures them that he hastens his coming.

He is not slack concerning the promise, even though to our impatience the time may seem long.

Especially in times of suffering and persecution, when the devil goes about like a roaring lion, when all the fury of the powers of darkness is let loose upon the church; in times when the ungodly mockers prosper and their eyes stand out with fatness, while the punishment of the righteous is there every morning; in times when the righteous are in distress and tribulation and pressed from every side, so that they cry out, "How long, O Lord?" and no answer comes from heaven, and the Lord seems not to care, and all things remain as they were from the beginning—especially in such periods it may appear to us as if the Lord is slack concerning his promise.

We would forbear no longer. How then can the Lord tolerate the wickedness of the ungodly and their persecution of the righteous?

We would make an end of things and cause righteousness and justice to appear gloriously over all the workers of iniquity. How then can the Lord abide in silence on the throne of his glory in heaven?

The Lord is longsuffering over us.

He is not slack concerning his promise. If you count his forbearing immediately to realize his promise as slackness, you do not understand him, and you ascribe to him what is unworthy of his name.

There is a different reason that he does not inaugurate the final realization of his kingdom and eternal covenant at once. He is longsuffering over us.

Do not miss the meaning of these words. He is longsuffering over us, over his people, over those who look for the hope of his coming, over his eternally beloved church. To read this as if the text spoke of a longsuffering of the Most High over the wicked is to change the word of God, and to deprive these words of their precious comfort for the waiting and hoping people of God; it is to cast the bread of the children before the dogs and to let the little ones go hungry. Not over the wicked, not over the scoffing enemy the Lord is longsuffering, but over his children. His forbearance is over the wicked, meaning that he would strike them down into perdition immediately, were it not his unchangeable purpose to realize all his counsel. But his longsuffering is over his beloved people. Thus according to these words of Peter, the Lord is longsuffering over us. Thus it is in the conclusion of the parable of the unrighteous judge: "And shall not God avenge his own elect, which cry day and night unto him, though he bear long with them [be longsuffering over them]?" (Luke 18:7).

Longsuffering over us.

Precious word of blessed comfort!

It implies, first, that the almighty, triune, covenant God remembers his people constantly in everlasting, unchangeable, and unfathomable love. He forgets them not for a moment. A mother might forget her nursing babe. Although she might forget, the Lord never forgets his beloved. They are dear to him; they have a constant place in his heart; he has engraved them in the palms of his hands.

It implies, second, that because of this everlasting love he is concerned about them as they are in the world. He is not indifferent regarding their suffering and distress, but is keenly sensitive with respect to all their afflictions. Those who touch his people touch the apple of his eye.

So it cannot be counted slackness if he does not immediately deliver them out of all their troubles and realize the promise of his coming and the final glory of his kingdom. In his everlasting love he longs to save them to the full and would avenge them quickly.

He is, however, longsuffering over them.

As the husbandmen longs to gather the precious fruit into the barn and would do so immediately, but is longsuffering over it until the proper time of the harvest, so the Lord would gather his people into his everlasting home and make them partakers of the final glory of his kingdom without delay, were it not that the harvest must be ripe and all his good counsel must first be fulfilled.

Humanly speaking, for the term *longsuffering* is human, the Lord restrains the promptings of his love until the hour of deliverance has fully come.

Until then the promise of his coming must wait for its realization.

Neither is he slack in bringing about that proper hour. In his longsuffering over his people, he hastens to their deliverance.

Behold, I come quickly!

Yea, come, Lord!

❖

The promise of his coming.

Blessed promise!

Rich in assurance of unspeakable glory. Certain of its fulfillment, as all the promises of God are in Christ yea and amen.

Hastening, always hastening on, throughout the ages of history, toward its final and complete realization in the day of Christ.

Drawing nearer, always nearer, as the years roll by, in all the events of history, in the fulfilling of the full measure of iniquity by its workers and in the continual ingathering of the elect, until the body of Christ, in which his fullness must dwell and his riches be displayed forever, will be complete.

Then the day will arrive.

Then, when all the chosen of God have been born, have come to repentance, have served the purpose of God's counsel, the exact hour will strike of the realization of the promise of his coming. Not before. Then without delay.

For God is not slack concerning his promise.

He is longsuffering as the husbandmen over the fruit of the land. Therefore he wills not that any should perish, but that all should come to repentance.

All. Every last one. Not one may be missing in that day.

How foolish, how utterly contrary to the meaning of the text, how absolutely impossible is the interpretation that would make "all" inclusive of every man in the universalistic sense. Foolish, because it is contrary to the plain teaching of the word of God. Contrary to the evident meaning of the text, because the Lord is not longsuffering over all, but over us, the people of his free and sovereign love, and all is as comprehensive as us. Impossible, because it is given as a reason that the Lord abides and does not immediately fulfill the promise of his coming. He wills that all should first come to repentance. He wills not that any should perish. Until all will have been saved, he will not come again. But never would he come again if his glorious revelations must wait for the salvation of all men without exception.

All, however, must come to repentance, that is, all those whom the Lord loved in everlasting love and sovereign grace and ordained unto eternal glory, predestinated to be made like unto the image of his Son, the Lord Jesus Christ.

For such is the will of the Father, who chose them and predestinated them and gave them to Christ, that of all these he should lose none, but should save them all and raise them in glory at the last day. Such is the will of our blessed savior, who received his own from the Father and shed his lifeblood for them on the accursed tree to redeem them from the guilt and power of sin. Such is the will of the Spirit of grace, who is given unto them to make them partakers of all the blessings of salvation in Christ Jesus.

Not one of them may perish, can perish, will ever perish!

For they are not an arbitrary number of individual believers, without unity of thought and divine plan. They constitute one whole.

They are the one flock of the good shepherd. They constitute the one glorious body of the Lord Jesus Christ, in the whole of which the glory of the riches of God's grace must shine forth forever, each individual member of which must serve his own purpose in his own divinely ordained place in the body, to add to the luster of that glorious grace. They are a holy temple in the Lord, God's dwelling place, and every individual stone is necessary, according to God's everlasting counsel, to complete the beauty of the whole.

Hence God wills not that any should perish, but that all come to repentance.

And he is longsuffering over us.

Oh, never count it slackness of the Lord, if it should seem as if he is long in coming.

He is hastening on through the ages to reach the consummation of his blessed counsel.

He abides to save us all!

29

Long Patience

"Nevertheless the Lord raised up judges, which delivered them out of the hand of those that spoiled them. And yet they would not hearken unto their judges, but they went a-whoring after other gods, and bowed themselves unto them: they turned quickly out of the way which their fathers walked in, obeying the commandments of the Lord; but they did not so. And when the Lord raised them up judges, then the Lord was with the judge and delivered them out of the hand of their enemies…for it repented the Lord because of their groanings."—Judges 2:16–18

Sad summary this is of Israel's history.

And, alas, of the history of God's church in the world throughout the ages.

And lest we should exalt ourselves, also a sad summary of the individual child of God, of you and of me.

A history weary with the mournful monotony of its ever-recurring phases, like the endless sameness of the waves of the ocean rolling over the smooth slope of the sandy beach.

The children of Israel did evil in the sight of the Lord…And the Lord delivered them into the hand of their enemies who spoiled them…And the Lord repented because of their groaning…And the Lord sent them judges who delivered them…And they would not hearken unto their judges…And they did evil in the sight of the Lord more than their fathers…And the Lord delivered them up…And they groaned…And the Lord repented and he delivered them…

Sin and backsliding…retribution and chastisement…repentance and groaning on the part of Israel…deliverance and respite… and then the whole cycle happens all over again.

On and on!

As the sun draws the vapor from the ocean in cloud vessels, and they carry the water to the tops of the mountains, there to empty themselves in pouring rains, forming streams and rivers that carry the water back to the ocean...Ever recurring; never finished process.

A history weary with the monotony of its constant return to the same phase.

And its apparent vanity.

❖

Marvelous revelation of God's long patience!

His longsuffering with Israel of the old dispensation, with his church throughout the centuries, with you, and with me.

Such is, no doubt, the central thought of this sad summary. It reveals the marvelous long patience of Jehovah, the God of his people, in all the brightness of his unchanging love, against the dark background of Israel's obstinacy, of your sin and my sin, of the constant backsliding of his chosen church.

Frequently Scripture speaks of the longsuffering of the Most High. The Lord is slow of anger, long of passion, longsuffering over his people. Often this wondrous virtue of Jehovah is mentioned in immediate connection with other perfections of his glorious and adorable being, such as grace, mercy, loving-kindness, and truth. Sometimes Scripture explains more fully that God is longsuffering to us because he does not will that any should perish, but that all should come to repentance; that he will avenge them speedily, although he is longsuffering over his elect who cry unto him day and night.

Sometimes Scripture does not specifically speak of this long patience of Jehovah, but merely causes us to feel that it only is the reason that Israel is cast into the crucible of affliction and suffering, yet is never consumed. Thus is the passage in Judges 2:16–18.

The hand of the Lord was against Israel...and they repented... were delivered...sinned again...were chastised once more...cried for help...the Lord repented and delivered.

Just repeat this story again and again, and you have the content of the book of Judges.

Again, only repeat this same monotonous and apparently

endless strain, and you write the history of the church of Christ in the world.

Times change, conditions alter, different persons appear on the stage of this history as generation after generation passes away....

But the same drama in all its acts and scenes is enacted. And through it all shines the long patience of God.

Wonderful longsuffering of Jehovah!

❖

Longsuffering. Do not say forbearance.

These are not the same and may not be confused, although they have an element in common.

They are alike in that both are a revelation of the long passion of God concerning his revelation in history. The Most High need not hasten; he can afford to wait until the appointed end is attained.

They differ in that longsuffering is the long passion of love, while forbearance is the long passion of wrath. Longsuffering is God's long passion over his people, whom he loved from before the foundation of the world, whom he ordained to be made like unto the image of his Son, whom he forms and redeems and sanctifies until they are without spot and blemish, in order that they should declare his praises. Forbearance is God's long passion over the ungodly, whom he hated with sovereign hatred and ordained as vessels of wrath, and whom he fits unto destruction, in order that his power and wrath and righteousness is revealed in them. Longsuffering is God's long passion to save, to save all, to save fully. Forbearance is God's long passion to destroy, to hurl into perdition all who exalt themselves against him and his holy name, to destroy all, to destroy fully.

You entertain a stranger in your home. He moves about freely in your dwelling as if he were the owner of your house. He helps himself to your food and drink; he clothes himself with your garments; he sleeps in your bed. And you charge him nothing at all.

Yet he assumes the attitude of wanton ingratitude over against you, his benefactor. From morning until night he acts as if you were not in the house. He neither thanks you nor even speaks to you. He goes to the neighbors to slander you and to drag your name through the mud. He orders your servants about as if they were his and maltreats them as he pleases. He begins to beat your children, to persecute them, to kill them. But you must have him in your house until a certain time, until he serves a certain purpose. Your attitude toward him is expressed as, "I bear with you as long as necessary, and then you go!"

Such is forbearance.

Such is also the forbearance of God, his long passion of wrath over the ungodly.

For is not the ungodly that stranger in God's house? Does he not eat God's food and drink God's drink and breathe God's air and cover himself with God's garments? No, more, does not he himself with all his powers belong to God, with his body and soul, with his mind and will, with all he is and possesses? Does he not move about in God's creation as if he were sole and rightful lord of all? Does he not act as if God were not? Does he not say in his heart, "There is no God"? Does he not hold the truth in unrighteousness and, knowing God, refuse to thank and to glorify him as God? Does he not exalt himself against the holy one, and does he not persecute his children in the world and kill them all the day long? Did he not even crucify the Lord of glory?

And does not he nevertheless serve God's purpose until God's appointed time?

Does not God assume the attitude over against him that he will bear with him until the measure of iniquity is filled, and no longer?

God's long passion of wrath.

His forbearance of the ungodly.

But different it is with respect to his long passion over his people. It is not forbearance, the long passion of wrath. It is longsuffering, the long passion of unchangeable love.

A surgeon is called upon to perform an operation on his own child, his flesh and blood.

The condition of the child is such that although the operation is necessary because it is the only means to save the child's life, it is impossible to administer an anesthetic. In full consciousness and sensibility the child must endure the agony caused by the surgical knife. The child is bound upon the operating table. The father cuts into his own flesh and blood. The child screams, and his screams cut into the father's heart. The child begs his father to stop, implores him to hurt him no more. And the father's heart bleeds with grief. Yet he continues. In spite of the awful agony of this child, of his cries and prayers, the father continues to work over the son of his love until the operation is finished.

Such is longsuffering.

And such is the longsuffering of the Most High over his people.

His long passion of love, when apparently deaf to their cries he operates on them and casts them into the crucible of suffering and agony unto their final perfection.

Longsuffering. Do not say forbearance.

❖

God loves his people.

He loves them with an everlasting love.

Only remember that God's love is perfect, always a love of self, because he is the highest and only good, the implication of perfection. The bond of perfectness with him is love.

He ordained his own as a perfect people. In sovereign causal love he chose them, perfect, holy, without spot and blemish. As such he has them and beholds them in his eternal counsel. And as such he loves them, has his delight in them, seeks them, and has fellowship with them, the fellowship of perfect friendship.

Israel was his people.

The church throughout the ages of history is his people.

However, that people, that church, as it actually and historically exists in the world, is not perfect as in the eternal pattern of them in the sovereign counsel of God. Far from that perfection they are by nature. Not only are not all Israel that are of Israel, and not only is there an ungodly and reprobate carnal seed with Israel, with the church of all times, but also the spiritual children are still far from perfection. Due to this carnal element as well as to the sins of the elect, they often forsake the Lord who formed them and hanker after other gods. An evil disease, the fatal disease of sin and corruption, cleaves to God's people as they exist and become manifest in the world.

And God loves them.

Because he loves them and would lead them to the eternal perfection of his tabernacle, so that they can be his sons and daughters forever and he can walk among them as their God and bless them, he operates on them.

His is the operating hand.

The instruments are the enemies who spoil them, who would surely destroy the church if they were not the operating instruments in the hand of Jehovah to serve only his purpose. Wherever Israel turned, as they bowed before Baal and Ashteroth, the hand of the Lord was against them for evil. The people groaned, for the enemy was cruel and rejoiced in causing them to suffer. For a long time the Lord kept silence and refused to listen to their cries. Although he loves his people and hates their enemies, yet he was silent and in spite of their cries, continued to chastise them. He was longsuffering over them.

Until they groaned to him. Until they let go of Baalim and Ashteroth and repented of their sins.

Not all repented, but the Bochim, the weepers, the remnant according to the election, wept before the Lord in true penitence and implored his mercy.

Then the Lord repented. Not as if the Lord is mutable, but in his eternal mercy he grieves when his people suffer.

And he delivered them. For a time he sent respite.

Until they turned back once again. Then he stretched out his mighty operating hand to cut into the flesh and blood of his son Israel.

For God loves his people from before the foundation of the world.

Loves them with the love of perfection.

He is longsuffering over them.

❖

Sad summary.

A historical account, wearying because of the ever-recurring phases of sin and repentance, chastisement and deliverance.

And they sinned and followed after Baal and Ashteroth…And the Lord delivered them into the hand of their enemies…And they groaned and repented of their evil...And the Lord repented and sent judges to deliver his people...And they sinned again...And so on and on...

Will the end never come?

Will that people never be perfected?

Will they always return to their sinful ways and make themselves abominable in the sight of God because of their backsliding and idolatry? And if they would return to their sinful ways, will the Lord finally destroy them?

Oh, they would, and the Lord would have to destroy them if their salvation depended on them and their walking in the way of the law, for the law cannot make those who come to it perfect. The Bochim, the weepers among Israel, would finally realize that one greater than the law must come, one greater than all the judges would have to arise to deliver them forever, one who could take all their sins upon himself and bear them away forever.

And he came.

For his people God delivered him to the death of the cross.

He was longsuffering over his only begotten Son.

Until all was finished.

Glorious victory!

30

A Shelter in the Time of Storm

"The LORD is good, a strong hold in the day of trouble; and he knoweth them that trust in him."—Nahum 1:7

GOOD is the Lord!

Suddenly these words appear in the midst of most awful threatenings of wrath and vengeance. These words come upon us unexpectedly, as the single shaft of sunlight piercing for a moment the dark and threatening clouds and cheering the earth with a message in gold, as a sudden lull in the storm that promises that soon the darkness will roll away and the light will shine again.

Jehovah had been depicted by the prophet in all the fierceness of his anger against the wicked. He is jealous and burning with zeal for the maintenance of his holiness. He is a God who revenges and is furious in his anger. Wrath is heaped up for his enemies; the vials of his anger are filled and he will pour them out. He will not acquit the wicked. He comes in the whirlwind. In the storm he descends. The clouds are like dust that he raises by his furious coming. By his rebuke and through the fire of his hot anger, the sea and the rivers are dried up. Bashan and Carmel languish. The mountains quake for fear. The hills melt. The earth is burned at his presence. The world and all its inhabitants are consumed. Like molten fire his fury is poured out. In his anger the mighty rocks are thrown down.

Terrible in his wrath is Jehovah!

Who can stand before his indignation? Who can abide in the fierceness of his anger?

Then, suddenly, "Good is Jehovah, a stronghold in the day of trouble; and he knows those who trust in him."

Fear not, you children of the Lord, you who trust in him, for the anger of his countenance does not burn against you. When you behold the Lord descending as furious anger, do not tremble and be amazed, neither let your heart be filled with doubts and misgivings and evil thoughts of the Lord your God, for the Lord is good. And because he is good he must be the furious avenger of evil, and he cannot acquit the doer of iniquity.

Oh, Jehovah is good.

He is good not in the weak, miserable, and sinful sense that wicked and corrupted minds frequently imagine him to be, as winking at sin and loving the wicked and the righteous alike, causing everyone to be full of bliss and joy. For his goodness is righteousness, holiness, and truth. His love is purer than the snow before it is soiled through contact with the earth. He is in himself goodness, and there is no evil in him. Such is his being; such is his nature; such is his mind and will. Such is all his life and activity.

As he is good in himself, so he is good to all his creatures, the supreme goodness, the sole fount of whatever good exists anywhere. Another source of goodness there is none. Beside him there is no God and no good. To live apart from him is death. It is good his face to see. Whoever in any sense separates himself from Jehovah must experience isolation and being severed from the sole source of all goodness.

He is good unchangeably, for his name is Jehovah, I AM. He is therefore goodness absolute, the uncaused cause of all goodness. There is no source other than himself or deeper than his infinite being from which he derives his goodness. Neither is there in him variableness or shadow of turning. He is the ever-active power of goodness, yet his power never diminishes. He is the continuously overflowing fount of goodness, yet there is in him no decrease.

Because he is unchangeably good, he is furious in his anger, and he cannot acquit the wicked. Because he is good, he always does good. Because he is righteous, he always executes righteousness. Because his love is pure and righteous, holy and just, he cannot tolerate the wicked in his presence and receive the doer of iniquity into his communion.

His anger burns against the wicked because he is holy in his love.

Good is the Lord!

❖

Jehovah is good.

In his goodness he loves the righteous.

The righteous are those whom he knew in love from before the foundation of the world and whom he chose in Christ in order to lead them to glory.

The righteous are those over whom Jehovah manifested his love when he sent his beloved into the world in the form of a servant, although he was Lord of all. He revealed his unchangeable and unfathomable love when in the form of a servant his Son humbled himself to the deepest reproach and pains of hell, having taken upon himself the sins of those whom the Father had given to him, and by his suffering and humiliation made reconciliation for them.

They are those whom by the wondrous power of grace the Father draws into living fellowship with his Son, Jesus Christ, by the power of his resurrection regenerating them unto a living hope, pouring forth into their hearts a new life and a new hope, calling them by the almighty voice of his word, and translating them from darkness into light. Thus he makes them righteous. He delivers them from all the power of the devil. He liberates them from the law of sin and death. And he creates in them a new heart with a new desire to walk according to all of his commandments. They are those who love his precepts and keep them. Oh, they often blunder and stumble in the way, for the power of sin is still within them and often seduces them from the path of the Lord's commandments. Perfection they have not reached. But they hate and abhor evil and detest the ways of the evildoer. While often they must humble themselves in sorrow and penitence before their Lord in Christ, yet they struggle and carry on the battle, the light of hope in their eyes that they will walk in perfectly white garments of purest holiness.

To them Jehovah is good. Good as the unchangeable I AM.

His relation toward them is his everlasting covenant.

Even as his perfect goodness becomes manifest in his wrath and vengeance over the wicked, so he reveals that he is good by loving the righteous and filling them with everlasting bliss and joy.

They need not fear in the day of his wrath, for when destruction is upon the earth, the Lord is a stronghold to his people.

When storms of trouble rage, the good Lord is a shelter to those who love him.

Oft through the storm they must go.

For the way to glory is a way of suffering and trouble. There is no other way. He who would be victor must fight. It was the good Lord's good pleasure that the children of his love should appear for a while in the world of darkness as children of light, to the glory of his wondrous grace. Because of this they must often suffer, for as the darkness is judged by the light and condemned, the darkness hates the light and always exerts itself to extinguish it. Besides, the good Lord sends judgments of destruction and desolation upon a world of darkness that rises against him and against his people. And in that world are also his people. They too partake of the suffering of this present time to which the world is subject because of sin. With the whole creation they groan. Of the world's sorrow and grief, sickness and pain, war and famine, desolation and death they partake.

But the good Lord is to them a stronghold in the day of trouble.

He is a fortress where one finds safety in the hour of danger.

A shelter in the time of storm.

Not so that protected by his mighty care, they need not suffer according to the flesh. They must. But as they are protected by their mighty Lord, all things must work together for their salvation, and their enemies must be instrumental unto their salvation.

How safe they are in the impregnable stronghold.

A shelter of almighty love.

Good is Jehovah. Loving the righteous.

A stronghold in the day of trouble.

A shelter in the time of storm.

The Lord is good!

❖

How worthy of the most perfect trust is the good Lord.

For those who put their confidence in him will never be ashamed. He knows them.

In its deepest root confidence is an act of love, an act of the love the good Lord spreads abroad in the hearts of those whom he loves.

Hatred does not trust, but can only be filled with distrust and dark apprehension with respect to its object. But love is trusting. It is like the little child clinging to father and feeling safe in the hour of danger.

Confidence is the assurance that the one in whom we trust loves us. So is trust in Jehovah. The love he spreads abroad in our hearts does not first witness within us that we love him, but that he loved us, loved us first, loved us from before time began, loved us with a great love. The love with which we love God never will be more than a response to the love with which he loved us, a response drawn forth by his almighty grace. Thus confidence must center in the cross. There it finds the strongest testimony that the good Lord loved us. There is its greatest, most wondrous manifestation. Looking at the accursed tree, the believer is assured that Jehovah loved and loves him, and that he can surely surrender himself to the good Lord as a stronghold in the day of trouble. There is no fear in love.

Trust is the firm assurance that the good Lord is Jehovah, faithful and true, who never changes, with whom there is no shadow of turning. As long as there is fear in our hearts that the Lord might change or alter his attitude toward us, we cannot have perfect confidence. But our God is Jehovah, more changeless than the rock. Although we change frequently and often sin against him, always we can turn to the immutable love that manifested itself in the blood of the cross. Looking at Calvary, and remembering that he loved us and surrendered his only begotten Son for us while we were yet sinners, we will approach him with quiet confidence and seek shelter with him in the time of storm.

To confide is to be assured that he in whom we put our trust is strong and mighty to help in the day of trouble. Love may be so fervent and faithful, but if it is lacking in power to help, we cannot find a safe shelter in it. The love of God is as infinite in power as it is unfathomable in depth. He is as strong to help as he is full of mercy. Surely no trouble can overwhelm us, no enemy can destroy us, and no danger can come near us, when we seek our refuge in him who revealed his power over sin and death and hell in the sacrifice of his beloved. The cross and the resurrection of Jesus Christ are the signs of God's almighty power to save and to deliver us in the day of trouble.

Hence that trust of love, whereby we know that he loves us and that his love is faithful and true, strong to save, to protect, and to deliver, seeks refuge in him and feels assured that the devil and all of our enemies are powerless to hurt us.

Neither is there any danger that the Lord will cast us out. For he knows those who put their trust in him. He knows them with a knowledge of love.

He knows them in distinction from the ungodly, upon whom he pours forth the molten fire of his wrath and furious anger. Although he comes in fury upon his enemies, so that the mountains languish and the hills melt, and all the earth quakes and trembles because of the fury of his wrath; and although they who trust in him are right in the midst of the raging storm of his judgments over the ungodly, yet will he be a stronghold in the day of trouble to those who seek refuge in him. In the general upheaval caused by his fierce wrath, no harm will come near them.

He knows them in their needs and troubles. He knows the way in which they must be led to inherit the city that has foundations, the incorruptible treasure that is kept in heaven for them. He knows their weaknesses, fears, all their wants, and how to supply them.

He knows them because he chose them. His knowledge is before they were. They are his handiwork. And he remembers that they are dust.

Thus they walk their way and fight their battles, assured that all is well.

Leaning on the Lord, they have peace and joy in their strong and faithful Lord even in the midst of trouble.

For a shelter in the time of storm is Jehovah.

Good is the Lord!

31

God's Blessing, Sure and Constant

"Thy blessing is upon thy people."—Psalm 3:8

GOD's blessing is his creative word of goodwill over us.

One who blesses, according to the picturesque literal signifi-cance of the original Hebrew, speaks a good word over him who is blessed, whether it be in the form of a mere wish, as we frequently do with respect to one another, or in the form of a prophetic read-ing from the counsel of God, as the old and dying patriarchs did over their sons.

Peculiarly divine is the power to bless.

Man's efforts to bless man are impotent. He may bestow many gifts upon his fellow man, but blessing is not in things, and though he enriches his neighbor with abundance and wealth according to this world, he still is powerless to bless his brother. He may express all the good wishes of a kind and loving heart upon him, but his word cannot realize the thing it conveys; it is impotent to create the thing it ardently desires; it is powerless to bless.

He is no source of blessing, for he is not the fountain of good.

A divine prerogative and power it is to bless. God speaks and it comes to pass. His word is a creative word. He speaks before things are, and they are caused. His word calls the things that are not as if they were. So we understand by faith that the things that are seen are not made of things that do appear. When he speaks well upon a creature, the blessing comes; when he speaks ill, who will prevent the certain curse?

His blessing is upon his people.

His powerful, almighty, creative word for their good is constant-ly upon them, proceeds toward them from his mouth continuously, surrounds them, meets them in the way, guides them by day, watches over them by night, is in them to fill them with good things, dwells with them in their homes, permeates their food and drink, keeps their enemies from harming them, makes them step upon the serpent and the young adder, turns all the evil for them into eternal good, causes those to be their servants who rise up against them, guards them in danger, strengthens them and makes them invulnerable in battle, comforts them in sorrow, makes them patient in suffering, and follows them all the way to the eternal inheritance that is prepared for them from before the foundation of the world.

For only what is good and truly a blessing is conducive for our everlasting salvation!

Whether anything is a blessing or a curse (and it surely is one or the other) is a question that may be answered only in the light of eternity.

The human criterion of blessing and good is false. It is earthly, temporal, subjective, and shortsighted.

We are inclined to judge all things in the light of this world and of the present time, frequently of the immediate present. Of eternal values and of ultimate ends we are apt to lose sight. The fulfillment of our desires and the realization of our aspirations we consider a good. Failure to reach the desired end, disappointment with respect to our personal wishes, things that are contrary to the longings of the flesh, we deplore as evils. We confuse blessing with success and look upon prosperity as a good, long for it, aspire after it, pray for it, strive for it, and stand weeping and wailing and murmuring against our lot when our chastisement is there every morning. We forget that what appears to us to be a good may be an evil in disguise, and what presents itself to our earthly perception as a present evil may be a means to our eternal glory. Foolishly we inquire whether the road is smooth without caring about the direction, and carefully we would avoid the rougher and steeper stretches of the way, though without them we cannot reach the promised heavenly country.

The man of the world prospers in his business, accumulates much wealth, and claims that a kind providence is blessing all his efforts—and everybody is inclined to believe him. We forget that the almighty word of the Most High may be in his goods, cursing him to damnation.

When the farmer's fields yield well and an abundant crop he harvests, so that he must increase the capacity of his barns, he is considered a well-blessed man. We seem oblivious to the reality that the Lord might take his soul from him and cast him into eternal destruction.

In these so-called bad times of depression, our souls are inclined to bewail the passing of the wave of abnormal prosperity of recent years. Barely is the hand of the Lord touching us and we are inclined to pray to heaven for prosperity. We can hardly be taught to see that the good times were bad and the bad times are better than the good times for the people of God.

According to the world, a nation is blessed when it prospers and grows mighty. An army is blessed when it claims victory. A church is blessed when it grows in numbers.

Always the same false standard of blessing and good is applied: the standard that is earthly, temporal, and carnal.

But God's blessing is not so.

It is upon his people to their eternal salvation. It is upon them when every word he speaks over them flows from his everlasting good pleasure unto their eternal glory, from his counsel of salvation, from his eternal thoughts of grace and mercy and peace upon them.

When that word is spoken upon them, it causes what it expresses. It changes every apparent evil into an eternal good, for it is the cause that all things work together for good to those who love God, to those who are called according to his purpose.

The irresistible operation of God's unchangeable, efficacious, almighty, all-comprehensive grace, through every means, in every way, in all the experiences of this present time—that is blessing.

God's blessing is his creative word of grace.

❖

Thy blessing is upon thy people.

The text is concise and draws the line sharply.

God's blessing is singular, not plural; it is one, not many, even though in the singleness of the blessing of Jehovah there is a plurality of manifold riches and graces.

It cannot be divided or distinguished into a general and a

particular, a common and a private blessing, for God is one, his everlasting counsel is one, his word is one, his blessing is one.

Even as the blessing is one, so the object upon which it is bestowed is one. Thy blessing is upon thy people. It is not a blessing that is upon all men. Neither is it one blessing for all men in general, and another for his people in particular. The blessing is inclusive of all his people; it is exclusive of all others. The curse follows all others to the grave.

Thy blessing is upon thy people.

It could not be otherwise. There can be no blessing of Jehovah upon the ungodly, nor can the blessing of our covenant God fail, even for the slightest conceivable moment, to be upon his people. It is upon them surely, constantly, without fail, uninterruptedly, for blessing is the word of Jehovah that proceeds toward the objects from his eternal counsel of goodwill and sovereign grace.

Therefore the recipients of his blessing can be only those whom he has determined to love and to ordain unto eternal glory in the everlasting likeness of his only begotten Son.

God's people are not self-determined, but divinely chosen and ordained. They are God's people because he sovereignly ordained them to be such in his eternal thoughts and purpose. It is the counsel from which the word of his blessing must proceed to all who are truly blessed, that ordained them to everlasting bliss in his tabernacle, to be partakers of the divine life through his Son, and to rejoice forever in his blessed covenantal friendship. It is the counsel in and by which he determined upon all things that are and will be.

The chief purpose of God's counsel is the self-glorification of his adorable being, the manifestation of the glorious virtues of his divine nature. That all-dominating purpose he counseled to realize in the fullness of glory manifested in the Lord Jesus Christ, in whom all the riches of the Godhead dwell bodily. The more complete radiation of that blessed glory he counseled to issue forth in the members of that body of which the Lord Jesus Christ is ordained to be the eternal head. All things in heaven and on earth and in the abyss are by that counsel so arranged that they must be means to the realization of that eternal purpose of the glory of God in Christ, radiating through the members of his body.

Nothing is excluded; the counsel is all-comprehensive.

Nowhere in that counsel is there a mistake; the counsel is full of eternal wisdom.

It all moves and works around and toward the one purpose: the eternal glory of Jehovah, the manifestation of the fullness of God in Christ, the eternal salvation of the people of his choice. Good and evil, grace and sin, friend and enemy, angels and devils, godly and ungodly, prosperity and adversity, health and sickness, joy and sorrow; whether the way is smooth and even or rough and almost impassable; whether we sing songs of joy in the daytime or cry for grief in the darkness of the night; whether we are surrounded by peace and plenty or whether the enemy harasses and persecutes us; life and death—all things are sovereignly and with infinite wisdom so determined in the everlasting counsel of the Most High that they must be infallible means to reach the one purpose: the highest manifestation of the glory of God in and through the salvation of his people in Christ.

Every word spoken by the Almighty proceeds from his eternal counsel and must be a realization of it.

Other words he never speaks.

Hence every word that leaves his lips tends to the realization of his counsel, moves toward the final manifestation of his glory, and works together for the ultimate realization of the salvation of his people.

Hence his blessing must be upon his people. It could be on no other.

Forever impossible it is that the blessing of the Most High would fail for even a moment to be upon his people. Every word of God upon his people is a word of blessing, working toward their everlasting joy in God's covenant.

Thy blessing is upon thy people.

It is the people whom he redeemed by the word of reconciliation. He spoke the word and Immanuel, God with us, dwelt among us. He spoke again and all the enemies cooperated to shed the blood that must redeem his people. He spoke once more, and redeemed they were in the glorious resurrection and exaltation of the Lord Jesus Christ.

The central word of blessing has been spoken upon them.

How shall he then fail to speak every last word of his counsel of salvation? How shall he not with him also freely give us all things?

God is for us. Who shall be against us?

They are the people whom he delivers by the recreative word of his almighty grace. By nature they are darkness, but by the word of his blessing he makes them children of light. They who were no people become his people who gladly confess that they are children of the living God.

Only in the way of that people, in the way of light, in the way of the Lord, can one truly say that the blessing of the Lord is upon him.

For God's blessing is upon his people!

❖

God's blessing is a constant, ever-present reality, for it is upon his people.

The text does not say that ultimately God's blessing will be upon his people, though now it is upon the godly and the ungodly in common.

It does not implore, "Oh, that God's blessing may be upon his people, though in the present time it so often leaves and forsakes them."

It is positive and expresses a present, a sure, a constant fact. The blessing of Jehovah is always, is now, is every day and every moment, is in every way and in every experience upon his people.

Quite contrary to experience this would seem, when we regard the things that are seen. How directly in conflict with the life and way of Asaph, the author of this psalm, how contrary to his experience, as he relates it in this song, seems the assertion that God's blessing is upon his people! Asaph complains that they are mightily increased who trouble him, that the number of those who rise up against him is great, that the taunt of his enemies is constantly in his ears, who say that there is no help for him in God. Contrary this seemed to the experience of Asaph for a while, when he looked at the things that are seen and considered that the ungodly all around him were prospering, that their eyes stood out with fatness, and that they knew no bands in their death, while his own punishment was awaiting him at every dawn. So it seems always, if we regard the things that are seen and have no eye for the hidden blessing of God's almighty and gracious word over his people. How are they afflicted who are called the children of God! How all things seem to turn against them! Not only do they receive their goodly portion of the sufferings and ills of this world, but also they often are the reproach of all, and their enemies seem to triumph over them.

Small wonder, considering the things that are perceived in this world, looking at them with an eye of the flesh, judging them in their own mind and according to the standard of this world, that there are those who would change the words of the psalmist and maintain that God's blessing is promiscuously upon all. It is not particular but general; it is not peculiar but common, even as are the experiences of this present life.

Small wonder that some of God's children complained that there is no knowledge in the Most High, that his way is not equal, and that the ungodly are the objects of God's richest blessing.

God is God who hides himself.

His ways are in the deep. His paths are frequently untraceable; his wisdom is unsearchable always.

Therefore we look not at the things that are seen, but at the things that are not seen; we regard not our earthly experiences to judge our God and his work in the light of them, but rather with the eye of faith look at him first, then at our way.

Then we know that he is unchangeable in his counsel of love.

And trust that his blessing is upon us in time and eternity.

32

Tender Watchfulness

*"For the eyes of the Lord are over the righteous, and his
ears are open unto their prayers: but the face of the Lord is
against them that do evil." —1 Peter 3:12*

WHAT comforting assurance for the righteous!

What cheering encouragement for them, inciting them to persevere in well-doing in the midst of a world full of darkness and evil.

The eyes of the Lord are upon, are over them; his ears are always
open unto their petitions and cries; his face is against those who
do evil. With such an attitude of the Lord of heaven toward them
and against their enemies, they are perfectly safe, and the way of
righteousness is assuredly a blessed and sure way.

This statement seems to be contrary to all appearances and to
everyday experiences and to be in conflict with everything the eye
sees in this world, for the way of the wicked is broad and even,
and the path of the righteous, rugged and narrow. Prosperity is the
seeming good fortune of those who do evil; adversity is the lot of
the righteous. Often those who care for neither God nor his people
wallow in wealth; while for those who walk not after the flesh but
after the Spirit affliction is present every morning with the rising of
the sun. Those feast, these starve; those sin, these groan. In the light
of actual facts in life, one would seem constrained to contradict the
apostle and to maintain that the face of the Lord is against those
who do well, while his eyes and ears have favor toward the wicked.

How paralyzing, how discouraging, how spiritually enervating
is the very thought for the righteous in the world.

But no.

God forbid!

This cannot be, for the Lord is righteousness, and righteousness the righteous Lord loves.

His eyes are assuredly over the righteous in tender care, and his ears are on the alert for their every prayer, while his face is against those who do evil.

Now, always, constantly, everywhere...

At every step, at every twist and turn of the road...

Blessed knowledge of faith!

❖

Did you never marvel at the courage of the saints?

Are you never astonished at their boasts, though weakness and helplessness appear in all of their features, as they are encompassed by enemies stronger and mightier than they?

Does it not sound like sheer vanity to stand alone in the midst of thousands and shout, "I will not be afraid of ten thousands of people, that have set themselves against me round about" (Ps. 3:6)? Or is it not madness to ring forth the challenge, "Though an host should encamp against me, my heart shall not fear" (Ps. 27:3)?

Where is the secret of the saint's power? What is the explanation of this superhuman courage that will never be daunted?

It is right here: The eyes of the Lord are over him, and he knows it; the ears of the Lord are inclined to his faintest groan, and he is assured of it; the face of the Lord always spells destruction to those who do evil, and in this he is confident. Without this assurance his valor would be vanity, his daring would be recklessness, and his courage in the midst of overwhelming enemies would be akin to insanity.

He is strong in the Lord.

The picture of this life you see in Israel's plunging through the Red Sea. Madness it seemed for Moses to lead that helpless multitude of men, women, and children into that threatening deep. Madness too it seemed for that persecuted crowd to follow their leader and deliverer from bondage into the sea before them. For dark was the night, and they knew not how far the path, struck through the surging billows, would extend before their feet. The fierce wind howled and the waves foamed and roared, spitting their spray upon the poor refugees, eager to spring upon them and swallow them up into death. Close upon their heels pursued the revengeful Egyptians, raving furiously because of the death of their firstborns. A last act of despair it seemed to plunge into that yawning deep.

Yes, but from the light side of the fire-pillar the eyes of Jehovah, kindly and encouraging, smiled upon his people, lighting their path through the dark night and assuring their hearts of victory. From the dark side of the cloud-pillar God's face frowned a terrible threat of destruction to the pursuing enemy host.

The eyes of the Lord were in watchful care over the righteous.

His face was in threatening indignation against the wicked.

Thus it ever is.

Do you still marvel at the boldness of the righteous? Though weak and alone, he can be bold as a lion.

For God is with him.

Blessed assurance!

The Lord's eyes upon us. And his ears open unto our prayers.

There is in these words the alert vigilance of a divine heart full of most tender love and care.

Did you never see a mother watching by the bedside of her sick darling? Sleep cannot touch those eyes, constantly fixed in anxious watchfulness upon the face of her babe; the slumber of weariness cannot still the keen alertness of that mother's ear, quick to perceive the merest groan from the sickbed. The faintest whisper she is prompt to hear; the slightest stir she is on the alert to notice. Nothing concerning the child of her love escapes her attention; upon him all her attention is concentrated. Why this quick and keen perception of eye and ear? Whence springs this anxious watchfulness and tender care?

Behind those wakeful eyes and keen-edged, high-strung ears there beats a heart of most tender love.

It is love that keeps open those eyes and holds them riveted upon its object. It is love that causes those ears to be keen to notice the faintest cry from her darling.

Strange how in common, everyday life and circumstances many objects pass within the range of our vision without drawing the slightest attention on our part; how many a sound beats upon our ears without being even so much as noticed by us. We see, yet we do not perceive; we hear, yet we do not notice, all because there is little or no interest in the objects of our vision and hearing. They leave us cold. We are not concerned about them. They cross our way and are forgotten without leaving an impression. But let the object have the love of our hearts, and let the sound heard strike the love-chord in our souls, and how keen are the eyes to see, how alert the ears to hear!

So the eyes of the Lord are open upon the righteous, and his ears are on the alert to hear the prayers of the righteous, because he loves their appearance and their cries strike the love-chord of his heart divine.

They are the righteous.

Righteous are they before him judicially, for he declared them free from sin and guilt and clothed them with a righteousness not their own, but his; and they washed their garments by faith in the blood of their redeemer. But righteous they are also actually, spiritually, with regard to the inmost spiritual principle of their lives. They are not only redeemed, but also delivered by the wondrous power of his grace. The bonds of sin and death were broken, and they have been set free unto righteousness. The love of God has been spread abroad in their hearts, and partakers they became of a new life, the life of God, through the resurrection of the Lord Jesus. Risen with him, they are righteous in their inmost life. Though often they stumble, they walk as righteous, as children of light, fleeing what is evil and rejoicing in well-doing, manifesting in their lives the life of God.

This is why the world hates them. Because they are righteous and walk as such.

This is why the world reviles and persecutes them. For righteousness' sake.

This is how they suffer. For well-doing.

Their prayers are often groans.

This is why the Lord loves them. This love of the righteous Lord for his righteous children keeps his eyes open over them and his ears keen and quiet to catch every sound from their lips.

Never he slumbers or sleeps. For not a wink do they escape his attention. Their every step he watches with most tender care. Their every sigh he hears with keenest desire to help and to save.

The righteous walk their way under the loving vigilance of the Lord their God.

He is their almighty aid.

Faithful and true.

❖

Why should they not boast? Why should they not triumph, even though a host encamps against them?

Is not the face of the Lord beaming with tender love upon those who walk in the way of righteousness, but against those who do evil, threatening constant destruction upon the enemies of the righteous?

The righteous need fear only one thing: to set their feet in ways of wickedness. Even when the enemy raves and does wickedly; even when the wicked foams in fury against them, reviles and speaks all manner of evil against them, they must not revile. They must fear to meet evil with evil. They must and do dread being seduced into ways of darkness and evil, for the face of the Lord is against those who walk in these ways.

This is comfort to the righteous.

For the wicked are their enemies. Primarily they are wicked with relation to the Lord. He is not in all their thoughts. His ways are not in their hearts. Their meditation is enmity against him. Children of darkness are they who sleep not unless they have done evil. They increase their guilt and heap up treasures of wrath. They abhor the ways of the righteous. As they hate him, the righteous God, so they hate them, his righteous children. They despise their profession and will not hear it. They detest their ways and will not suffer them to walk in them. They hate their light, their Christ, their cause. They make them suffer and fill them with reproach and shame. They would lead the righteous as sheep to the slaughter.

God's face is against the wicked.

His face is the reflection of his heart, and there is nothing in the heart of the righteous Lord that favors those who do evil. He is a light and there is no darkness in him. He is a consuming fire to those who hate him and his children. This terrible divine displeasure and opposition are perfectly reflected in his face.

And his face is his presence. His omnipresent presence. His ever-active presence.

When God is against us, this implies that his omnipresent presence turns against us, acts against us, threatening, discomfiting, and destroying.

Here, there, yonder, everywhere.

Now, then, always, every moment, eternally.

Frowning us into outer darkness!

Things may not appear so in the world, and the wicked may not notice this reality of the Lord's attributes, so full of woe to them and of gladdest comfort to the righteous. Reality is such nonetheless. For the eyes of the Lord are over the righteous in most tender watchfulness, his ears are open upon their prayers in keenest alertness, and his heart is filled with love to them. But his face frowns upon those who do evil.

Yet a little while and the full reality of this will be manifest, when the end of the way will be reached, and all the weary night of life's journey will be past, when the present joy of the wicked will be turned into everlasting weeping and gnashing of teeth, and the present grief of the righteous, into eternal gladness. Then it will be manifest to all not only that it will be true then, but also that it was always true, even in the darkest hours of the righteous.

Against the wicked is the face of the Lord.

And over the righteous are his eyes. To their prayers his ears are open.

To save them to the full.

Hallelujah!

33

Guidance and Glory

"Thou shalt guide me with thy counsel, and
afterward receive me to glory."
—Psalm 73:24

How blessed is the man whose God is the Lord!

How happy is the soul that is spiritually acquainted with the unspeakably rich comfort, embracing time and eternity, life and death, that is contained in these words of the psalmist.

Thou shalt guide me with thy counsel implies all the soul can desire for the present.

Thou shalt receive me to glory embraces all the soul can make the object of its hope for the everlasting future.

Thou shalt guide me with thy counsel and afterward receive me to glory, or in order to receive me to glory afterward, implies all that can satisfy the soul with regard to the direction of the way in which it is guided.

Oh, to appropriate these words and to make them our own! To receive them into our hearts and to take them upon our lips as the expression of our deepest confidence! No, do not change them to eliminate their personal note. Do not alter them into a mere piece of cold dogmatism, so that you would say, "The Lord will guide his people with his counsel and afterward receive them to glory." This also is true, and a precious truth it is for those who know the Lord. But it does not bring the truth as close to your heart and mine as do the words of the psalmist in the way he puts the truth, "Thou shalt guide me and receive me to glory."

To make them our words we must look directly at God, at Jehovah, at the unchangeable rock of our salvation. We must look at him with the steadfast eye of faith, with the tranquil look of confidence in these words, with simple and childlike trust that loves and is conscious of being loved, that is weak but leans on the strong one, with the longing look of hope for the glory that will be revealed in us. Then, with that look in our eyes fixed on Jehovah, in that disposition of our hearts and minds, we express it just in that form, "Thou shalt guide me with thy counsel, and afterward receive me to glory."

Oh, how blessed. How full of peace, satisfaction, submission and surrender, quiet trust and confidence, and all that is to be desired in time and eternity!

A guide we need for the present.

The traveler in a strange mountain country needs a guide. He knows not the way and would be hopelessly lost should he venture out alone in the labyrinth of winding and climbing trails and mountain paths. There are lurking dangers of sudden precipices and hidden ravines with which he is unacquainted and in which he would find his death, should he spurn the aid of a guide. The guide knows and will lead him safely.

So we do not know life's way.

There are ways that seem broad and smooth and others that appear narrow and rough, but whether the one or the other is the better we cannot judge. There are wide and beautiful roads of joy and gladness, of prosperity and wealth; and there are dark trails of sorrow and grief, of suffering and pain, whose gloom appears like the shadow of death. But which to choose we would not know, even were it left in our power and to our wisdom. And there are dangers in the way. There are false guides whose direction would lead us without expectation in broad and seemingly happy roads that lead to destruction. There are slippery places, hidden from our view, on which if we set our feet we would be hurled into certain desolation. There are enemies who lurk to seek our destruction, who like wild beasts would eat our flesh.

How sorely in need are we of a guide!

The psalmist had felt this need.

For a while he had mistrusted the guide of his life. In ways narrow and steep, rough and dark, he had been led, while others were allowed to travel royal highways, smooth and wide. These lived in ease and splendor and knew no bands, or pangs of conscience, in their death. These were the godless, the wicked who oppressed the people of God and spoke blasphemously against the God of heaven. Pride compassed them about as a chain. Yet their prosperity was constant, and never were they in trouble. But the psalmist washed his hands in innocence, and his delight was in the law of the Lord. Yet a way of unchanged suffering and grief had been mapped out for him; his punishment was waiting for him at every dawn of day. And for a while his confidence in his faithful guide had been severely shocked. He had been inclined to oppose his own judgment to that of his guide. He had relinquished his hold upon the hand that led him and became dissatisfied and fretful. Other ways, better roads he would choose for himself.

But his guide had been merciful to him.

When his feet had struck one of the slippery places and he had nearly perished, his merciful guide had taken him into his sanctuary, in order from the viewpoint of that holy place to see the smooth and wide roads of the wicked in contrast to his narrow way. He had seen how the end of those is destruction in a moment, while the outcome of his own dark way was eternal light and joy in glory.

He had seen his foolishness.

He had humbled himself before the Lord who led him and vowed that he would never distrust the Lord again.

He had felt how blessed he was with Jehovah holding his right hand, and in the consciousness of his blessedness he had cried out, "Thou shalt guide me with thy counsel, and afterward receive me to glory."

How blessed is the man whose God is the Lord!

❖

Thou shalt guide me.

How safe am I, if these words are my confession.

The safety of a traveler depends upon the trustworthiness of his guide. For to that guide he surrenders. He submits his own judgment to that of his leader. He travels in unknown regions, blindly to an extent, following his director. Three things are greatly necessary in the guide: He must know the way; he must be powerful to protect his follower; and he must be favorably disposed to the one he guides and intend to lead him safely to the destination.

One who does not know the way cannot lead others.

One who is himself weak and helpless cannot protect others in the presence of dangers.

One who is our enemy and ill disposed toward us cannot be trusted to lead us safely on.

Thou shalt guide me with thy counsel.

How safe is the traveler, the pilgrim, whose guide is Jehovah!

He knows with a perfect and eternal knowledge the way and the destination, for he guides with his counsel, according to which he fixed the end of my way in eternal glory. "For whom he did foreknow, he also did predestinate to be conformed to the image of his Son, that he might be the firstborn among many brethren" (Rom. 8:29). In his eternal good pleasure he fixed the end of all his people and determined the particular place in glory that I will occupy when I reach the end of the way.

There is more. Not only did he establish the end by his eternal counsel, but he also determined the way that must lead there. Every curve in the road, every narrow stretch and steep incline, every hour of suffering and tribulation, of grief and sorrow, every shadow of darkness through which I must pass, he knows because he so determined the way before the world was, in order to lead me on to eternal glory.

And he is powerful to guard me in the midst of danger.

For God Almighty he is.

There is no way too steep for me to climb if his strong hand upholds me and lifts me up. There is no darkness so thick and black that his light is insufficient to lead me on. There is no ravine so deep that, should I stumble and fall, his might could not save me. There is no enemy who is so strong that he can overcome me and cause my death and destruction, if Jehovah chooses to protect me. All the power of the world is insufficient to prevail against his power. All the assaults of hell and the devil are in vain when the Lord of hosts is the fortress of my life, my strong tower and refuge.

There is still more. He guides me by his counsel, but by that same counsel the enemy is placed on my way, and according to Jehovah's counsel all the forces of opposition operate. They do nothing against his will. They only execute his good pleasure. And as they execute the everlasting counsel of my guide, I am assured that they must all cooperate for my salvation.

And well may I entrust myself to Jehovah.

Not only does he know the way, and not only is he able and strong to lead and to protect me in the midst of hosts of enemies who seek after my soul, but he also loves me with immutable love. Well may I feel that I can safely lay my hand in his and confidently press closely to his side. For he loved me before the world was, I know not why. He loved me when I was in sin and rebellion and lifted my fist in his face. He loved me with a love that is faithful and true and far surpasses the bounds of all human comprehension. And he manifested his love when I was still a sinner, a child of wrath, as were also the others. He revealed how he loved when he sent his only begotten Son into the world, when he sent him into my shame and into death, when he sent him into the accursed death of the bloody tree of Calvary.

That love he also spread abroad in my heart. In that love of his, spread abroad in my heart, I love him and feel that he loves me.

And feeling that he loves me with an infinite love...

And knowing that he is strong...

And assured that he knows the way...

I entrust myself to him and, looking at his face, confidently express, "Thou shalt guide me with thy counsel. Lord, all is well."

❖

And afterward...

Thou shalt receive me to glory.

When the pilgrim's journey is ended, when the last curve has been rounded and the last incline has been climbed, when the last dark valley of this strange country has been passed through, then, oh, then I will see that my trust in him was not in vain, that he knew the way, and that the end of it all is glory.

Afterward...

Immediately afterward. For he has his house prepared for me, a house of many mansions. And in it he will receive me. He will open its gates and welcome me, his pilgrim child whom he loved for his own name's sake, and press me to his heart, and clothe me with new garments, and give me a scepter for the sword, a crown for the helmet, a palm branch for the pilgrim's staff, and dry my tears and receive me into his glorious house. There is the Lord who loved me unto death. There are the saints who have trodden the way of suffering and trouble before me. There are the angels who so often served and guarded me in the way. There is no sin, no darkness, no sorrow and grief, no enemy, and no battle. There is perfection, the beauty of holiness, the blessedness of heavenly fellowship. There is light, the perfect light that beams from the countenance of him who loved me. There is everlasting glory.

Thus it will be immediately afterward...

And afterward...

Still afterward.

For even then, at my entrance into the house of many mansions, all is not finished. My body is still left behind in the dust of death.

Afterward Jehovah will also receive my body into glory. He will raise it and glorify it. He will change its weakness into strength, its corruption into incorruption, its mortality into immortality. As we have borne the image of the earthly, so shall we also bear the image of the heavenly.

And afterward...

He will make all things new and deliver the creature from the bondage of corruption, that it may partake of the glorious liberty of the children of God. In the united and glorified heaven and earth he shall spread his tabernacle over me, all over, forever and ever.

Thou shalt guide me with thy counsel.

Lord, teach me never to distrust thy guidance again. Teach me to surrender, to cast myself on thee, for near thee all is well, I know.

I know the way leads there.

I know that sorrow and trouble and affliction, that darkness and danger and death, that enemies and battle and struggle, that my punishment every morning, all belong to the way in which Jehovah guides me that I may be taken to glory.

Teach me perfectly to trust.

For blessed is the man who trusts in thee!

34

Satisfied in Glory

*"But my God shall supply all your need according to his riches
in glory by Christ Jesus."—Philippians 4:19*

MY God.

Emphatically the apostle speaks of his God.

Evidently the reason is that he still has in mind the gift the Philippians sent to him while he was in bonds for Christ's sake. Generously the saints in Philippi had remembered him. It had been a gift of their love in Christ, given for Christ's sake, to one of his servants.

Hence he says, "My God." Just as if a son would say to his benefactor, "My father will reward you." Or as the ambassador of a king would assure him who had been of succor to him in the strange country, "My lord and king will remember you."

So the apostle is still thinking of the gift from the viewpoint of the abounding fruit—abounding unto an eternal recompense for the givers.

What you did to me you did to my God.

He will reward you.

Supply your need.

My God.

❖

Blessed promise.

In glory he will supply all your need.

Thus the text must be understood. It has respect to the final reward of the people of God, to their state of eternal and heavenly glory, for only then will their whole need be perfectly supplied and they will be satisfied with God's likeness forever.

Wrongly the words have been read as if they expressed that

God, according to the riches of his glory in Christ Jesus, would supply all the needs of his people, and as if the needs had reference to their earthly sustenance.

Rightly the meaning of the word of God here is expressed in the far more significant and blessed promise: In glory my God shall supply all your need, according to his riches, by Christ Jesus.

Then, in glory, their capacity for God's riches will be enlarged.

Then he will manifest to them all the riches of his grace.

Then they will be satisfied.

Glorious reward!

❖

Blessed satisfaction.

Your need he will supply in glory.

All your need: your whole need.

Need is not identical with desire, although in the perfection of glory the two will fully accord with each other. In glory we will always know and always desire exactly what we need, and our need being constantly supplied, our desire will continuously be satisfied.

Desire is the subjective conception, the feeling we have of our need and the longing to have it satisfied.

Need is the objective want of our being and nature. Our desire is determined by the condition of our heart and mind and need— by our being. Need is that for which our being, as it was formed by the hands of the creator, really calls; it is that which must be supplied for our well-being. A plant, according to its being and its well-being needs the soil, the rain, and the sunshine. A bird needs the air. A fish needs the water. Man needs God.

That man needs God is determined by man's being. God made man to be God's image-bearer. He made him a rational, moral creature with a mind, a will, and a spiritual soul—a creature who in his nature is adapted to live in the fellowship of God's covenantal friendship; to know him and to be known of him in love; to enter into his secrets; to understand his works, will, and counsel; to will his will; to love him with all his heart, mind, soul, and strength; to stand at the head of all created things and with them all to serve God and to be blessed by his grace; to taste his goodness and to acknowledge it; to glorify him; to thank him forever; to be God's eternal friend-servant; to dwell in his tabernacle; to see him face-to-face; and to be satisfied with God's likeness.

Man's need is one: the living God.

Hence the singular: all your need, your whole need. God's fellowship, loving-kindness, and the consciousness of his favor—this is the need for which his being cries.

All other needs are determined by, are subservient to, and are concentrated around that one need.

If that need is not fulfilled, he really needs nothing. Unless that need is fulfilled, the supply of all other desires curses him, makes him walk in darkness, causes him to work out his own destruction, and leads him to hell.

For that one need he needs all things—spiritual and material, eternal and temporal. He needs the knowledge of the living God, the light of life. He needs righteousness before God, the sole basis on which he is able to meet his God, to dwell in his presence, and to be the object of his favor. He needs holiness to seek always the living God and to consecrate himself and all things to him only. He needs all things as a means to serve and to glorify him who is blessed forever.

What he needs he lost!

He lost God's image—knowledge, light, truth, righteousness, holiness—and became darkness, a foolish lover and pursuer of the lie, perverse in all his ways, corrupt in heart and obdurate in mind, holding the truth in unrighteousness and serving the creature before the face of the creator, lusting after the things of the flesh, a lover of evil and an enemy of righteousness, seeking his own destruction. He lost God, his loving-kindness and fellowship, and he became an exile and the object of the awful, always-operating, ever-present wrath of God that besets him and pursues him even into outer darkness. So miserable and foolish he has become that he never realizes or acknowledges the wretchedness of his loss, that he no more desires what he needs, but instead lusts after those things that must inevitably destroy him.

Thus he needs forgiveness.

He needs the righteousness of God in Christ Jesus by faith.

He needs deliverance from that terrible power of darkness, of the lie, of corruption, of sin and death, of the devil, of this present world. He needs new light, new life, new righteousness, new holiness.

He needs God in everlasting mercy.

God will supply your whole need.

To supply means "to fill." Your whole need he will perfectly fulfill.

The promise is to the church, to the redeemed people of God. In principle they have received the supply of their need through grace in Christ Jesus, for they have been delivered, liberated from the shackles of sin and corruption. Their sins are blotted out, and they receive forgiveness, the adoption unto children, and righteousness by faith in Christ. Their darkness is dispelled, and they walk in a new light; their eyes have been opened, and they see; their ears have been renewed, and they hear; they know their need and desire the perfect fulfillment. They are poor in spirit; they mourn; and they hunger and thirst after righteousness.

For still they are far from perfection. A small beginning they have, the firstfruits of the Spirit, by which they are saved in hope, and by virtue of which they long for the full and final harvest of eternal glory.

And God will supply their whole need.

The time will come when they will not hunger and thirst; when they will not mourn; and when constantly they will be satisfied—filled with all knowledge of God, righteousness, and holiness forever.

So they will know as they are known.

See face-to-face.

Be satisfied with his likeness.

Glorious blessing!

❖

Riches of grace.

In glory and according to his riches, God will supply our whole need.

In glory! Frequently the word of God speaks of this glory that God has prepared from before the foundation of the world for those who love him, for his own in Christ Jesus. Always it refers to the future of the Messianic kingdom.

That kingdom will be a kingdom of glory.

All the citizens of the kingdom eternal will then be glorified. Its glory will shine not merely around them, will not only and chiefly be in their environment. It will be in them. Their beings, their souls, and their bodies will be glorious.

Glory is the manifestation, or the radiation, of goodness, of great goodness, of goodness on a high plane. God is infinitely glorious, for he is infinitely good. He is goodness, perfection, and the fount of all goodness. Hence all glory is eternally his, whether it is the glory that is eternally immanent in his adorable being, the glory as he beholds it from eternity to eternity, or the glory that radiates forth from him in all the works of his hands, the glory that dwells especially in Christ and through Christ in the church. In the eternal kingdom all will be a manifestation of the glory of God in Christ Jesus. As far as heaven is above the earth, as far as the excellence of Christ is above that of the first Adam, so far will the excellent glory of that kingdom be above the beauty of the first paradise.

In that glory God will supply all our need.

Our need will be greater than before, because we will be glorified. There will be new capacities to fill: new capacities of knowledge and light, of righteousness and holiness, of life and blessing, of fellowship and love.

A new, heavenly, eternal capacity for the living God.

He will fulfill our need not once, but constantly. We will not hunger or thirst, but eternally will drink from the fountain of the water of life freely, will be nourished with the hidden manna, and will eat of the fruit of the tree of life, for the tabernacle of God will be with men, and all things will be made new. God will dwell with them and they will be his people, and God will be with them and be their God. God will wipe away all tears from their eyes. There will be no death, no sorrow, no crying, and no pain, for the former things will have passed away. There will be no curse, for the throne of God and of the Lamb will be in the new Jerusalem, and God's servants will serve him. They will see his face, and his name will be in their foreheads. There will be no night there; they will need no candle or light of the sun, for the Lord God will give them light. They will reign forever and ever.

Then, then they will be satisfied!

When God will have supplied their whole need, in glory.

And according to his riches.

In glory and according to his riches belong inseparably together. In glory denotes the eternal, heavenly capacity of the whole need of the children of God in the kingdom that is to come. According to his riches points to the only source from which their need can be supplied, as well as to the standard of measure according to which it will forever be fulfilled. There will be a blessed capacity for the riches of God that must be filled, and there will be an inexhaustible source of riches to fill it.

According to his riches.

God is rich!

With him there is an infinite store of goodnesses, of bounties and blessings, of things to make happy and to rejoice in forever.

He is rich in himself. Infinitely rich he is in light and life, in knowledge and truth, in righteousness and holiness, rich in the fellowship of his blessed triune covenantal life. Most blessed is he forever.

And rich he is for his people, for to the glory of his grace in the beloved, he has ordained for them from before the foundation of the world a rich inheritance, an inconceivably great store of spiritual, heavenly riches, joy unspeakable and full of glory.

Those riches will be the source of our eternal supply. They will be the standard according to which he will fulfill our whole need.

All the riches of God will be poured out upon us.

No good thing will he withhold.

Glorious hope!

❖

By Christ Jesus, or literally in Christ Jesus. Of God in Christ.

Thus it is now; thus it must be; thus it will be forever in the glory of the eternal kingdom.

In Christ, for he is the meritorious cause of all the riches of grace with which God will supply our whole need in glory. On our part there is nothing to boast. We lost the riches we had possessed. We forfeited forever the riches of God's goodness. Impossible, wholly impossible it is for us to regain them. Worthy of wrath and death we made ourselves. All we could do, and did, was daily to make ourselves more worthy of wrath and death. But Christ, God's

Christ, opened for us inexhaustible stores of greater divine riches of grace than ever we possessed or could have obtained without him.

Abundant mercy.

In Christ, for he is the head of his body, the church. On him are the riches of God poured out first and centrally. To him they are given as the head. He became the quickening spirit, that he might pour out the riches of God's grace on those who are of him. He is our manna. He is the living reservoir of the water of life from which we will drink forever.

In Christ.

Yet of God. For even Christ is of God.

God the fountain. Of him are all things, and through him, and to him.

To him be the glory forever!

Amen, yea, amen!

35

With Whom We Have To Do

"For the word of God is quick, and powerful, and sharper than
any two-edged sword, piercing even to the dividing asunder of
soul and spirit, and of the joints and marrow, and is a discerner
of the thoughts and intents of the heart. Neither is there any
creature that is not manifest in his sight: but all things are naked
and opened unto the eyes of him with whom we have to do."
—Hebrews 4:12–13

FOR...

For the word of God is quick, and powerful...

This little word "for" signifies that we should pay special attention to the statement that follows, because it contains a powerful incentive to heed the exhortation that precedes and obey it with fear and trembling.

This exhortation, which in some form or other occurs repeatedly in the epistle to the Hebrews, is that we must labor and give diligence to enter into the rest that in the new dispensation still remains for the people of God.

It is addressed to those who have a place in the house of God, the house over which the Son, the glorious apostle and high priest of our profession, is anointed as Lord. In that house his voice is heard. Always his voice demands of those who dwell in the house of God that they give diligence to enter into the rest of God, into his covenant, for the covenant of God is the rest that even now remains. Truly, into that covenant the people of God have entered. In principle they have been received into the rest of God. Yet here in this world, and in the body of this death, they are still in the midst of the unrest of sin and death. Their life is in a tension. Constantly they must fight the good fight. Always they must give diligence to enter into the rest, to fight against sin, to crucify their old nature, to forsake the world, and to walk in a new and holy life.

Give diligence, therefore.

Labor to enter into the rest of God.

Very painstakingly, with holy fear and trembling, work out your own salvation.

For in the house of God, you are in the sphere of the word of God. And that word of God is quick and powerful. It is sharper than any two-edged sword; it pierces even to the dividing asunder of soul and spirit, and of the joints and marrow.

It discerns the thoughts and intents of your hearts.

All is exposed and naked before his eyes.

With him we have to do.

❖

Wonderful word of God.

Wonderful because that word is not an *it*, but a *he*: he with whom we have to do.

Through this word we have to do with him who speaks it!

Thus this marvelous passage of Holy Writ must be understood.

Men have thought upon these amazing words and pondered the question what might be meant by this word of God that has such mighty power. Variously they have answered this question.

It has been concluded that this word of God is the gospel as it is contained in the Holy Scriptures and as it is preached by and in the church of Christ in the world. Is not the author of this epistle speaking of the house of God, where the voice of the Son of God is heard? And is not the Bible the word of God as it is delivered to the church and as it is proclaimed and heard in the house of God? To this word of God as we have it in the Scriptures and as it is preached by men, the text must have reference.

Nor can it be denied that there is truth in this interpretation. There is no word of God heard in the church except what is proclaimed according to the Scriptures.

Yet there is no less truth in the objections that are raised against this view by those who insist that the text does not refer to the Bible, nor to the preaching of the gospel by men, but to the eternal Logos, the Word of God become flesh, crucified and raised from the dead, and exalted at the right hand of God, the quickening Spirit, the living, mighty, and glorious Christ himself. However true it is that the contents of the Holy Scriptures and the contents of the word preached according to the Scriptures always judge and discern the thoughts and intents of the heart, it cannot be said of either the Bible or the preaching, apart from the living Christ, that it is quick and powerful and piercing to the dividing asunder of soul and spirit. If the preaching of the word by men were meant, what is said of its piercing and discerning and judging power could not be applied to it. Men hear the word preached and criticize it, judge it, oppose it, cast it from them in disdain, and refuse to become doers of the word. Besides, does not the text itself sufficiently make plain that the reference cannot be to the Bible, nor to the preaching of the word by men, but to the personal Word himself, when it declares that there is not any creature that is not manifest in *his* sight, but all things are naked and opened before the eyes of *him* with *whom* we have to do?

Yet without the word of God as revealed in Holy Writ and as proclaimed in and by the church, there is no word that is heard.

No word is heard without the Scriptures; no mighty word, without the living Christ who speaks.

The two must be combined.

They are inseparable.

Separate the personal Word, the Son of God become flesh, who died and was raised, and who is glorified in the highest heavens, from his word in the Scriptures as it is preached in the church, and what you have left is a word of man, powerless to pierce the heart of man, to convict and to save.

Again, despise the Scriptures and separate them from the living Christ and you must be hopelessly lost in the thick fog of false mysticism, in which you hear the siren song of many voices, but into which the voice of the living Lord does not penetrate.

In the house of God we have to do not with an *it*, but with a mighty *he*.

The word of God is the Son of God speaking.

Its contents are in the Holy Scriptures, and it is proclaimed through the preaching of the word by men. Nevertheless, it is he, the living Lord, who died and was raised, who received the promise of the Holy Ghost, and who through and in that Spirit dwells in his own house, who speaks and whose voice is heard in the church.

It is the sharp, two-edged sword that proceeds out of his mouth.

See that we despise not him who speaks.

Labor to enter into the rest.

❖

Mighty word of God!

Quick and powerful it is.

Quick signifies living.

With heavy emphasis, according to the original, this virtue of the word of God is mentioned first. Living is the word.

Because it is living, vibrating with the life of him who speaks it, it is powerful, that is, energetic. The word is a current of living power. It is not like the word of man, which communicates to you the thoughts and desires of its subject, but is powerless to lord it over you; which tries to persuade you, but must wait for your consent; which attempts to convince you, but must submit itself to your judgment and determination. The word is living and energetic. Never does it reach you in vain. Always it accomplishes that for which it is sent. It saves or it damns; it quickens or it kills; it brings you to contrition or it hardens. Whether its effect in and upon you is that you brokenheartedly humble yourself in dust and ashes or that, in the vain imagination of your haughty heart, you reject and oppose it and raise your rebellious fist against him who speaks—always it is the effect of that living and energetic word.

That word darkens and illuminates, it blinds and it gives sight to the blind, it hides and it reveals.

It is a savor of death unto death, as well as a savor of life unto life.

It is a quickening flame and a consuming fire.

Vibrant it is with the power of eternal election and of reprobation.

Moreover, it is the word of your Lord, and as such it judges you. As a judging word it penetrates into your inmost being, into the most secret recesses of your heart, to expose them to the light of sovereign and most indubitable righteousness and justice, to discern them, and to pronounce upon them the judgment from which there is no appeal.

It is compared to a sharp, two-edged sword and found to be sharper than it. Without respect of persons, this word cuts through the outer surface of your appearance, of the conventional words you speak, of your lying and deceitful smiles and tears, of your outward actions and apparently good deeds, in order to penetrate into your deepest existence, your thoughts, your desires, your aspirations, your real purposes and motives, into the heart whence are the issues of life. In the finest and tiniest fibers of your nature it cuts, to distinguish, to separate, to expose them. It pierces even to the dividing asunder of soul and spirit, and in each of these it finds its way into the joints and marrow, that is, into each secret inclination, and desire, and motive. There is in us a life related to this present world in all its relationships, a soul life, with its thinking and willing, its seeing and hearing, its love and hatred, its joy and sorrow, its pleasure and pain. And there is in us that which is related to God, a spirit life, also with its joy and sorrow, its pleasure and displeasure, its love and hatred. Into the joints and marrow of each of these this word of God pierces, distinguishing and exposing whether your joy is joy in God or joy in the things of this life, whether your repentance is truly sorrow after God or sorrow of the world, whether you seek the things that are above or the things that are on the earth.

Always it judges, for it discerns the thoughts and intents of the heart.

The heart has its thoughts, and the heart has its considerations, intents, purposes, and motives.

The heart is the deepest in man, from an ethical, spiritual viewpoint. It is the center of his love and activity as a moral being, created to be God's image-bearer and to be motivated in all his life and acts by the love of God. From the heart are the issues of life as far as their relation to the will of God is concerned. There are found the deepest answers to the questions concerning the reason and purpose of all your actions: why and unto what end you laugh or weep, you sing or curse, you labor and struggle, you pray and give alms, you worship and do well. In your heart is found the answer to the question, what is your worth in relation to God and man?

The thoughts and intents of the heart.

Discerned they are, one and all, by the word of God.

That word is your judge.

In the light of the perfect will of God, that word makes separation between the truth and the lie, light and darkness, righteousness and unrighteousness, and it pronounces God's verdict upon the hidden things of the heart.

It knows no respect of persons.

Nor is there any appeal from its judgment.

Powerful word of God!

❖

With him we have to do.

As we dwell in the house of God, the word of God comes to us.

Always it speaks to us through the Holy Scriptures, through the preaching, through instruction in the catechism room, through personal exhortation and admonition. In the sphere of that word we live. From earliest childhood we carry it in our mind. It is always with us. Whether we sit in our house or walk by the way; whether we labor in the factory or sit in our office; whether we lie down or rise up—always that word of God is with us, living, energetic, penetrating, piercing into the dividing asunder of the soul and spirit, of the joints and marrow, discerning, judging, condemning, justifying, quickening, killing.

Through that word, as it is spoken to us, as it reaches us and is always with us, we have to do with him, with the speaker, the living Christ, the Lord of the house of God.

With him, the Word, the Son of the living God.

We have to do with him exactly because his word is the word of the Lord. It is not a philosophy that is submitted to our criticism, nor an invitation we may kindly accept or politely decline, nor even a doctrine that we may learn to know and to the truth of which we may consent. His word is a word of life and death. It concerns us personally. Through this word we have to do with him as our Lord, who owns us because he purchased us with the price of his precious blood; whose servants we are, whose mind is our mind, and whose will is our law; who is responsible for us, and to whom we are responsible. We have to do with him, the Son of God, because he demands the obedience of faith and love, that in his house we walk as children of light.

With him we have to do.

See that you refuse not him who speaks.

His speech is clear: Give diligence to enter into the rest; love the Lord your God with all your heart, and with all your mind, and with all your soul, and with all your strength; forsake the world, crucify your old nature, and walk in a new and holy life.

Say not in your heart that you can hide from him with whom we have to do, or walk in his house with a lie in your right hand, for there is no creature that is not manifest in his sight, but all things are naked and opened unto his eyes.

Give diligence therefore to work out your own salvation.

With fear and trembling.

As before his eyes!

PART VI

God's Goodness
Responded To

36

All of Him

"Wherefore David blessed the LORD before
all the congregation: and David said, Blessed be thou,
LORD God of Israel our father, for ever and ever. Thine, O
LORD, is the greatness, and the power, and the glory, and the
victory, and the majesty: for all that is in the heaven and in
the earth is thine; thine is the kingdom, O LORD, and thou
art exalted as head above all. Both riches and honour come of
thee, and thou reignest over all; and in thine hand is power
and might; and in thine hand it is to make great, and to give
strength unto all. Now therefore, our God, we thank thee, and
praise thy glorious name. But who am I, and what is my people,
that we should be able to offer so willingly after this sort? for all
things come of thee, and of thine own have we given thee. For we
are strangers before thee, and sojourners, as were all our
fathers: our days on the earth are as a shadow, and
there is none abiding."—1 Chronicles 29:10–15

ALL of him, none of self.

This confession is essential to real thanksgiving.

Oh, it is easy to rejoice in an abundance of things, of earthly bounties, of food and drink, of health and strength, of position and honor, of might and power, of victory and peace, and to confuse such carnal joy with the real joy of gratitude.

It is quite conceivable that on Thanksgiving Day we exalt ourselves in sinful pride, boast in the things we possess and enjoy, attribute them in our deepest heart to our own ingenuity and efforts, and thus boast in our own worthiness, while perhaps we acknowledge that the Lord came to assist and to crown our worthy efforts. Thus imagining that we can remunerate the Lord of all for all his benefits, we bring to him the sacrifice of the wicked and become abominable in the sight of him to whom belongs the earth and the fullness thereof, the world and they who dwell therein.

Thanksgiving indeed implies joy and gladness of heart, but not in the abundance of earthly things. Our joy is in God who is really God, the Lord of all, who reigns in the heavens above and on the earth beneath, who does all things well; who is, moreover, the God of our salvation in Christ Jesus our Lord, who forgives all our iniquities, who heals all our diseases, and from whose fatherly hand we receive all things—rain and drought, fruitful and barren years, health and sickness, joy and sorrow, life and death—and who causes all things to work for our salvation.

To give thanks means, to be sure, that we point to blessings received and that we count them one by one, but not so that we exclude from these benefits anything that we received from the hand of our heavenly Father in this valley of death, so that we speak of "many things to be thankful for," while we know not what to do with those experiences that were contrary to our earthly desires; but so that we consider all things by faith and in the light of his promise, as gifts of his grace for which he is to be praised and adored.

To give thanks means that we praise him and glorify his holy name because of the abundance of his mercy over us, but again, not in the vain imagination that by doing so we add anything to his glory and oblige him to us, but in the deep sense that even our thanksgiving and praise are gifts of grace, an unspeakably great privilege that he bestows upon us and for which we owe him thanks.

Thus it implies that we deeply humble ourselves before him who is God, the Lord, and acknowledge that we are wholly unworthy of all his benefits.

To acknowledge him as God alone, and to prostrate ourselves in adoration before his throne—this is thanksgiving.

All of him, none of self.

❖

None of self.

This is the deep note that pervades the praise of David in his thanksgiving.

The king of Israel is old, and his days are well-nigh fulfilled. Yet a little while, and he will be gathered to his fathers. Still he is concerned about the house of God he had so strongly desired to build in Jerusalem, but which work had been taken out of his hands by the word of God through the prophet and assigned to his son who would succeed him on the throne of Israel. However, having set his affection on the house of God, he had collected a huge store of materials—gold, silver, brass, iron, marble, precious stones, and wood in abundance—so that in the days of his son the work of building God's temple could proceed without delay. And of his own personal possessions he had added to this store three thousand talents of gold and seven thousand talents of refined silver.

The people had joined him and had willingly offered for the Lord's house. For this the king's heart overflows with joy in the Lord and with praise to the God of Israel. He recognizes in their willing offerings the grace of God over them.

There is in it none of self.

There is nothing about which to boast.

Even of this pure joy of giving willingly with perfect hearts, they were unworthy: "Who am I, and what is my people, that we should be able to offer so willingly? for all things come of thee, and of thine own have we given thee. For we are strangers before thee, and sojourners, as were all our fathers: our days on the earth are as a shadow, and there is none abiding."

Let us translate the king's profoundly humble acknowledgment in terms of our thanksgiving. "Who are we that we are able to praise and glorify thee, O Lord, and to bring to thee so willingly our gratitude with joyful hearts? It is all of thee. Everything that we receive from thy fatherly hand, the knowledge that everything comes from thee as our gracious God in Christ our Lord, the assurance that everything thou doest is well-done and that thou causest all things to work together for good to those who love thee, our joy and peace, and our willingness to offer our praise and thanksgiving unto thy holy name—it is all of thee!"

The blessings we count are thine.

The grace to remember them and to praise thee for them is thine.

And who are we?

Strangers and sojourners in the land.

As strangers in the land, we possess nothing. As sojourners, who tarry but for a day, we have a right to nothing. Our day is as a shadow, for we have sinned, and we move about in the midst of death; there is nothing abiding.

Who are we?

What else are we than guilty and corrupt sinners, who in ourselves are worthy of death and damnation, unworthy and wholly incapable of the joy of offering praise and adoration to the Most High, exiles from the house of God?

Oh, in all our thanksgiving there is none of self.

It is all of the God of our salvation, who revealed himself to us in the face of his Son Jesus Christ as our reconciler and redeemer; who blotted out all our iniquities through the blood of the cross; and who, by the power of his wondrous grace, drew us out of the mire of sin and into the glory of his fellowship and called us out of darkness into the marvelous light of his tabernacle, in which we rejoice in him and praise his holy name with thanksgiving.

None of self. Nothing but sin and guilt and corruption.

None of self. Not even our praise and adoration of his holy name. It is his gift to us.

O Lord, who are we?

❖

All of him.

And therefore unto him.

To acknowledge this in our hearts, and to declare this before his face with holy reverence—that is thanksgiving.

For remember, he is God.

He is not a man, that you can recompense him for all his benefits. He is the absolutely self-sufficient Lord of heaven and earth. His are all things. All the gold and silver, the cattle on a thousand hills, you yourself, your body and your soul, your mind and your will, all your power and talents, are his. He is infinitely glorious and perfectly blessed in himself.

What then would you give him or do for him?

Ever he is the giver, never the receiver.

The overflowing fountain of good is he, and we can approach him only to drink from that fount.

What then will we render unto the Lord for all his benefits?

Nothing, absolutely nothing! How else shall we bring the offering of our praise and thanksgiving to him than by humbly and reverently acknowledging that he is all?

So does the king in his beautiful hymn of praise. He simply exalts the name of the Lord.

> *Blessed be thou, LORD God of Israel our father, for ever and ever. Thine, O LORD, is the greatness, and the power, and the glory, and the victory, and the majesty: for all that is in the heaven and in the earth is thine; thine is the kingdom, O LORD, and thou art exalted as head above all. Both riches and honor come of thee, and thou reignest over all; and in thine hand is power and might; and in thine hand it is to make great, and to give strength unto all.*

All of him!

This is the keynote of this beautiful ascription of praise to the Most High. This must be the sole theme of our thanksgiving to him, of whom, and through whom, and unto whom are all things.

Nor is such praise a mere abstraction, an ascription of glory to some unknown god, which we have learned by heart but which has little real and concrete meaning for our conscious lives. On the contrary, it implies that we know the name of the Lord as he has revealed it to us and that by faith we have seen the revelation of his name as it concerns us. Thus we know whereof we speak and are impelled to prostrate ourselves before him, to express what lives in our hearts of the glory of that name, and to ascribe to him blessedness, greatness, power, glory, victory, majesty, dominion, and exaltation over all.

Does not the king speak of the glorious name of God?

"Now therefore, our God, we thank thee, and praise thy glorious name."

The glorious name of God.

What else does it mean than that he has revealed himself to us in all the glory of infinite might and dominion, majesty and greatness, grace and mercy, righteousness and truth, so that we can know him and ascribe glory to his holy name? What else does it mean than that he made himself known not only as our creator, who calls the

things that are not as if they were; but also and above all as our redeemer, who loves us with an everlasting love, who revealed his love
and the mighty power of his grace to us in the face of Jesus Christ,
his only begotten Son in the flesh, crucified and slain and raised
on the third day; as the one who blotted out all our iniquities, who
clothes us with an everlasting righteousness, and who purposes to
lead us to the everlasting glory of his heavenly tabernacle?

His glorious name!

What else does it mean than that we now behold all things in
the light of that glorious revelation of himself in the face of Jesus
Christ our Lord, whom he raised from the dead?

Do we not know him, as we behold his glory in the grace of
Jesus, as the one who created all things with a view to the heavenly commonwealth of his eternal kingdom, in which Christ will
be fully revealed as the firstborn of every creature, having the preeminence over all?

Contemplating his revelation in the name of Jesus, are we not
assured that he governs all things with a view to the realization
of his everlasting tabernacle, the full manifestation of all the glory
of our Lord Jesus Christ, and the final glorification of his beloved
church in him?

The glorious name of our God!

Do we not see all our present way through the valley of death,
all our experiences in this world, all that comes to us by his fatherly hand, in the light of his glorious name: joys and sorrows,
prosperity and adversity, riches and poverty, health and sickness,
life and death; and are we not assured that all of these things are
ours, blessings of his grace to us, and that all must work together
for our salvation?

Now therefore, our God, we thank thee and praise thy glorious
name.

For that thy name of salvation is near, thy wondrous works
declare.

We thank thee.

To thank the Most High presupposes a joyful consciousness of
having been blessed, of having received benefits, of receiving nothing but good things from him. It means that we point out these
blessings, according to the picturesque Hebrew expression, which

means "to throw out the hand," "to point" to something, "to indicate" blessings we received, "to call attention" to them as revelations of the goodness and glory of the Lord our God.

Thus we praise him.

We praise him because in all things we received out of his hand we recognize his glorious name, his power, his everlasting love and mercy over us, his wisdom, the wonder of his marvelous grace in Christ Jesus our Lord.

We praise him by glorifying his virtues, as revealed in all his benefits.

And by declaring his glory to him and to men.

All of him.

❖

Joy in the Lord!

Such is the gladness of true thanksgiving.

This rejoicing is possible only in the conscious acknowledgment that we are nothing and that God is all.

Notice that this is the essence and ground of the joy and gladness of the king and of the people, as expressed in this inspired praise and thanksgiving: "Then the people rejoiced, for that they offered willingly, because with perfect heart they offered willingly to the LORD: and David the king also rejoiced with great joy" (1 Chron. 29:9). They rejoiced in the Lord, for they were glad because of the grace bestowed upon them to offer willingly unto the Lord their God.

It is the joy of the experience that the God of our salvation is our God for Christ's sake.

The joy of the consciousness that we drink from the fountain of good.

It is a joy pure and undefiled.

And enduring forever.

37

Glory to the Only Wise God

*"Now to him that is of power to stablish you according to my
gospel, and the preaching of Jesus Christ, according to the
revelation of the mystery, which was kept secret since the world
began, But now is made manifest, and by the scriptures of the
prophets, according to the commandment of the everlasting God,
made known to all nations for the obedience of faith: To God
only wise, be glory through Jesus Christ for ever. Amen."*
—Romans 16:25–27

AMEN. So let it be.

Glory be to the only wise God through Jesus Christ!

Let the church on earth, called through the gospel unto the obedience of faith, fall down in adoration and glorify him for the revelation of his marvelous wisdom. Let the redeemed and glorified
church in heaven, the spirits of the saints made perfect, cast their
crowns before him who sits on the throne, and rejoicing, sing that
he is the alone wise God. Let the myriads of angels, always eager to
look into these things, now say that they have beheld his wondrous
works, all revealing his infinite wisdom.

When the divine counsel is realized, when the last elect has been
perfected to fit into his own place in the glorified body of Christ,
when the new heavens and the new earth, in which righteousness
dwells, have been created, when the new Jerusalem, adorned with
the glory of God, beautiful as a bride prepared to meet the bridegroom, has descended out of heaven on the new earth, when the
covenant of God is perfected and the tabernacle of God will be
with men forever—then let all the new creation sing the only glad
song on the one glorious theme: God is the only wise!

Forever!

Let all hell acknowledge that sin is exposed as utter folly, that God's wisdom is infinitely perfect.

Amen, yea, amen.

❖

God, the only wise.

Through Jesus Christ.

Thus the last part of this beautiful doxology should be read. The apostle does not mean to say that glory ought to be given through Jesus Christ to the only wise God, but that he has become revealed to us as the only wise God through Jesus Christ.

This revelation of his wisdom through Jesus Christ, through whom we behold him as the only, the perfectly, the infinitely wise God, must impel us to bring to him the glory that is due unto his name.

It is not an abstract, dogmatic knowledge of the divine wisdom that will ever bring this doxology to our lips. We must see his wisdom, not merely learn a doctrinal formula declaring that God is all-wise. We must be brought under the spell of that amazing wisdom, not merely repeat a logical proposition. We must behold that glorious wisdom of our God in its most central and perfect manifestation, that is, through Jesus Christ, in order to join in with the apostle in this song of praise: Glory be to the only wise God!

The wisdom of God is revealed everywhere, in all the works of his hands.

Wisdom is the marvelous virtue of the Most High that is displayed in the perfect harmony and adaptation to one another of all things, so that each creature in the whole cosmos has its own name, occupies its own place, serves its own purpose, and is perfectly adapted to serve that purpose; and so that the individual purpose of each creature is subservient to the purpose of the whole: the revelation of God's name and the praises of his glorious virtues. There is wisdom in the firmament with its myriads of twinkling stars, pouring forth their speech into the silent night; in the circuit of the golden sun, going forth as a bridegroom coming out of his chamber and rejoicing as a strong man to run a race; in the clouds that fill their vessels over the ocean to empty them over the dry and thirsty fields; in the seed that falls into the earth and dies in order to bring forth fruits, thirty, sixty, and hundredfold; in the chirping of the sparrow, the cry of the young raven, and the sweet notes of the nightingale; in the mountains and vales, woods and meadows, meandering brooks and majestic streams; in the howling storm, the roaring thunder, the flashing lightning, the raging sea, the softly whispering zephyr; the gently dropping dew, the cedar of Lebanon, the lily of the valley, the blooming rose; in day and in night, in summer and in winter, in times and in seasons for all things; in the eye adapted to receive the light, in the ear that hears, in the mouth that speaks and the voice that sings, in the colors of the spectrum, and in the notes of the octave—harmony, adaptation, purpose, and revelation of divine wisdom everywhere as far as eye can see.

Frequently the psalms sing of this wisdom of the Most High. They love to enumerate the mighty works of God in creation and bless the name of him who covers himself with light as with a garment and stretches out the heavens like a curtain; who lays the beams of his chambers in the waters; who makes the clouds his chariot; who walks upon the wings of the wind; who sends the springs into the valleys, which run among the hills and give drink to all the beasts of the field; who waters the hills from his chambers and causes the grass to grow for the cattle and the herb for the service of man, wine that makes glad his heart and oil to make his face shine; who provides nests for the birds and houses for the storks, and a refuge for the wild goats and for the conies; who appointed the moon for seasons and makes the sun to know his going down; who causes darkness to descend, wherein all the wild beasts of the forest creep forth, and makes his sun to rise upon a new day, that man may go forth unto his work and labor until the evening.

The psalms end in the glorification of that only wise God, revealed in all the works of his hands: "O Lord, how manifold are thy works! in wisdom hast thou made them all: the earth is full of thy riches" (Ps. 104:24).

Everywhere the voice of wisdom.

Yet there is another note in these works of God, apparently contradicting this testimony of God's wisdom, mocking it.

It is the note of death and destruction.

The note of the bondage of corruption.
The cry of vanity.

> One generation passeth away, and another generation
> cometh: but the earth abideth forever. The sun also riseth,
> and the sun goeth down, and hasteth to his place where
> he arose. The wind goeth toward the south, and turneth
> about unto the north; it whirleth about continually, and
> the wind returneth again according to his circuits. All the
> rivers run into the sea; yet the sea is not full; unto the place
> from whence the rivers come, thither they return again. All
> things are full of labour; man cannot utter it (Eccl. 1:4–8).

> The whole creation groaneth and travaileth in pain togeth-
> er until now...For the creature was made subject to vanity
> (Rom. 8:22, 20).

There seems to be no conclusion.

There is no design. There is no end, or *telos*. All things appear
foolish and purposeless.

Mockers have said with wicked audacity that if they were to
make a world, they would vastly improve upon God's world.

And there is no answer.

Until you look at Jesus Christ.

Leave him out of consideration, out of the scope of your vision,
out of your worldview, and you cannot find the conclusion of the
matter. Then the sole conclusion appears to be in the slogan, "Let us
eat and drink, for tomorrow we die." But behold him, and all things
change. Contemplate him, in the purpose assigned to him, in the
center of all things, at the head of all things, and you will fall down
in adoration before the only wise God. For he is the firstborn of
every creature and the first begotten of the dead; by him and unto
him were all things designed and created.

The wisdom of God through Jesus Christ.

Give him his place in the scheme of all things. Him, the incarnated Son of God, Immanuel, God of God and man of man; him,
the crucified one, in whom God reconciled the world unto himself;

him, the risen Lord, glorified in the highest heavens, exalted at the right hand of God.

See Jesus, crowned with glory and honor, and you see all things in a different light.

In the light of his face all things—and now absolutely all—sin, death, suffering, and vanity not excluded, become manifestations of divine wisdom.

All things, nothing excluded, must serve the purpose of the highest realization of God's eternal covenant.

The most glorious revelation of his name.

The name of the alone wise God.

Through Jesus Christ.

❖

The divine mystery.

A mystery is not something that is contrary to our understanding, some incomprehensible thing that we cannot know, that we cannot grasp, of which our human understanding cannot lay hold, but it is that which by our understanding we can never reach, that far transcends our common experience, is outside of the scope of our earthly perception, and is made known unto us by the grace of divine revelation.

Jesus Christ.

Eye has not seen; ear has not heard; in the heart of man it was never conceived. Yet it is *the* answer to all questions, the solution of all problems, the sole conclusion of the matter. How then can human philosophy give us an answer?

The mystery of God.

Jesus Christ.

From times eternal, from ages of yore, this mystery was hidden in God, in his eternal wisdom and incomprehensible counsel. Even in the centuries of the old dispensation it was hidden. There was the word concerning its coming manifestation, but it had not come. There were the shadows, but the body was not yet. There was the promise, but it was not fulfilled. Even as the pale light of the moon at night assures us that the sun still shines and that it will presently shine forth in all its glory, so in the ages of the old dispensation there were glimmerings of the light that would shine when the mystery would be revealed, yet the mystery itself was hidden.

But now it is manifested.

The answer is given. The solution is offered. The conclusion is reached.

Manifested is the mystery that was hidden. There is a difference between revelation and manifestation, though the two are closely related. To reveal is to unveil, to expose to view by taking off the cover; to manifest is to break through, even as the sun breaks through the clouds on a dark and stormy day.

The mystery was manifested.

The Sun of righteousness broke through our darkness, the darkness of the shadow of death, of guilt and sin, of corruption and vanity.

In the historic fullness of time, the mystery of God was manifested in the incarnation of the Son of God, his sojourn among us, his speaking of the words of eternal life, his descent into the lower parts of the earth on the accursed tree, yea, into the depths of hell; his glorious resurrection unto life and justification, his ascension into the highest heavens, his being exalted as Lord and Christ, his return in the Spirit.

We see Jesus.

The mystery of God.

Eye has not seen; ear has not heard; never could it have arisen in the heart of man.

The wisdom of God.

Through Jesus Christ.

❖

Amen. So let it be!

Glory be to the only wise God through Jesus Christ!

Witness of it, church of Jesus Christ in the world; sing of it; shout aloud. For thereunto were you called out of darkness into his marvelous light, that you should show forth his praises.

Sing of it, be witnesses of this marvelous wisdom. For you have been made to see this mystery of wisdom that was hidden from times eternal. It was not only manifested in the fullness of time, but it was also made known unto you. Through the preaching of the gospel, which the apostles began according to the commandment of God, and through the prophetic writings that they used as means in the proclamation of the gospel of God concerning this mystery, the mystery was made known to all nations and made known also to you.

Through that gospel, by the Spirit of grace, you were brought unto the obedience of the faith. The faith of Jesus Christ. The faith that is revealed in and through him. The faith that God was in Christ reconciling the world unto himself, not imputing their trespasses unto them. The faith that he died and rose again, never to die again. The faith that is the victory over the damnation of our guilt, over the corruption of our sin, over the dominion of death. The faith that in the name of Jesus there is redemption, even the forgiveness of sin, righteousness, and eternal life. Unto that faith you were brought into obedience, so that you believed, repented, were justified, were enlightened and sanctified.

In that faith and obedience he, the only wise God, is able to establish you through the same gospel and preserve you though all hell should rise against you.

Until that day.

And why?

Why this hidden mystery and the manifestation of it? Why all these problems of sin and death, of corruption and vanity, and the answer to them all in Jesus Christ? Why these Scriptures of the prophets, predicting the coming manifestation of the mystery, and the preaching of the gospel, the message that now the mystery is manifested? Why this bringing of the church unto the knowledge of this mystery and unto the obedience of faith?

There is only one answer: glory to the alone wise God.

Oh yes, it is *the* answer.

That we behold his marvelous wisdom and are brought under the spell of it forever.

That we proclaim it now and forever.

Glory to God, the only wise.

Through Jesus Christ.

Amen, yea, amen!

38

Glorifying God with One Accord

"Now the God of patience and consolation grant you to be like-minded one toward another according to Christ Jesus: That ye may with one mind and one mouth glorify God, even the Father of our Lord Jesus Christ. Wherefore receive ye one another, as Christ also received us to the glory of God. Now I say that Jesus Christ was a minister of the circumcision for the truth of God, to confirm the promises made unto the fathers: And that the Gentiles might glorify God for his mercy."—Romans 15:5–9

GOD is glorious!

His alone is the glory, even as his is the kingdom and the power.

Excellent is he in goodness. He excels in infinite perfection. He is uniquely good, incomparably perfect in truth and righteousness, in power and holiness, in wisdom and knowledge, in love and grace and mercy and loving-kindness.

The holy one of Israel.

To whom will you liken him? There is none on earth, neither is there anyone in the heavens whose name can be mentioned in one breath with his name. The glory of the sun is darkness in comparison with his glory. In the presence of even a little of that glory the holy angels cover their faces and can only shout, "Holy, holy, holy!"

Where is there a power like unto his power, where a majesty like unto the majesty of the Most High? What wisdom can be compared with his, or where is the knowledge that would match itself with the infinite knowledge of the omniscient one? Who can boast of a love that is ought else than a mere reflection of a drop from the infinite ocean of love that is he, or who can boast of life that is more than a drop from the eternally sparkling fountain that is God? Can there be holiness anywhere that is not a mere response to his holiness, or is there righteousness among the creature of which he is not the criterion? Can man ever be gracious otherwise than as a little mirror of his boundless grace, or is the creature ever clothed with a beauty that is not a faint reflection of the infinite pleasures that are at his right hand? To whom then will you liken God?

He is the incomparable one. To compare him is to deny him. To present him on a par with the creature is blasphemy.

The excellent, the absolutely excellent, the infinitely excellent, the alone excellent is he!

The manifestation of the divine excellence—the incomparable goodness of the all-transcending perfection of God—is divine glory.

Glory, his glory, excellent glory is revealed. For he willed to make known his excellent goodness, to manifest his transcendent glory, that we can behold it and wonder, that we can see it and tremble with rejoicing in the Lord our God, that we can taste it and be blessed, that we can adore it and worship. All the works of his hands proclaim that glory, pour forth speech, in the heavens above and on the earth beneath, in the deep silence of the night and in the bright glory of the noonday, whispering in adoration or singing with joy, testifying of his excellent wisdom, might, goodness, and majesty. Do not the heavens declare the glory of God? Does not day unto day utter speech and night unto night show knowledge?

Speech of him.

Knowledge of his excellence.

Quite distinctly of his perfections they speak. Quite clearly they witness of none other than of him alone. There is no danger of confusing his glory with the glory of the creature. There is no room for the mistake of losing sight of the divine excellence in the midst of the virtues of things that are made.

When you behold the work of God, radiating his power and goodness and wisdom, you recognize at once that it is his and that no one can even approximate the wonder of it. You can compare the proudest work of man's hands with the humblest work of God, and the former falls within the scope of your own power and understanding, while the latter remains forever a wonder, excellent, unique, inimitable, and incomparable. For a moment you can adore a smoothly running and gracefully lined and beautifully finished automobile, place it on exhibition at the fairs of the world, and boast of the ingenuity and progress of man. Yet what is a car in comparison with even a blade of grass, a flower of the field, a grain of sand? You consider man's work, and you know it is numbered, and always it bears the number of mere man. You consider God's work to be excellent and recognize it as divine, separated by an infinite chasm from the grandest work of man. You let your eyes rest on the most glorious product of man's power and ingenuity, but soon you grow weary of looking, and you turn to something else; but never can your eyes grow weary of seeing, never can your mind become exhausted of contemplating the works of God.

Of God.

Of the mighty creator and sustainer of all things!

Yet more glorious than this glory that is revealed in creation is the glory that is manifested of him as the God and Father of the Lord Jesus Christ. For the God and Father of Jesus Christ is he. To be sure, within the holy mystery of the divine Trinity the first person is the Father in relation to the second; yet the triune God is the God and Father of Jesus Christ, the Son of God in human nature. He ordained him, he formed him, he revealed all his power and glory in him, who is the firstborn of every creature and the firstborn of the dead, the revelation of the God of our salvation.

The glory of the God and Father of our Lord Jesus Christ!

What glory is like the wonder of all wonders, the incarnated God, Immanuel, creator and creature, Lord and servant, omnipotence and weakness, infinitude and finitude, eternity and time in one? What glory is comparable to the wonder of the cross, God in human flesh bearing God's wrath, fulfilling all righteousness, satisfying all justice, reconciling the world unto himself, redeeming his people by his own blood, God in us forsaken of God? What love is like the unfathomable love that became manifested when in due time Christ died for sinners? What mercy can be compared to the divine mercy that entered into our darkness and death and filled us with eternal bliss? What power is as mighty as the power of God that raised Jesus from the dead and gave him a name that is above all names?

Excellent is he.

The holy one of Israel.

And the excellence of his power and might, his holiness and

righteousness, his justice and truth, his love and grace and mercy and all his wonderful goodness is become manifest.

Revealed in the face of Jesus Christ our Lord.

Glorious indeed is God!

❖

Glorify him then, O church of Christ!

Say it, sing it, sing about it, for you have seen and tasted his great goodness, that he is glorious, that he is boundless in love, infinite in grace, unfathomable in wisdom and knowledge, unlimited in power, excellent in all his virtues.

Say it to him in thankful worship and adoration.

Witness of it to one another as you speak of the wonder of his grace.

Sing it aloud before all the world, before the holy angels who see his face and before the devils who tremble before him, that his alone is all the glory.

Glory to God in the highest!

Glorify him with one accord.

With one mind and with one heart and with one mouth.

Let the church of Christ be one grand chorus of many voices, each one singing in his own place his own part, yet all uniting in the harmony of the one theme: Glory to the God and Father of our Lord Jesus Christ. There is none like him who raises the dead. Let all take part in this glorification of the God of our salvation, redeemed from Jews and Gentiles, small and great, parents and children, young and old, men and women. Let none be silent, but all show forth the praises of him who called them out of darkness into his marvelous light. Glorify him always. In the midst of the church and in the world, on the Sabbath and during the week, in your homes and everywhere, with your mouths and in your walk, glorify him with one accord.

Let no dissonance mar the beauty of your praise.

For it is of the excellent glory that you sing, of the glory of the incomparable God. Let there be nothing of man in your glorying.

All of him, nothing of self.

Such is your calling, your sole calling. For what would you do for him, or how would you remunerate him, or what could you bring to him who is the excellent one, the fount of all good, always the fount, one ever-overflowing fount, except to give him the glory that is due unto his name?

That he should be glorified, that his church should glorify him with one accord, is his eternal purpose.

It is the purpose of your redemption. It is Christ's purpose. For unto this end he became minister of the circumcision, that he might manifest the truth of God and that you should sing of it. A servant of the circumcision Christ became, but not merely in the sense that he became a servant of the Jews. That too. He came to seek and to save the lost sheep of Israel and to realize unto them the promise made unto the fathers, Abraham, Isaac, and Jacob. But he also became a servant *under* the circumcision, under the old covenant, under the law; a minister of the promise in the shadows of the law. As a minister of the circumcision he took upon himself the curse of the law, removed it by his perfect sacrifice, that he might redeem those who were under the law, and at the same time abrogate the law and the shadows, and extend salvation even unto the Gentiles.

Jew and Gentile he redeemed.

And he received us. Us, who were by nature children of wrath, enemies of God and enemies of him, who spent all our fury upon him and nailed him to the accursed tree. He received us when in eternity the Father gave us to him. He received us when he had to shed his lifeblood in our behalf. He received us when the Father drew us to him with cords of irresistible love. He received us when we came to him, drawn by the Father, with nothing in our hands to bring, guilty, damnable, wretched, dead through trespasses and sins, empty, hungry and thirsty, laboring and weary, toiling in vain and heavy laden. He received us and did not cast us off. He took us to himself forever, united us with himself, filled us with his marvelous grace, justified us, forgave us all our sins, cleansed and delivered us from the pollution and dominion of sin, set us free, made us living children of God, and gave us eternal life and glory.

He received us. Why? To the glory of God.

He became minister of the circumcision. Why? In behalf of the truth, of the unchangeable veracity, of the faithfulness of God. For the promise of salvation was made unto the fathers in times of old. Long they had waited for the fulfillment of that promise, the promise of all the mercies of David, of redemption and deliverance from sin and all the power of the devil and the bondage of corruption. Would God's promise fail? God forbid. The truth of God, and with that truth all the glory of his great goodness, must become manifest in the glory of God.

He became the end of the law and the Lord even of the Gentiles, to reveal unto them the salvation of God. Why? That also the Gentiles might glorify God for his mercy.

Thus he, the Christ of God, spoke already in the old dispensation, even "as it is written: For this cause I will confess to thee among the Gentiles, and sing unto thy name. And again he saith, Rejoice, ye Gentiles, with his people" (Rom. 15:9–10). In those olden times it was David who thus spoke. But it was Christ who even then spoke in and through him.

His purpose it is to glorify God.

To glorify him through the mouths of the millions upon millions of those whom he redeemed and received.

A thousandfold song of glorification, sung with one accord.

❖

Oh, to be likeminded.

Likeminded toward one another in and according to Christ Jesus.

For how shall we glorify God with one accord, with one mind and with one mouth, unless there is the unity of the Spirit that reveals itself in likemindedness according to Christ?

This likemindedness is not only a certain unanimity of thought and conviction with regard to the truth in Christ Jesus, so that we unite on the basis of the same confession. To be sure, it implies this. How shall we be likeminded at all if it is not in the bond of the truth? But it is more than this. It is to be one in the Spirit in the bond of peace. It is to be of the same purpose and aim. It is to strive unitedly, to pursue one and the same object and purpose. It is likemindedness that is rooted in the love of God that is poured out in our hearts. It is the denial of self and the love of God and of one another in Christ. It is the united subjection of self and our own purposes, and of all things that are in themselves indifferent and of no account, to the one great purpose of Christ and of the church: to glorify God with one accord.

Hence it is likemindedness according to Christ.

Christ is not only the motive power, but also the standard and criterion of this likemindedness. He is its scope. He is also its limitation. Let whatever is not of the Christ of the Scriptures be absolutely excluded from this likemindedness. What concord is there between Christ and Belial? But let us unitedly mind the things that are of Christ Jesus our Lord.

Oh, to be thus likeminded! For according to the text, this likemindedness is an indispensible requisite unto the realization of the only purpose of the church: the glory of God. God grant you to be likeminded according to Christ, that you can with one mind and with one mouth glorify God and the Father of our Lord Jesus Christ.

What an incentive!

Shall the song of that glorification of God be silenced in the church of Christ, redeemed by him and received by him for that very purpose, because of our personal differences and quarrels?

God forbid!

Rather, let all be subservient to the realization of that only aim: glorifying God with one accord.

39

Blessed Be He Who Blessed Us

"Blessed be the God and Father of our Lord Jesus Christ, who hath blessed us with all spiritual blessings in heavenly places in Christ: According as he hath chosen us in him."
—*Ephesians 1:3–4*

BLESSED be he who blessed us.

It cannot escape our attention that the same word is used twice: God blesses us, we bless him. Yet there is a profound difference in meaning between the two uses of the word.

God's blessing us and our blessing God are not mere reciprocal acts, so that the latter is a remuneration of the former, a returning of favors received, a reward of blessing he bestowed on us. God is God. We are always creature. God is the giver; we are always the receivers. God is the ever-overflowing fountain of all good; we are always the thirsty ones who drink from that fountain. This relation never ceases and cannot be reversed. Never does the moment arrive when he receives from us anything that is not truly his. When we bless him, we only express that we have tasted how good he is. Our blessing of him is only the expression of our consciousness of having been blessed by him.

His blessing then is first, always first, eternally first.

Even as "Herein is love, not that we loved God, but that he loved us" (1 John 4:10), so herein is blessing, not that we bless him, but that he blesses us.

His blessing us is the eternally operating cause of our blessing him. For his blessing, never ours, is causal, efficacious, divinely powerful, and effective.

To bless is "to speak well." Such is the literal significance of the graphic word that is here twice used in the original. When God blesses us, he speaks well of us, concerning us, to us, over us; when we bless God, we speak well of him, concerning him, to him. But his word is a word of power. He speaks and it is done; he commands and it stands fast. His word creates what it declares; it brings to pass what it expresses. But our word can only declare what already is and what has become an object of our knowledge and experience.

His speaking precedes the thing; our speaking follows it. He speaks, and what he speaks comes into being; we speak because we know that the thing is already.

He speaks well of us and to us, and as a result we are filled with all goodness.

We speak well of him because we taste that he is eternally good.

We speak because through his speech we know him.

Blessed be he who blessed us.

Even so, amen.

❖

How richly he blessed us.

In how marvelous a way he lavished his goodness upon us.

How fully and completely he filled us with his glorious benefits.

For he blessed us with all spiritual blessings in heavenly places in Christ.

In Christ he blessed us. This indicates the wonderful way in which he manifested all his great goodness and made us recipients of it. Another way in which to reveal *all* his marvelous goodness to the highest possible degree there was not. For Christ is the first-born of every creature and the first begotten of the dead; he is the image of the invisible God, and it was the Father's good pleasure that in him all the fullness should dwell.

When we are told that he blessed us in Christ, it is plain that he blessed Christ first. He spoke well of Christ, to Christ, chiefly, centrally, as the chief over his house, as the son in whom he is well pleased, as the obedient servant, as the head of the body, the church. The Father spoke his word of blessing in the amazing wonder of the incarnation, in the deep way of Christ's suffering, in his awful descent into hell, in his sojourn in Sheol; he revealed his word of blessing in Christ's glorious resurrection, in his blessed exaltation in the highest heavens, in the exceeding greatness of his power and authority over every name that is named. And he finished his word of blessing when the glorified Christ received the promise of the Spirit, that he might be the quickening Spirit, the life-giving head of his church.

In Christ God has blessed us.

Therefore these blessings with which he has blessed us are all the spiritual blessings in heavenly places.

Spiritual these blessings are because they are all the fruits of the Holy Spirit, the Spirit of Christ, and are wrought by him. Spiritual they are too because they are not natural; they do not change the essence of things, the essence of our being and of our relation to the world, but by them our spiritual, ethical nature is reversed and our relation to God is made perfect. They change our darkness into light, our love of the lie into love of the truth, our folly into wisdom, our ignorance into the knowledge of God, our guilt into perfect righteousness, our corruption into holiness, our unrest into peace, our sorrow into joy, our death into eternal life. They do not feed us with the bread that perishes, but with the bread of life; they do not enrich us with treasures on earth, where moth and rust corrupt, but with incorruptible treasures in heaven. They are blessings of grace and mercy, of righteousness and peace, of holiness and the love of God, of wisdom and knowledge, of meekness and patience, of joy and light, of justification in the midst of sin, of victory in the midst of apparently overwhelming enemies, of a blessed hope in the midst of despair, of unspeakable rejoicings in the midst of suffering, of glorious life in the midst of devouring death.

Blessings in Christ, in heavenly places.

These blessings are in Christ. From God, through Christ, in the Spirit they constantly flow toward us. Christ is in heavenly places and is therefore himself heavenly, raised far above the level of mundane, earthly relations. The blessings are like their source. In heavenly places they are, from heavenly places they descend, heavenly they are. They are not merely spiritual in distinction from natural and carnal, but they are also heavenly in distinction from the mere earthly. They do not merely restore, but elevate; they do not repair what was broken and spoiled, but they raise to a higher level, the level of heavenly perfection. For as far as Christ is higher than the first Adam, the heavenly blessings we receive from him are higher than all the things of the earth. To be born again is to be born from above, where Christ sits on the right hand of God in heavenly places. This rebirth is only the beginning of what will be perfected in the final resurrection and in the glory of the heavenly creation.

Blessed with *all* spiritual blessings.

In Christ.

In him is the fullness of spiritual blessings. All the fullness of the Godhead dwells in him bodily. No spiritual blessing is lacking. No blessing can be added. Over and above the spiritual blessings in Christ no blessing is conceivable. To be blessed in Christ is to be blessed fully, completely, perfectly.

And God has blessed *us* in him.

God caused Christ to merit eternal righteousness for us by his death and resurrection. In him we are justified. In him we have the adoption unto children. In him we are heirs, heirs of God and co-heirs with Christ. In him we have a right to eternal life and to the eternal inheritance.

He makes us partakers of these spiritual blessings.

For it is God who makes us one plant with Christ in the likeness of his death and his resurrection. It is he, the God and Father of our Lord Jesus Christ, who gives us the lively faith whereby we become partakers of him and of all his benefits.

In the blessed Christ he has blessed us.

Abundant mercy!

❖

Blessed is the God and Father of our Lord Jesus Christ.

Yea, blessed be he alone!

For he is the fount of all these glorious blessings, and there is none beside him. He alone is the author of this great salvation. To him be glory and thanksgiving forever.

To God triune, blessed forever, be all the praise.

He is the Father and God of our Lord Jesus Christ.

This relation of our Lord Jesus Christ to God triune has its deeper, its eternal cause in the holy Trinity itself. The first person of the divine family is the father of the second. And the Son, God of God, coequal with the Father and the Spirit, is the express image of the Father.

He is this in the divine nature.

Never can it be said that the first person of the Trinity is the God of the second person. Yet thus our text expresses the relation between Christ and the Father. Even though some would connect the words "our Lord Jesus Christ," we maintain that this is not the meaning, and that the text declares that the Father is also the God of Christ, our Lord. Besides, this is expressed more than once in Scripture. Christ Jesus our Lord therefore is not only the eternal Son, essentially divine, in relation to the first person of the holy Trinity, but he is also the holy child Jesus and the servant of the Lord, and the triune God is his God and Father.

He is this in his human nature.

The triune God is the God and Father of the Son in human nature.

The triune God ordained Christ to be the head of his church and the head over all things. God ordained him to be the firstborn of every creature and the first begotten of the dead. His good pleasure it was that in Christ all the fullness should dwell. God made the Son and perfected him as the captain of salvation in the incarnation, through his suffering and death, in the way of his resurrection and exaltation at the right hand of God in heavenly places, and by fulfilling unto him the promise of the Spirit.

Blessed be he, the God and Father of our Lord Jesus Christ.

He it is who has blessed us in Christ.

He did so freely, sovereignly, of his good pleasure, even as he has chosen us in him before the foundation of the world.

Eternally he elected us. God's election of his church does not fall in time. It does not belong to time and is not determined and limited by time, but is an eternal act of the eternal God. That he chose us "before the foundation of the world" (Eph. 1:4) does not refer to a certain moment preceding creation, as if the eternal one ever had been without his divine election. In eternity there is no time. For an eternal act there are no moments. "Before the foundation of the world" therefore only can express a logical relation in God's mind, a relation of order between election and creation. Election is first, the foundation of the world follows; the church is end, the world is means. Even as Christ is the firstborn of every creature, and all things are made through him and unto him—first even in relation to the church, so that the church exists for Christ's sake— so the church is first in relation to the foundation of the world, and all things exist for her sake and are adapted to her realization and perfection.

Eternally he has chosen us before the foundation of the world.

Even as this election is an eternal act, so it is strictly sovereign.

God's election is never a selection of the best. Thus men who do not fully grasp the truth that God is God would explain that God chose the best according to his foreknowledge. He chose whom he foresaw as believers, as obedient to the gospel, as persevering to the end. But the election of God is even before the foundation of the world, and all things are adapted to it. It is causal. It ordains the elect. That they are elect is solely due to an act of his sovereign will and in no wise to any foreseen or foreknown goodness or act on our part.

He chose us in in Christ Jesus our Lord.

God ordained Christ as the chief among the brethren, as the head of the church, in order that in him all the fullness of the invisible God might dwell and be revealed. In that Christ, in his sphere, he elected his church, all his people, giving them to Christ, giving to each one of them his own place in Christ, so that the whole of them might show forth the fullness of the glorious virtues of the Godhead as it is in Christ, that God may be all in all.

He predestinated them to be made like unto the image of his Son, each in his own way and according to his own position in him, that he might be the firstborn among many brethren.

Even as he chose us in him, so he blesses us in him.

Never without him.

In Christ we are juridically. He is delivered for our transgressions and raised for our justification. By faith we know that we are in him, and we are justified and have peace with God.

Even as he has chosen us.

In Christ we are organically. He lives in us and dwells in us, and we are delivered and glorified, begotten again unto a lively hope.

Even as God has chosen us, so he has blessed us.

In Christ. Freely, eternally, sovereignly.

Blessed be God!

❖❖❖

He has blessed us.

Let us now bless him, the God and Father of our Lord Jesus Christ. For such is his purpose.

He has made all things for his own name's sake: Christ, the church, the world, all things. All things are yours; but you are Christ's, and Christ is God's.

He has blessed us, that we might bless him.

Not as if our blessing of him could at all be like his blessing us. He is God. We are creature. He is the fount. We drink from him. Nor can we in any way remunerate him for the glorious blessings he has bestowed upon us in eternal and sovereign love. The very thought that we can remunerate the all- and self-sufficient one is blasphemous. What shall I render unto the Lord for all his benefits bestowed on me? Nothing!

But I can take the cup of salvation from which I drink, and by which I taste that he is the blessed one.

And call upon his name.

And say that he is good.

The blessed one forever!

40
Thou Hast Dealt Well

"Thou hast dealt well with thy servant, O LORD, according unto thy word. Teach me good judgment and knowledge: for I have believed thy commandments."—Psalm 119:65–66

LORD, thou hast dealt well!

This acknowledgment as a matter of experience dominates this entire section of the psalm.

There had been enemies, haters of God and of his word, who had forged a lie against the psalmist, hated him, persecuted him, and spoken evil against him falsely. The inspired psalmist, as the servant of the Lord, had been in distress, no doubt afflicted because of and by the hatred of the enemies of Jehovah. Of this affliction he speaks twice in this section.

However, in the midst of affliction and persecution by the enemy, the psalmist had not become unfaithful, had not departed from the ways of God's precepts, but had loved and kept them.

Through all his experiences, he had come to acknowledge that God is faithful, that his promises are sure, that his word is true, and that Jehovah always deals well with his servants.

Even when suffering and tribulation are our lot, even when the enemies rise up against us to destroy our soul, the Lord is good, and he causes all things to work together for our salvation.

Such had been the experience of the psalmist.

Looking back upon the affliction of the past, he now clearly discerns that it was good for him to be afflicted.

Lord, thou hast dealt well with thy servant.

❖

According unto thy word.

It is the word of the Lord throughout that he always deals well with his servants.

Particularly it is his word that even when he casts us into the crucible of trial and tribulation, through the suffering of this present time he deals well with his servants.

This the psalmist confesses.

In the first part of the text he speaks of experience. He is looking back. The immediate past had brought him suffering. He had been sorely tried. But the affliction is past for the moment. Now that it is over, he can and does testify from experience that the Lord had dealt well with him. He can see it now. Perhaps this fact had not always been so clear to him while he had been suffering, but in retrospect he discerns it clearly. Now he compares this experience with the word of God and acknowledges that the two are in harmony, that the word of the Lord is faithful and true: "LORD, thou hast dealt well with thy servant, according unto thy word."

This implies that the word of God assures his servants in this world that the Lord will always deal well with them.

And indeed it does.

When the psalmist speaks of the word of God, he does not refer to any special or particular revelation he had received, but to the entire revelation of God in Christ as it had always been addressed to all the servants of Jehovah; as it gradually increased and grew in riches and clarity; as the poet possessed that word of God in the Lord's testimonies that he knew and loved; as it was centrally and completely fulfilled in the fullness of time in Jesus Christ, in his incarnation and sojourn among us, in his word and work, in his death and resurrection and exaltation at the right hand of God, and in the pouring forth of the Spirit of the exalted Christ, the Lord of all; as the word directs the eyes of our hope to the final goal, to his coming again with power and glory to reveal his glory and to establish his eternal kingdom, in which the tabernacle of God will be with men.

The gospel. The gospel of the promise.

That word throughout, emphatically and in various ways, assures the servant of the Lord that God will always do well with him, will never leave or forsake him, will be a shelter to him in the time of storm and a strong tower into which he can always run and be safe, that he will sustain and keep him, that not a hair will fall from his head against the Lord's will, that he will bring it to pass, that he will cause all things to work together for his good, even and emphatically the apparently evil things of this present time, and that absolutely nothing, on earth or in heaven or in hell, can separate him from the love of God in Christ Jesus the Lord.

Such is the word of God.

It is a light in darkness.

It is a strong assurance of salvation in the midst of suffering.

A mighty consolation in the time of trouble.

The faithfulness of this word the poet had experienced. Of it he sings, "Thou hast dealt well with thy servant, O LORD, according unto thy word."

Let us not misunderstand this confession and give it an erroneous application. The psalmist does not have in mind any temporal or material good the Lord had bestowed on him. When he acknowledges that the Lord had dealt well with him, he does not mean that his pathway through life had been bright and rosy and that he had been spared suffering and affliction. The contrary is true. His way had not been materially prosperous. Emphatically he speaks of his affliction, but in and through his affliction the Lord had dealt well with him.

Nor does this well-dealing of the Lord refer to the past afflictions out of which the Lord had delivered him, so that at the present time his way is joyful and prosperous. On the contrary, he regards his affliction, the sufferings he had endured, as the Lord's dealing with him. Even though the enemies of the Lord had inflicted this suffering upon him, he realizes that the Lord had been dealing with him through the enemies. So the affliction had been a good to him. In the tribulation the Lord had dealt well with him.

Abundantly evident this becomes in the rest of the section.

Does he not clearly express that he regards the affliction itself as a good? Before he was afflicted he had gone astray, but now he keeps the word of God. It had been good for him to be afflicted. He had learned the statutes of the Lord.

The well-dealing of the Lord does not therefore refer to any natural, earthly, material, temporal good, but to the spiritual, heavenly, eternal blessings of the kingdom and covenant of God, as they will ultimately be realized in all their fullness in the final glory of God's heavenly house, the heavenly perfection of his eternal covenant of friendship.

This is the promise of the word of God throughout.

God's promise to his people is not that they will be excused from or spared suffering. On the contrary, they lie not only in the midst of death with the whole world and must therefore endure with the world general sufferings, but they must also expect the special tribulation that is the fulfillment of the sufferings of Christ: "In the world ye shall have tribulation" (John 16:33).

Ahead still looms the great tribulation that will leave no room in the world for the faithful.

But be of good cheer.

The Lord deals well with his servants.

Such is his word, the word of the revelation of his eternal counsel concerning our salvation.

In God's counsel he willed and arranged all things, even all the sufferings of this present time and all the powers of darkness that rave and rage furiously against the church, that they must all work together for the final salvation of those who love him, who are the called according to his purpose.

His counsel he reveals and realizes in time, so that all things are made subservient to the purpose of the final glory of his servants.

Always it is true that the Lord deals well with his servants.

According to his word.

❖

Thy servant.

Serious qualification indeed.

Not with all, not with the reprobate wicked, who depart from his ways and love iniquity, does the Lord deal well.

The contrary is true. Even their prosperity God designed to be slippery places on which they hasten to destruction. Even when they grow as the grass, it is so they may be destroyed forever.

He loves the righteous.

His servants.

They are those who love him, who stand in covenantal relation to him, who know him and keep his commandments, and who in this world represent the cause of the Son of God. To them, and them exclusively, he does good, and with them he deals well even in all the experiences and vicissitudes, all the sufferings and afflictions, of this present time.

Not as if they have anything of which to boast.

For they are not servants of Jehovah of themselves. On the contrary, they were children of wrath, even as the others. If God's well-dealing with his servants depended at all upon anything they are or accomplished, they could expect nothing else than eternal wrath, darkness, and damnation. But they are servants because God ordained them as such in his eternal good pleasure. This is why he could deal well with them when they were yet enemies and give his only begotten Son so they would not perish, but have life and become his servants.

Always he dealt well with them.

He forgave all their iniquity and cleansed them from all their guilt, clothing them with his own righteousness in Christ Jesus their Lord.

He quickened them together with Christ, calling them out of darkness into his marvelous light.

He changes them from servants of sin and the devil into his own servants by the wonder of his grace.

He preserves them by his power through the faith he gives unto them.

He makes them more than conquerors even in the midst of their enemies.

His servants they are, yes, but solely through his sovereign grace.

That no flesh should glory in his presence.

❖

Blessed acknowledgment!

For not a mere doctrinal statement is found in these words, but a glad, joyful, and thankful acknowledgment of Jehovah's faithfulness as the psalmist had experienced it.

Blessed are they who thus acknowledge and taste the goodness of the Lord.

More blessed still are they who are so taught and upheld by the grace of their God, that even while they are being afflicted, they can joyfully confess, "Lord, thou art dealing well with thy servant, according unto thy word."

This is the victory of faith.

The psalmist is speaking in retrospect. He had been afflicted, but the affliction is now past. He reaps and enjoys the fruit of tribulation. He experiences that it had been good for him to be afflicted. He receives the fruit of righteousness. He is sanctified through suffering. Before he was afflicted he had wandered, but now he keeps the word of his God. He is able to see the salutary effect of affliction as it is sanctified unto his heart by the grace of God. So, speaking in the past tense, he rejoices in the Lord and confesses, "Thou hast dealt well with thy servant, O LORD, according unto thy word."

How blessed to glory, even in the midst of tribulation.

Oh, it is not easy, but impossible for the flesh (and how mighty is often the flesh in us!) to rejoice in the well-doing of the Lord even when the way grows dark and all things appear to be against us. When we suffer not only the general sufferings of this present time, but also the tribulation that comes upon the servants of the Lord because they are his servants; when it seems as if God's cause in the world will suffer defeat and the wicked prosper; ah, then, we are so easily inclined to cry out in doubt and fear, "Is there knowledge in the Most High?"

The more faithful we are as servants of the Lord, the more we suffer affliction.

How can it be then that the Lord deals well with his servants?

Also, how often we too seek the "good" in the things of this present time, in the things that are seen, rather than in the spiritual things of the kingdom of God. For we are earthly, and our desires are after earthly things. The flesh darkens our understanding, so we do not clearly discern the good.

We glory also in tribulation, yes, but with fear and trembling.

If our faith is to be victorious in suffering and tribulation, well may the prayer of the psalmist be consistently in our hearts and on our lips, "Teach me good judgment and knowledge, for I have believed thy commandments." Daily we need judgment—clear and distinct spiritual discernment of the real, eternal, spiritual good, in order to be sober and to evaluate all things in the light of the eternal—and true, spiritual, and experiential knowledge of the eternal and spiritual good, in order to rejoice in the well-dealing of the Lord in the midst of trouble.

Then, and then only, faith can have the victory, and we can glory even in tribulation.

Blessed glorying!

41

Thanksgiving

"Bless the Lord, *O my soul: and all that is within me, bless his holy name. Bless the* Lord, *O my soul, and forget not all his benefits."*—Psalm 103:1–2

Bless Jehovah!

Beautifully and picturesquely the Hebrew poet expressed himself: "Kneel down in praise, O my soul, before Jehovah."

Praise and thanksgiving are not common deeds of mankind. Neither are they national performances in which all alike are able to participate, for they are preeminently the expression of the humble and contrite heart and soul.

How shall I, how shall you, how shall anyone as he is by nature truly praise the Lord, render unto him the thanksgiving that is acceptable to him and pleasing in his sight? True, we may have many possessions and be surrounded with the increase of the earth, with the gold and silver of the world, with fatness and plenty. Our hearts may rejoice in the abundance of our wealth. At the sight of our corn and wheat, of our cattle and sheep, of our oil and wine, we banish care and anxiety from our hearts and sing songs of gladness and joy.

But joy and gladness in the possession of mere things is no praise and thanksgiving.

If it were, how could thanksgiving ever be anything but a work of the rich and of those who have health and strength? How could the thousands upon thousands who suffer affliction and poverty, who labor and toil every day to earn their measure of wheat for a penny, who behold the bottom of their breadbasket every night; or how could they who seem to be born to be afflicted, whose chastisement is there every morning, who groan in pain and agony or are overwhelmed with deep sorrow of heart—how could they join in with our songs of praise and gladness? If rejoicing in things were thanksgiving, gratitude must increase according as wealth and riches are multiplied, and the indigent who must satisfy his hunger with a dry crust of bread must grumble in his poverty.

Or perhaps, at the sight of all our possessions, of the prosperity of our businesses, of the increase of our cattle, of the fruit of the field, we may acknowledge that providence did his part to cooperate with our honest efforts, so that while we diligently plowed and sowed, toiled and labored from morning until night, he sent his rain and sunshine from above and blessed our labors. We will remember our own goodness and wisdom, our own labors and toil together with the cooperation of the Most High. And we will stammer the thanksgiving of the Pharisee in the parable, looking down on the poor and miserable publican and crying out, "I thank thee Lord that I am not as he."

But remembrance of self and celebration of our own worthiness are the opposite of praise and thanksgiving and are an abomination in the sight of the Lord.

To bless the Lord is, in deepest root, to kneel before him. To kneel not merely with the body, but to come before him with our souls bowed down in humiliation. Praise and thanksgiving proceed from the consciousness of our insignificance, from knowing that we are nothing and God is all; that he only is the source, the fount of all good, and that we must always be filled with him; that he always overflows with goodness, and that we cannot remunerate him at all, and from the feeling that we are totally unworthy, that we are children of corruption and wrath by nature, who defiled our way a thousand times and who are deeply conscious that we cannot stand before the Lord of heaven and earth and appear in his sanctuary if he would mark transgressions. Praise and thanksgiving arise, furthermore, from the knowledge not that we possess many things and are surrounded with plenty, but that he is our God and we are his people, who are called by him out of darkness into his marvelous light so that we should declare his praises, whose sins he forgives, whose diseases he heals, whose lives he delivers from destruction, whose youth he renews like the eagle's, in order for us to dwell in his communion, to know him, to love him, to walk with him, and to be led by his hand. True praise rejoices not in things, but in the possession of the Lord, who causes all things to work together for good to those who love him.

Thus, humbly kneeling in a sense of our shame and unworthiness and of the goodness and grace of Jehovah, we feel ourselves in the presence of the Lord of glory and address him, adore him, extol his glorious wonders and virtues, and express that he is good.

This is why he appears before the grateful soul as Jehovah.

Jehovah is his holy name.

In that name he stands before the worshiping soul in all the glory of his goodness. That name expresses that he is the everlasting God, the absolute, the unchangeable, the uncaused cause of all, the source of all, who has no deeper source than himself, the faithful, the true, the glorious God. It also expresses that he is all that he is for his people, whom he loved, loves, and will love and never forsake, but will bless unto all eternity with his own friendship and communion.

It is the name he revealed in his only begotten Son, Jesus, Jehovah-salvation.

Him he gave in everlasting love. In him he stands before us in all the power of his boundless grace.

How shall he not with him freely give us all things?

Bless, oh, bless the Lord!

Jehovah, my God.

❖

O my soul.

Bless Jehovah!

The beauty of this psalm is that it is a thanksgiving proclamation that begins and ends with self. The poet addresses self, his own soul, inciting himself to praise and bless Jehovah; then he turns to the creatures around him, calling on heaven and earth to join in with adoration and glad thanksgiving songs; and he returns to self again and closes as he began, "Bless the Lord, O my soul."

Thus it is only proper.

Thanksgiving is primarily personal. The soul exercises personal fellowship, stands all alone before the Lord, and bows down in humble adoration. To be sure, it does not end there. The truly thankful heart, rejoicing in the possession of the Lord as God, overwhelmed with the sense of his goodness and loving-kindness over his children, will point to the many benefits that it received from his hand, will call attention to them as manifestations of his holy name, cannot rest until the attention of all the brethren, of all creation in heaven and earth, has been fixed on his blessed name and mighty works, and until all that breathes has been summoned to extol the wondrous name of Jehovah. But thanksgiving does not commence there. It starts with self. It does not turn to another first, neither does it commence by glorifying the holy name of Jehovah before the brethren on earth and the holy angels in heaven. It knows of a keen desire to be alone with God, to pour itself out before him, to tell of his wonders before his face, to address itself to him, and to express what it has tasted and what it still does taste of the goodness of the Lord.

Bless the Lord, O my soul! And until my own soul blesses him, I cannot call on others to join in outpourings of praise.

Thanksgiving is also a matter of the inner man. Not first the lips or the bended knee. Truly, that too. The truly grateful heart cannot keep silence. It is constrained to pour itself out in thankful adoration. But first and chiefly it is a matter of the soul, never a mere external formality in which there throbs no living soul. The Lord has respect not to the face but to the heart; all empty form is vain and abominable in his sight. He desires truth in the inward parts. The soul, the seat of life, the living man, must be busy in the praise of the Lord. So it is with everything within the soul. He who would acceptably praise and bless Jehovah must adore him with mind and will, with thoughts and desires, with inclination and longing, and with all his emotions; the praise of the Lord must captivate the most secret recess of his inner life. He must consciously, knowingly, willingly, lovingly, fervently, ardently, with all his powers, sing the praises of him who is worthy to be praised forever and ever.

All that is within me, bless his holy name!

It is the self-address of the heart that knows of a strong desire, of a fervent longing of the inner man to glorify its God. It is the regenerate man, possessing a beginning of the new obedience, having tasted that the Lord is gracious, who is here speaking to himself. He is addressing himself, inciting everything within him to praise and adoration of Jehovah, because he is conscious of his imperfection, of the power of sin within him that is loath to break forth in praise for the living God. It is the soul that on the one hand is conscious of a delight in the law of God according to the inner man, but on the other hand knows of another law in his members that wars against the law of the mind.

How often is he slow to acknowledge the goodness and glory of the Lord. How often has he been surrounded with the manifestations of Jehovah's holy name and never known it, never took notice, never broke forth in glad thanksgiving notes. O my soul, how ashamed ought you to be because of your ungrateful attitude so frequently assumed over against him whose loving-kindness and mercy are from everlasting to everlasting over you. Therefore, O my soul, bless the Lord.

Kneel down before him in shame and humiliation because of your laxity, lukewarmness, and indifference. Awake, O my soul, to the praises of your benefactor.

Taste that the Lord is good and gracious.

Behold his holy name.

And tell him. Bless him.

O my soul.

❖

Bless him.

Bless his holy name.

Forget not all his benefits.

These three constitute an unbreakable chain linking my soul to the living God and inducing me to praise and adore the Lord Jehovah.

Forget not all his benefits. A Hebrew way of saying, "Forget none of them, but remember them all."

God's benefits are all his deeds, all his acts with respect to his children. The root meaning of the original word is "deeds." Forget not all his deeds toward you, O my soul. Indeed, all his acts are benefits unto his children, whom he loved with unfathomable compassion from before the world was. He never harms them. Whether the way is light or dark, bright or gloomy, whether it is smooth and level or rough and steep, whether it leads through dark ravines or over mountain heights bathing in the bright gold of cheering sunlight, whether God sends prosperity or adversity, health or sickness, joy or sorrow, our lives in their courses and in all their vicissitudes are his deeds, and the various stretches and curves in the road are his acts.

Because they are his acts with respect to his children, they must be benefits. The great central deed is the benefit of all benefits: the gift of God's only begotten Son. From that one gift flow all other gifts. That one deed is at once the source and the great sample of all God's other deeds. For from it flows the benefit that God forgives all our transgressions, swallowing them in Christ's precious blood; that God heals all our diseases, bearing them all by Christ's stripes; that God delivers our lives from destruction, seeing that Christ entered into our deepest woe and brought life from death and heaven from hell; that God renews our youth like the eagles, for eternal youth and glory Christ carried from the grave with him into heaven to bestow upon his people.

These spiritual benefits are first because they are basic. He who cannot rejoice in them cannot rejoice in Jehovah, cannot praise him and break forth into glad thanksgiving. Without these benefits nothing avails; with them all is well. He who forgives all our iniquities and washes us in the blood of his beloved, who heals our diseases and delivers us to crown our lives with everlasting glory and blessedness, will surely make all things subservient to our salvation.

Forget not all his deeds.

Remember that all his deeds are benefits to you, my soul.

Then you will behold in all these benefits his holy name that surrounds you—accompanies you every step, is your everlasting good and protection, holds your hand and leads you through darkness and light, over mountains and through vales, when the way is steep and rough as well as over paved and level roads—and leads you to glory.

Forget not all his benefits.

Count them one by one.

Exercise yourself to keep them constantly before your mind, dwell on them, make them your meditation day and night, in cheer and in gloom, in joy and in sorrow, in the midst of the fat of the earth or with the dry crust between your teeth, for in them you behold his holy name, Jehovah, the faithful and unchangeable God of your salvation.

In that name you ascend up to him whom no eye has ever seen, but whom his people love and know.

Then, O my soul, you never need to be expelled from the company of those who praise the Lord.

All things are benefits. All must work together for your salvation.

You will see God in your prosperity. You will taste his goodness over you in affliction and sorrow.

Forget not all his benefits.

Bless, O my soul; bless, all that is within me!

Bless his name.

Bless him.

Hallelujah!

42

Heart Searching

"Search me, O God, and know my heart: try me, and know my thoughts: And see if there be any wicked way in me, and lead me in the way everlasting."—Psalm 139:23–24

PROFOUND supplication.

Cry of perfect agreement with and of wholehearted surrender to the ever-searching, constantly trying God.

Search me, O God!

The prayer is the ultimate outcome, the inevitable, final result of the poet's consciousness of the presence of that God whose knowledge is dear, extremely precious, yet far too wonderful for him.

In the light of the whole psalm, this cry for the Most High's heart-searching judgment might appear paradoxical. For is not the whole psalm the expression of an amazed consciousness of the presence of God as a searcher of the hearts and the reins? Is not this theme expressed in the positive statement of the first verse: "O LORD, thou hast searched me, and known me"? Why, if the poet is profoundly conscious of the Most High's searching and knowing him, would he conclude his adoration of Jehovah with this prayer for searching?

Though it may seem paradoxical to pray for what God is already and constantly performing within us, the two are in perfect harmony. The prayer is the inevitable outcome of the poet's consciousness.

Jehovah's searching presence.

Deeply conscious, conscious with fear and trembling, with wonderment and utter amazement, the poet was of this overpowering, soul-overwhelming presence.

Of this he had sung in the rest of the psalm. God searched him and knew him. From this searching and trying and knowing and judging God there is no escape. He besets us on all sides. He is near us every moment. He knows our every move. He watches closely our every act. He knows our sitting down and our rising up; our thoughts he understands afar off, even before they arise into our consciousness. Our path he compasses, and with all our ways he is acquainted. Before a word leaves our lips, he knows it. He surrounds us, is before us and behind, below and above, in heaven and in hell; from his presence there is no escape. On the wings of the morning we cannot flee from him; to the uttermost parts of the earth we may take our flight, but even there we meet him. The deepest darkness cannot cover us from before his face; in his presence the night shines as the day. Even when we were made, when we were quite wonderfully and curiously wrought, before our substance was fashioned, he was present with us, and his searching eye watched over the process of our formation.

How wonderful is that presence!

How amazing is the thought of his penetrating search of us!

Spellbound, wholly and awfully charmed, the poet had stood in that marvelous presence. He had felt something of the awe that the seraphim experience as they stand in the presence of his glorious majesty and cover their faces with their wings as they cry out, "Holy, holy, holy!"

Yet while the psalmist had stood in the presence and had experienced the penetration of those searching eyes of the judge of heaven and earth, something more than mere awe had filled his soul, something else than mere fear had caused his inmost being to tremble. He feared Jehovah, yes, but with the fear of love. He had not wanted to flee, but to remain. His awful experience of the presence was not like that of the ungodly, who at the sight of him who sits on the throne cry out to the mountains and rocks, "Fall on us, and hide us!" On the contrary, marvelously sweet was the presence to him; wonderfully precious to his soul were the thoughts of God.

Still more.

While trembling in awe in the consciousness of his holiness and of his penetrating search, the poet had felt a bond of friendship with that glorious holy one.

He knew himself to be in God's covenant. He would be of his party. He could agree with him, take his side, even in God's searching judgment of himself. He feels himself wholly in harmony with that searching, trying, judging presence that besets him on every side.

The poet longs with a profound yearning to be in harmony with Jehovah, to be like him, to be righteous as he is righteous, to be holy as he is holy, to dwell in the light as he dwells in the light, and thus to know him, to dwell in his house, to see his face, to taste that he is good.

In that longing he willingly submits himself to Jehovah's judgment, gives himself completely over to the search of his penetrating eyes, in order to know himself, condemn himself, cast himself upon Jehovah's mercy, be delivered from his evil way, and be guided by Jehovah in the way everlasting.

Thus the consciousness of God's presence presses from his heart this marvelous prayer.

Search me, O God!

I know that thou always dost search me, but now I long to be searched.

Know my heart!

I know that thou dost constantly know my inmost being, but now I deeply yearn to be known.

Try me, and know my thoughts, which I know thou provest even before I am aware of them.

See if there be any wicked way in me. For I would condemn it with thee, and I long to be delivered, O my God.

Lead me in the everlasting way.

Marvelous prayer!

❖

Bold request.

For the poet asks nothing less than that he before whom nothing is hid, who proves the reins and the heart, will cause the searching and trying light of his just judgment to penetrate even into the depth of the poet's existence.

Nothing in him must remain hidden.

Such is the meaning of the word "search." It signifies to bore through, to penetrate even to the bottom. Hence the poet speaks of the thoughts that lie behind the outward appearance. Know my thoughts, that is, my inner life, my plans and purposes, my desires and aspirations, my imaginations and reasonings, my inclinations and the motives of all my actions. So too he mentions his heart, the center of his whole existence from a spiritual, ethical viewpoint. Search me, bore through the surface of my life, penetrate into the depths of my existence, until thou dost know my heart, whence are the issues of life.

Let nothing remain uncovered.

Let me be utterly exposed before thy face, O my God.

What is more, thus exposed in his inmost being, the poet desires to be evaluated, to be tried, to be judged, by the holy one.

Try me.

And know me. Know my thoughts. Know my heart.

He voluntarily puts himself on trial before the tribunal of the only judge of heaven and earth. He implores the Holy One to apply to him the touchstone of his own righteousness, his perfect law. He beseeches his God to compare him, his nature, his heart, his thoughts, his inmost inclinations and desires and motives, as well as the words of his mouth and all his walk and conversation, with the holy law of love. Fully aware that Jehovah can and will be satisfied with nothing less than complete harmony of the whole man with his own righteous will, the will that we love him with all our heart and mind and soul and strength, and that the holy one is too pure of eyes even to behold iniquity, he takes his position before the tribunal of the Most High and prays, "Try me. And know me, my thoughts, my inmost heart."

He asks to be evaluated, to be known by God as to the ethical value of his inner life.

Know me. Determine what I am. Express a verdict as to my righteousness or unrighteousness. He desires to hear that verdict, to know himself in the light of God's own judgment over him.

Nor is this prayer a mere abstraction or a mystical desire that God may directly reveal himself and speak to him and cause the light of his righteousness to expose the inner recesses of his heart. On the contrary, it is a prayer that is heard whenever the child of God submits himself to the infallible judgment of the word of God as contained in the Holy Scriptures, and as God's own Spirit applies that word to his heart. Standing before and beholding himself in the mirror of the perfect law of liberty, his prayer is heard indeed.

Try me, and know my thoughts and my heart.

How is this possible?

Is not this prayer too audacious? Is it not an act of utter rashness to invoke the judgment of God upon us?

What motivates the poet? What gives him this boldness to beseech the righteous judge of all to search him to the depth of his being, try him, and express his righteous judgment upon him? Does he perhaps pray in the assurance of his own righteousness? Does he feel that he may freely present himself before him who searches the hearts and the reins, confident that he will find nothing worthy of condemnation? No, such a spirit of self-righteousness is contrary to the profound knowledge of and reverence for the Most High expressed in the entire psalm. Besides, does not the poet speak of the wicked way the Lord might find within him? Rather it is thus: In the light of the searching presence, the poet has already examined himself, and his examination of self yielded the result of the knowledge of many sins of which he is conscious. Now, realizing that his trial of himself is very imperfect, considering that in the depth of his heart there are other wicked ways of which he is not even conscious, he implores the Most High for more light, for more thorough searching of the heart, for a clearer and more penetrating exposure of the hidden sins within.

Bold prayer indeed for a sinful man!

But it is the boldness not of self-righteousness, nor of the rashness of blind ignorance, but of faith. It is the boldness of confidence of faith in Christ.

Except for Christ this supplication would be utterly impossible. Should a man who is a sinner invoke upon himself the judgment of him who is a consuming fire? Rather, should he not call to the rocks to fall on him and to the mountains to cover him?

But in Christ this prayer is possible.

In him we are confident that we will not come into condemnation. He is the revelation of the God of our salvation. He took upon himself all our sins, all our iniquities, all our condemnation. For them he offered the perfect obedience of love. There, in the darkness of desolation, he too cried unto his God and prayed, "Search me, O my God; try me, and know my thoughts and my heart; and see if there be in me, as I offer myself a sacrifice for the sins of my people, any wicked way."

He was answered in the resurrection.

No wicked way was found in him. His sacrifice was perfect, without blemish.

He was justified before the tribunal of God as the head of all his own.

And they were forever justified in him. He was raised for their justification.

He was exalted at the right hand of God and was given the Spirit of promise. In that Spirit he dwells in all his own, calling them out of darkness into the marvelous light of the God of their salvation, bestowing upon them the adoption unto children, the forgiveness of sins, and eternal righteousness.

In that Spirit they have confidence to pray, "Search me, O God."

In that Spirit they know that with God there is forgiveness, so that he is feared.

Longing to obtain forgiveness, to obtain it ever again, to taste of its sweetness ever more deeply, they have boldness to place themselves willingly before the tribunal of the God of grace in Christ Jesus their Lord, praying for his searching judgment.

Bold supplication indeed!

But it is the boldness of faith.

Through Jesus Christ.

❖

And lead me.

To be sure, also the desire expressed in the last part of this prayer motivates the poet.

It is not only the consciousness of forgiveness and the desire to drink of the blessed fountain of redemption more deeply that cause him to implore his God to search him, to try him, to know his thoughts and his heart, but he also longs to be delivered from every evil way and to be guided in the way everlasting.

How could it be different?

Is not faith in the Lord Jesus, by which we long for, pray for, and are confident of forgiveness, rooted in the love of God shed abroad in our hearts, the love wherewith he loved us even unto the death of his Son? Do we not, through that love wherewith he loved us first, also love him? How then can this faith, rooted in love and operating through the love of God, ever be satisfied with forgiveness alone? How can it ever rest until the perfect deliverance from all the power and dominion of sin will be accomplished, and we will be like him, to dwell in his tabernacle forever and to see him face-to-face?

Hence see if there is any wicked way in me—the way of an idol, the secret inclination to follow after vanity, to deny the living God, to serve the lust of the flesh and the lust of the eye and the pride of life.

Discover that evil tendency in me, not merely so that I may have forgiveness, but that I may know the evil, fight it, and be delivered from it by thy grace.

And lead me in the way everlasting.

This is the way of the righteousness of the kingdom of heaven. Everlasting because it is the way of the righteousness of Christ, through his death and resurrection, into the everlasting light of the tabernacle of God with men.

I am weak and helpless, prone to wander.

Lead me, O my God!

43

When Thou Shalt Enlarge My Heart

*"I will run the way of thy commandments, when thou shalt
enlarge my heart."—Psalm 119:32*

WHEN thou shalt enlarge my heart.

Apparently strange and impossible desire!

More than a mere fact, but also the expression of an intense
longing we must see in these words of the poet.

He longs to run the way of God's commandments, for in him
there is that which greatly loves the word of God and deeply delights in his statutes. Therefore it is his earnest desire that his heart
be enlarged, for he understands that such enlargement of his heart
is indispensable to his running the way of God's precepts.

He finds his heart too small, too narrow.

The heart is man's spiritual, ethical driving power, that mysterious, hardly conceivable yet very real, almost indefinable yet clearly
experienced center of his human life and existence that determines
the spiritual, ethical direction, the yes or no, the good or evil, the
truth or falsity of all his actions and their direction with a view
to God and his will. The heart determines the nature, motive, and
purpose of his walk and conversation, his speech and deeds, his
seeing and hearing, his joy and sorrow, his pleasure and displeasure,
his desires and aspirations, his choices and decisions, yea, even of
the deepest inclinations of his being before they cross the threshold
of his consciousness. There in the heart of man are the roots, the
springs, the hidden and mysterious sources, of all his activity.

From the heart are the issues of life.

Not from a natural perspective, for the seat of man's thinking
and willing is not his heart, but his soul. But spiritually and ethically the heart is the center, the fountain, the driving force, of all man

does, feels, enjoys, loves, hates, admires, seeks, flees, worships, curses, chooses, and rejects. In his heart is the either/or, never the both/and. There is the love of God or the enmity against God. There are the roots of the fear of Jehovah or of rebellion against him. There are the beginnings and principles of wisdom—the knowledge of God, righteousness, and holiness—or of folly, the lie, iniquity, and corruption. From the heart arise good thoughts, imaginations, desires, volitions, words, and deeds; or from the heart arise evil thoughts, imaginations, desires, volitions, words, and deeds.

Never both at once.

Does a fountain send forth at the same place sweet water and bitter? Can the fig tree bear olive berries? Can a vine bear figs?

Neither alternately good and evil. It is always either/or. And as the heart is, so is man.

"When thou shalt enlarge my heart."

The child of God, the Christian, is speaking. He is conscious of having become a new creature through the grace of God who called him out of darkness into his marvelous light, by which he received a new heart instead of the old and the controls of his life were transferred to a new directing power, the law of the Spirit of life in Christ Jesus. Of all this the speaker is conscious, for he desires from God not a new heart, but that his heart may be enlarged. To enlarge one's heart signifies to make it more spacious, to create more room in it, to give it more receptivity, more power to act, a bigger place in one's life.

But how can the poet even conceive of the desirability of an enlargement of his heart, unless he is assured that his heart has been renewed? The evil heart can also be enlarged. Often, in fact always, it is. The enlargement of the evil heart means a greater capacity for evil, for enmity against God and rebellion against the Most High, for hatred and envy, for love of the lie, of iniquity and unrighteousness, for the lust of the flesh and the lust of the eye and the pride of life. The result of such enlargement is that one runs the way of sin and darkness and destruction. How far this is from the intention of the poet!

My heart is the new heart.

When the grace of God touches the heart, it is changed, wholly and radically changed, completely reversed, driven by a new power, actuated by a different law, the law of the Spirit of life. Whatever fearful contrasts and contradictions the Christian finds within himself, however deeply he experiences his present imperfection, so that he often hates what he does and does what he hates, he is not and knows that he is not a man with two hearts. He is conscious of having one new heart that is filled with the love of God in Christ Jesus.

He is a new creature.

Old things have passed away; all things have become new.

He is pure of heart. And he delights in the law of God according to the inward man.

Of that delight the poet sings throughout this psalm. Of it he sings in this particular section. He prays that God's law will be graciously granted to him; he chooses the way of truth; he lays Jehovah's judgments before himself. He sticks to God's testimonies, and he longs to run the way of God's commandments.

Such are the desires, the issues, of his heart.

But it appears that his heart is so small. And he finds another law in his members, oppressing his heart, preventing its free expression, its unhampered activity. His soul cleaves unto the dust; he realizes that he is weak; his soul is melting for heaviness.

Not a better, but a larger heart he desires. More capacity for the love of God, an increase in the spiritual receptivity for the things of God's kingdom; more knowledge of God, more righteousness and holiness, more sorrow over sin, and more delight in God's precepts.

Less death and more life.

Less of darkness and more of light.

Enlargement of the heart.

❖

When thou shalt…

The poet is waiting upon God.

For he realizes that salvation is of the Lord, and that if his heart is to be enlarged, God must work within him.

It is not a resolution that he expresses, "I will enlarge my heart." It is no vow that he pledges before the face of Jehovah, that henceforth his heart will be larger. He realizes that he has no power over his own heart. The God of his salvation must do it. And thus it is. Only God's sovereign, irresistible grace can change the heart when it is motivated by enmity against God, when its imaginations are at all times only evil. Only he, who by the marvelous power of his grace renews us, radically reversing our hearts, is able to enlarge them and to make us grow in the knowledge and grace of Christ Jesus our Lord. He is the sole author of our salvation from its inception to its culmination.

He does so by his Spirit.

That Spirit is the Spirit of Christ, the Spirit of adoption, whereby Christ himself dwells in our hearts and we cry, "Abba, Father." By that Spirit he renews us and continually dwells in us. By that Spirit he opens our hearts wide, so that we hunger and thirst after righteousness and more righteousness, so that we long for and are receptive to the things of the kingdom of heaven, for the love of God in Christ Jesus, for the forgiveness of sins and the adoption unto children, for the knowledge of him in all the preciousness of his grace, for sanctification of life and delight in his precepts. Even as he enlarges our hearts and increases their capacity for the grace of God, so he fills them, always, constantly, and out of him we receive grace for grace.

Even unto the end.

He works within us to will and to do of his good pleasure.

Mark well: He does so.

Fail not, while you emphasize that the poet acknowledges his utter dependence on his God for the work of salvation to its end, to notice two other elements. The one, which you cannot fail to notice, is that he earnestly desires this enlargement of the heart, and that even his longing is a manifestation of the heart-enlarging grace of God already operating within him. The other is that he appears to be perfectly confident that Jehovah will surely enlarge his heart. His attitude is not that of a dead, careless, or hopeless surrender to the inevitable. He does not coldly and indifferently walk in the way of the flesh, saying that since only God can enlarge his heart he can sin until it pleases the Lord to do so. Neither does he express doubt as to whether Jehovah will be pleased to enlarge his heart. On the contrary, with earnest desire he longs for grace and more grace, and with perfect confidence he looks forward to the realization of his desires and the answer to his prayer, "When thou shalt enlarge my heart."

Such is the way of God with his children.

He enlarges their hearts in the way of their longing, which only he creates; in the way of their prayers, which only he works in the heart; in the way of constant heart-exercise, of which he is the author.

To be sure, he does it, not we. He alone enlarges our hearts, not he and we in cooperation with him.

He who glories, let him glory in the Lord.

But to be sure, let him glory.

Many profess to believe in the sovereignty of God's grace who never glory in the Lord at all. They never seek and they never find, though they pride themselves in their seeking. They never ask and they never receive, though they appear to be forever asking. They never strive and they never attain because they do not strive. Never is their heart enlarged; never do they glory in the faithfulness of the Lord who fulfills all his promises to his people; never do they sing the song of thankful joy and praise because the Lord has heard that prayer. They confess that the Lord *must* do it all, but to them he never accomplishes his work of grace; they emphasize that he who glories must glory in the Lord, but they never glory.

In the meantime they walk in darkness, in unbelief, in the service of sin, in the ways of their carnal minds. Until it pleases the Lord to enlarge their hearts.

Dark souls.

Be not deceived by them.

Do not attempt to rouse them from their spiritual lethargy by denying that God must indeed accomplish all of salvation, and by assuring them that they also must add their share and perform their part. That God is the sole author of salvation and that man has no part in this work of God at any stage of its development, is surely the truth.

The error of these sickly souls does not lie in their confession of this truth.

Rather they must understand not only that God *must* accomplish salvation, but also that he surely *does* perform it unto the end;

that when he begins and continues to accomplish his wonderful grace in our hearts, we do not and cannot remain coldly indifferent, waiting in an attitude of sickly passivity, but we respond with all our hearts, long for salvation and for more of it, seek it, hunger and thirst after it, open our hearts to his saving influences, walk in the ways in which we expect them, and exercise ourselves in faith and sanctification.

God enlarges our hearts in the way of spiritual exercise.

It is even so with the wicked. In the way of sin and the exercise of the sinful heart in sin, God even enlarges the heart of the natural man, so that he increases in capacity for evil. The more he seeks and satisfies himself with the lust of the flesh, the more he craves it, and the more it requires to satisfy his lust.

When God enlarges the heart of his child, he does so not without, but through the heart-exercise of the renewed and sanctified saint, longing and yearning, praying and seeking, searching the word, dwelling in the midst of God's people, fighting the good fight, walking in the way of his good commandments. Thus the saint goes from strength to strength, rejoicing in the Lord and confiding in his promise.

Until he appears before God in Zion.

To be satisfied with his likeness.

❖

I will run.

Such will be the fruit of this enlargement of the heart.

This fruit—that he will run the way of God's commandments— is the object of the poet's longing, the reason he desires God to enlarge his heart.

To run that way, with all the emphasis on the running, is his purpose, his goal.

The way of God's commandments is the objective standard of our lives as God wills them, as they are pleasing in his sight, as they are in harmony with his precepts. His will covers our lives in all their phases and relationships—the lives of our bodies and souls, of our intellects and wills; our lives in relation to spouses and children, to employers and employees, to fellow saints and the world; our lives always and everywhere, on Sunday and during the week, in the church and on the street, in the home and in the shop. The way of God's commandments makes of our lives a divine calling and makes us his friend-servants every moment of our lives in the world.

That way I would run.

To *run* is the same as to *walk* in the way of God's commandments, but with great emphasis. To run in the way of God's commandments is to live not only according to some but according to all of God's commandments, willingly and readily to subject all my active life—within and without, in private and in public, in the church and in the world—to the will of God, because I love him with all my heart, mind, soul, and strength; to do this without murmuring, eagerly, zealously, with a glad heart, rejoicing even in tribulation for his name's sake, overcoming the world.

Now I so often hesitate, am reluctant, and stumble in the way of God's commandments.

Yet I long to run.

And run I will, I know.

When thou shalt enlarge my heart.

44

Open Thou My Lips!

"O Lord, open thou my lips; and my mouth shall shew forth thy praise."—Psalm 51:15

OPEN *my* lips.

The prayer of the psalmist is definitely in the singular.

Emphatically personal is this outcry, personal in its longings to proclaim the praise of Jehovah, in its profound sense of unworthiness and incapability of praising the Lord, in its consciousness of lips that are irrevocably sealed unless they are opened by the grace of the God of his salvation.

But the prayer and praise that leave our lips on Thanksgiving Day are a united expression of the whole church.

On that day we gather to unite in grateful praise.

We unite, let it be clearly understood, not as a nation, but as the people of God. It is not the wicked and the righteous, unbelievers and believers, who meet on that day before the throne of grace to pour out their hearts before the Most High. Even though the occasion for this day is the end of harvest; even though it is true that the Lord caused his sun to rise over the righteous and wicked alike, and sent rain on the just and the unjust; even though on this day we are therefore emphatically reminded of the truth that in this world there is something promiscuous in God's providential dealings with men, so that the righteous and the unrighteous have all things in common, and the unrighteous even receive more of earthly riches and abundance than the righteous; yet even on Thanksgiving Day the distinction between those who fear the Lord and those who fear him not is not obliterated, but clearly maintained, and it is only those who fear the Lord who unite in praise.

To give thanks one must not taste things, but the favor of the Most High.

For the wicked this is impossible. They taste many things, but not the grace of God. Even in their prosperity the favor of Jehovah is not upon them; his face is against those who do evil. Even in their abundance they receive no token of God's loving-kindness toward them, for he is angry with the wicked every day, and when they prosper he sets them on slippery places, so that they can be cast down into destruction.

Even on Thanksgiving Day, though it is proclaimed by the president of our nation, the truth remains that there is only one access to the throne of grace and that the way into the inner sanctuary leads along the blood-sprinkled way, through the veil, that is, the flesh of Christ that was broken for us. But in Christ the unbeliever has no part. Even on Thanksgiving Day the sacrifices of the wicked are an abomination to Jehovah, and it is only the prayer of the upright that is his delight. Even on the day of national rejoicing, the wicked open their lips to eat and to drink, but the prayer that their lips may be opened unto the praise of the Lord is foreign to them.

How then can they praise him whose favor they do not taste?

How can they give thanks to him whose truth they hold under in unrighteousness and for whose glory they care not? Is it not true that even on Thanksgiving Day:

> *Thus speaks the Lord to wicked men:*
> *My statutes why do ye declare?*
> *Why take my covenant in your mouth,*
> *Since ye for wisdom do not care?*
> *For ye my holy words profane*
> *And cast them from you in disdain.*
> *Consider this, who God forget,*
> *Lest I destroy with none to free;*
> *Who offers sacrifice of thanks,*
> *He glorifies and honors me:*
> *To him who orders well his way*
> *Salvation free I will display (Psalter 138:1, 4).*

But unite we do as God's people in Christ, the church of the living God, in order that "the abundant grace might through the thanksgiving of many redound to the glory of God" (2 Cor. 4:15).

All unite.

Unite so that in oneness of heart and mind, in the one Christ by the one Spirit, without a single discordant note, we sing the praises of the God of our salvation.

The content, the ground, and the object of our thanksgiving must be such that not one of the saints, no matter what his station and position in life, no matter what his earthly way and lot may be, is excluded.

It must at once embrace and transcend all things.

Embrace all things, for the Lord reigns over all.

On Thanksgiving Day, or on any other day, you dare not find the reason for your praise in an abundance of things, in earthly prosperity and joy. You dare not let mere things be the measure of your gratitude and adoration. If you do, you must divide your things and your experience into two classes and pile them into two heaps. You will regard the one heap, the pile of what you consider "good things," with a certain carnal joy and conclude that you have still many reasons to be thankful, while with regard to the "evil things," you will desperately attempt, at least for one day, to forget them and to smother the murmur of rebellion that rises in your heart.

How small the pile of "good things" then becomes for some of us.

Who, even in the midst of the present prosperity, is able to forget that it is war prosperity? Who, as we take our places at the family table covered with abundance, can fail to see the empty place of husband or son or brother who is perhaps even in that very moment in the heat of battle, homesick, miserable, in fear of death, utterly perplexed because of the "hell" that is let loose all about him? Who, even for one day, can be oblivious of the place that is left empty forever, concerning whom we received the formally cold but for us heartrending report: "We regret...Killed in action"?

Where then, if things are the ground of your thanksgiving, is your joy and peace?

No, we will not divide our experience into two piles, but our thanksgiving will embrace *all things*. But while it embraces all of the experiences and vicissitudes of this life, it will transcend this *all*. For with all things, we will lift up our hearts to the God of our salvation and understand and acknowledge that all these things come to us not by chance, but by his fatherly hand.

Peace and war, joy and sorrow, prosperity and adversity, plenty and scarcity, sickness and health, life and death—they are all his work.

Considering that they are the work of the God of our salvation, we know that they are good, though we understand it not. Knowing that he does whatsoever he has pleased, we are prepared to praise him in all his works.

And so we unite in thanksgiving.

Yet if we are thus to embrace all things in our adoration, if we are thus unitedly to transcend them all and to rejoice in the loving-kindness of our God in the midst of sufferings, we should humble ourselves before the throne of grace and implore him for his mercy.

Before we unite in thanksgiving, we should enter our closets and each in his position utter this intensely personal prayer, "O Lord, open thou my lips!"

❖

"That I may show forth thy praise."

Such is the purpose of the prayer for the opening of our lips.

To be sure, the showing forth of the praise of God is also the result, the fruit, of the grace whereby our lips are opened. The psalmist, no doubt, also intends to confess that he is incapable and unworthy of showing forth the praise of Jehovah, unless the Lord by his irresistible grace opens his lips.

Yet that which is the fruit of God's grace is also the purpose of the psalmist's prayer, the end that he has in view and that he longs to attain, so that the prayer can be rendered thus: "O Lord, open thou my lips, in order that my mouth may show forth thy praise."

To show forth the praise of the Lord is true thanksgiving.

Let us beware, lest our deceitful hearts substitute anything else for this showing forth of his praise. Beware, lest you imagine that in any sense you could remunerate him for all his benefits to you. What would you give him? He is the ever-blessed God, the fullness of all good, the absolutely self-sufficient Lord. He is the sole proprietor of the whole universe, the creator of the heavens and of the earth. The silver and the gold, the cattle on a thousand hills, and the earth and its fullness belong to Jehovah. Always he speaks:

> I will receive from out thy fold
> No off'ring for my holy shrine;
> The cattle on a thousand hills
> And all the forest beasts are mine;
> Each mountain bird to me is known,
> Whatever roams the field I own.
> Behold, if I should hungry grow,
> I would not tell my need to thee,
> For all the world itself is mine,
> And all its wealth belongs to me;
> Why should I aught of thee receive,
> My thirst or hunger to relieve? (Psalter 137:4–5)

Beware, lest your evil imaginations make you feel pious and religious in the thought that you give him something when you offer him a dime of his own dollar. Beware, lest you become abominable in his sight when you foolishly would pour a little drop back into the fountain from which your cup was and always is filled. You can give him nothing! He is always the giver, never the receiver. He is the ever-flowing fount of all good. Even your thanksgiving is his gift to you, not yours to him. As soon as you have rendered thanks unto his holy name, you are already under obligation to fall back on your knees and thank him for your gratitude.

To show forth his praise—that alone is thanksgiving.

His praises, you understand, are his marvelous virtues.

God is God.

And he is the Lord.

And he is good.

He is the implication, the fullness, of all infinite perfections. He is a light, and there is no darkness in him at all. He is pure and infinite goodness. He is righteousness and holiness, truth and faithfulness, love and grace and mercy and loving-kindness, justice and power and might, the only potentate of potentates, the only Lord, who dwells in the light no man can approach unto, the creator and redeemer, who calls the things that are not as if they were, and who quickens the dead.

This praise he reveals to us in many praises in all the works of his hands.

He reveals them in creation, for the heavens declare the glory of God and the firmament shows his handiwork; day unto day utters speech, and night unto night shows knowledge. He reveals them in the works of his providence even in this cursed world, in which all things are made subject to vanity and as we lie in the midst of death. He reveals his praises in rain and sunshine, in devastating floods and scorching heat, in abundance and famine, in prosperity and adversity, in peace and war, in health and sickness, in joy and sorrow, in life and death. He reveals them to his people centrally in the death and resurrection of his only begotten Son, through whom he revealed his everlasting love and purpose of salvation, and in the light of whose cross and glory you are assured that all other things will be added unto you and will work together for your salvation.

That is his praise revealed in many praises.

Show them forth!

Point to them. Include them all. Exclude none of them. Do not put your things on two piles to praise him for some of them, but point to them all and confess that they all show forth his praise, that they all reveal that the Lord is good, and that his mercy endures forever. Say it to him in adoration and worship. Tell it to your children, to one another. Declare in all the world, before a boasting and vaunting and wicked world that speaks of chariots and of horses, that the Lord is God, that he reigns over all.

And that he is ever good.

Unto this you were called.

He called you out of darkness into his marvelous light, that you might show forth his virtues.

His marvelous praises!

❖

Lord, open thou my lips.

How else will we ever declare his praise?

Oh, how utterly impossible this is without his grace! On the one hand, with our natural eyes we do not see his praise. We see war and destruction, madness and confusion, suffering and death; we see that the wicked prosper, that the righteous suffer, and that the ways of the Lord are not equal. On the other hand, we are carnal and sinful by nature and are neither worthy nor capable and willing to show forth the praises of the Most High. We are inclined rather to rejoice in things and to rebel when things are against us.

Thanksgiving, the showing forth of the praise of Jehovah, is the fruit of his marvelous grace in the beloved.

Lord, open thou my lips!

My lips, yes, but from within. Open my heart, whence are the issues of life. Work mightily, constantly, and irresistibly in my inmost heart, so that I have eyes to see thy glory and thy everlasting mercy over me in *all* things and a will to adore thee and to joy in thee.

Then, and then only, my mouth will be opened.

To declare thy glorious praise.

Forever!

45

Reverent Circumspection

"Keep thy foot when thou goest to the house of God, and be more ready to hear, than to give the sacrifice of fools: for they consider not that they do evil. Be not rash with thy mouth, and let not thine heart be hasty to utter any thing before God: for God is in heaven, and thou upon earth: therefore let thy words be few."—*Ecclesiastes 5:1–2*

WHEN you enter the house of God...

For this occasion the word of God in this connection sounds a threefold warning.

The house of God to which the text refers was the old dispensational temple, the sanctuary of Israel, where the people of God went to worship, to offer their prayers, to bring their sacrifices, and to pledge and to pay their vows.

In the new dispensation this sanctuary is no longer on earth; it is in heaven. The blood of Christ has sprinkled the way that leads into the inner sanctuary of God, the veil of his flesh was rent, and the way into the presence of God is made manifest. There in the sanctuary, our eternal and holy high priest appears before God in our behalf, and with our eye of faith fixed on him, we may walk the blood-sprinkled way and boldly enter through the veil into the presence of the Most High, confident that we will be received.

Yet the threefold exhortation of God is still important and to the point.

All three warnings are comprehended in one: "Keep thy foot." Do not blindly rush into God's sanctuary, as if you were entering your neighbor's house, but rather be circumspect and prepare yourselves properly to meet your God.

Applied to your worship, this signifies, first, that it is better to hear than to bring the sacrifices of fools. Remember when you sacrifice that your offering is presented to the living God. You cannot pretend to do him a favor. You dare not assume the attitude of the donor. Beware lest you feel that with your gift on the altar, you can add to his riches, so that he ought to be pleased with the outward offering. The earth is the Lord's and the fullness thereof. All the gold and silver in the world and the cattle on a thousand hills are his. Let therefore your sacrifice only be a token of humility and deep contrition, an expression that it is your delight to hear his word and to keep his commandments, if he will give you grace. For it is better to hear than to give the sacrifice of fools. To hear and to obey the word of God is better than sacrifice.

Second, the principle that you should keep your feet and not madly rush into the presence of God implies that you should pay your vows.

Vow and pay. Defer not to pay or vow not at all.

For you are making your vow to the living God, and he has no pleasure in fools.

Last, when you pray, be not rash with your mouth, so that you speak thoughtlessly, oblivious of the one you are addressing; nor let your heart be the criterion of your prayer and madly make you utter many words. Rather, when you utter your prayers before the Most High, let the knowledge of him and the consciousness of being in his presence control and determine your attitude and every word you speak.

You are speaking to God.

God is in heaven; you are on the earth. Therefore let your words be few.

Let the fear of the Most High motivate your heart and mind.

Holy circumspection.

❖

God is the Lord.

This is the emphatic and primary significance of the reminder that he is in heaven and that we are on earth.

To be sure, he is not confined to heaven; omnipresent is he. On the earth as well as in heaven his presence fills all things. Nothing excludes him. Moreover, he is the infinite one who transcends all that is called creature, who cannot be measured by space; the eternal God, whose beginning or end cannot be discovered, who transcends all time. The heaven, yea, the heaven of heavens cannot contain him.

When the word of God makes the distinction between his being in heaven and our being on the earth, it would have us remember that he is the Lord, the absolute Lord, the sole ruler and proprietor of the whole universe, and we are living on his footstool.

Heaven is his throne.

When you prepare to enter into his sanctuary and to appear in the presence of God, when you are about to open your mouth in prayer and to utter your petitions before his face, you must do so in the clear and profound consciousness that you stand face-to-face with the potentate of potentates, the only sovereign of the whole universe, the heavenly majesty. He is the creator of the heavens and of the earth. They owe their existence solely to the marvel of his power. They came into being when he called the things that were not as if they were. There was no one with him.

He is the sole proprietor. The earth is the Lord's and the fullness thereof, and he does with all things according to his good pleasure. The heavens and the earth, the clouds and the rain and the sunshine, the rivers and the valleys, the mountains and the hills, the cattle and the beasts of the forest, the soil you plow and the seed you sow and the power you employ to do it, the air you breathe and the water you drink and the bread you eat, the clothes that cover your nakedness and the fire that makes you comfortable in the cold of winter, your silver and your gold, all the means wherewith you toil and labor, yea, you yourselves with body and soul, with mind and will and heart, and with all your power and ingenuity—all are his.

He is in heaven, you are on the earth.

Beware, when you present your petitions to him, lest you should speak with the pretension of having any right or claim to even the smallest speck of dust. Remember that you have sinned against his majesty and that if he would mark your transgressions, you would be cast into everlasting desolation.

Be not rash with your mouth, and speak not as if he were the caretaker of your property.

Let not your heart be hasty to bring before him your carnal requests, as if he existed to prosper your cause, a kind providence whose sole purpose it must be to fill you with prosperity and plenty.

He is the proprietor, you are his property.

In the heavens is he, while you are on the earth.

Therefore let your words be few.

He is the Lord!

❖

The sole governor is he.

Alone he is enthroned in the heavens.

All the reins of the government of the entire universe are in his hands. There is no one with him, no one who gives him counsel, no one who shares the government with him, who has the prerogative, the authority, the wisdom, or the power even to be his advisor.

God is in heaven, we are on earth; he is the governor, we and all things are the ruled.

This implies that he moves as by his hand every creature in all the living universe and directs it according to his will.

Whether you see the sun rise every morning exactly at its appointed time, or whether you watch a lonely white cloud drift, apparently quite arbitrarily, across the blue firmament; whether you marvel at the beauty and exact position of each sparkling and twinkling star in the dark heavens, or whether you see the swift meteor flash across a section of the sky; whether you consider the spring rain or the summer drought, the sprouting grass and herb or the golden grain ready to be harvested; whether you listen to the soft murmur of the brook or to the roar of the mighty ocean in the storm; whether you hear the cry of the raven or the song of the meadowlark—all you perceive is moved and directed as it were by his hand. The bullet that seeks its target, the shell that bursts to spread death and destruction, the bomb that is dropped from the plane, the torpedo that makes its treacherous course through the dark waters, as well as the thoughts and plans of mighty man who invents and prepares them for their destructive work—all are directed as it were by his hand.

When you are healthy and well, it is his hand that makes you so, but when sickness enters your home, it is by his hand that it is sent; when you harvest an abundant crop, it was his gift to you, but when the almost-ready harvest is destroyed by hail, his hand alone directed the path of the hail; when there is an abundance of supplies in your cellars, it was he who filled them, but when the bread basket is empty, it was also his hand that emptied it. When your son gets through this dreadful war without a scratch, or when he is wounded or killed on the battlefield, it is God who directs it all. The message that is delivered at your door, "We regret to inform you that your son was killed in action," is brought to you by his hand.

Prosperity and adversity, sickness and health, fruitful and barren years, life and death, peace and war—they are all his. He determines when and what will be the outcome of this war.

God is in heaven, he alone does, and he alone is able to rule.

He is the Lord.

Be not rash with your tongue when you pray, and be not hasty to utter a thousand requests that might arise from your heart.

When he sends heavy rains at the time of harvest or drought in the springtime, do not instruct him to change his government; when sickness enters your family, do not request that he remove it; when war ravages the whole world and his judgments are in the earth, neither clamor for peace because you do not like war and judgments nor instruct him as to whose cause is righteous and must have the victory; when hundreds and thousands of young men are killed in battle, do not insist that your son or husband must be kept unharmed.

Rather, say, "O God, thy will be done. Give us grace to will that will."

He is the Lord.

Besides, that he alone governs all things implies that he directs all the history and movement of all the universe to his own end.

Things do not move at random. They are all directed according to an eternal purpose. The plan of all things is in heaven, in the divine mind, in eternity, in the immutable decree of the Lord of heaven and earth.

And you know, for in his grace he assured you of it, that as far as those who love him are concerned, that purpose is everlasting glory and salvation.

Is not that sufficient?

All things work together for good to those who love him, who are the called according to his purpose. Would you insist that he change that purpose because of some individual experience that is not to your liking, some suffering sorrow that he sends you here on the earth?

Would you rather commit it all to him?

God is in heaven, and you are on the earth; therefore let your words be few.

Oh, let them be as many as you please, pour out your hearts in an abundance of words, if you mean to praise and adore and glorify him and acknowledge that he is the Lord, for of his wondrous works there is no end.

But as far as the details of your life and way are concerned, leave them to him.

Be not rash with your mouth.

God is the Lord!

❖

He alone knows.

Yes, also this is implied in the reminder that he is in the heavens and that we are on the earth.

He knows all. We do not understand his way or work, except in as far as it pleases him to make them known unto us.

> Jehovah from His throne on high
> Looks down with clear and searching eye
> On all that dwell below;
> And He that fashioned heart and mind
> Looks ever down on all mankind,
> The works of men to know (Psalter 87:1).

Yes, and he looks down not only on the works of men, but on all things to know them. He looks from his throne on high and looks

down. God is in heaven. His perspective is heavenly, that of the
Lord of heaven and earth who created all things, who possesses all
things, who does with all things according to his good pleasure, and
who directs them according to his sovereign counsel. He knows
them not by studying them and watching their courses, but from
his eternal good pleasure and wise decree. He knows them in their
relation to one another and in relation to the final and all-comprehensive purpose they must serve and reach. He knows them all,
and he knows them in their minutest details. He knows exactly
what must happen in the affairs of the world and in your and my
individual experiences.

Father knows. We do not.

We often look at things from the infinitesimally small and narrow viewpoint of our own earthly and carnal wants and desires, in
order then to determine and tell the Lord in heaven what should
be done.

We are creatures of the dust. We are on the earth, we are of
time, of yesterday. We are of space, hemmed in on every side. We
see very little, almost nothing, except what it pleased the Lord to
reveal to us of his counsel: his general purpose of salvation.

Shall we then give him counsel?

We need give him no information in our prayers. He knows.

Be not rash with your mouth.

God is in heaven!

❖

Soli Deo Gloria!

That is the end. For God is in heaven.

He alone is the purpose of all things. All things are and must
be of him, and through him, and to him. Have your delight in that
purpose, and approach him with fear.

With reverent circumspection.

46

Remember Thy Word

*"Remember the word unto thy servant, upon which thou hast
caused me to hope."—Psalm 119:49*

THE word unto thy servant.

Almost it would appear from his personal application of the
word of God to himself that the psalmist refers to a special word of
God that had been addressed only to him.

Yet he would be mistaken who would thus understand the
meaning of the word of God here. The psalmist employs various
terms to denote the same word of God. He speaks of God's statutes
and his ordinances, of his law and his precepts, but always he refers
to the revealed word of God, revealed not personally to him and for
his benefit, addressed not to him individually but to all the servants
of Jehovah of all ages and out of every land; the word of God to his
people in this world; the word as it is essentially always the same,
but as it grows in riches of knowledge and wisdom, of salvation and
blessedness, as the promise of the gospel is being realized, and as
the church of the new dispensation possesses it in all its fullness of
glory radiating from the face of Jesus Christ.

Of that word the psalmist sings.

That word he applies to himself individually and personally, as
if it had been addressed to him privately, as if in it he were mentioned by name: the word unto thy servant.

He had heard it.

Through it the Most High, the Lord of heaven and earth, the
amen, the faithful and true, whom no man has ever seen, had spoken to him. And he knew it. So confident he felt that this word of
God had been addressed to him personally, that its blessed contents were promised to him, that in simple and childlike faith he

could appeal to it as "the word unto thy servant" and on the basis of it plead, "Remember."

Nor could anything less intimate, less specific than this personal hearing of the word of God suffice the people of God in this world.

Not as long as we read the Bible as a word of God to his people; still less while we hear it as a general offer of glory and salvation to all without distinction. Only when we perceive it and receive it in the depths of our souls as the word of our God to us is it truly to us a power of God unto salvation. Nothing less will suffice. How could it? Is it not on the sure basis of his word that we speak of our only comfort in life and death; that we boast of the things that are not seen; that we defy the seen and heard things in this world that always contradict the profession of our faith; that we glory in righteousness in the midst of sin and corruption and insist that we are justified before God, though all things, the devil, the world, and even our own consciences witness against us; that we profess to be heirs of all things, even though we are the most miserable of paupers in the world; that we glory in life although we die; that we boast of victory although we are defeated; that we count all things as dung for the excellency of Jesus Christ; that we would rather suffer the loss of all things than to lose the hope that is not seen?

How then can anyone so believe, so profess, so hope for things not seen, so boast and glory and rise in the face of all his opponents, mockers, deriders, persecutors, unless he has heard that word of God as addressed to him in person?

Nor is it impossible for us so to hear the word of God that we lay hold of it and respond, "The word unto thy servant."

For that word as we possess it in Scripture, universal though its sounding forth is, is always definite and distinctive in its content, both as to its promise and as to those to whom the promise is given.

That word is a promise, always a promise. The psalmist conceives of it as a personal promise of the Most High to himself. Is not this perfectly clear from the entire section introduced by the appeal, "Remember the word unto thy servant"? The psalmist speaks of suffering and affliction, of the house of his pilgrimage, and of the night. He complains that the proud have had him greatly in derision. Yet he speaks of joy and hope, of comfort in his affliction, and of songs that he sings in the night. Whence are his joy and cheer and the hope and comfort in the midst of suffering? They are in "the word unto thy servant, which thou hast caused me to hope." Is this not also evident from the words of verse 49? No doubt, when the psalmist addresses the Most High, "Remember the word unto thy servant," he means, "Be mindful of thy promise unto me, O Lord."

The word of God is a word of promise.

It is the promise of the sure mercies of David—sure because he who promised is faithful and true, never forsakes his word, but realizes it to the full. He is the omnipotent one, who alone created and alone moves heaven and earth, and so moves them that they must all be conducive unto the realization of the promise. It is the promise of full and glorious salvation, the forgiveness of sin, the adoption unto children, the deliverance from all corruption and death, the inheritance incorruptible and undefiled and that fades not away, the glory of God's everlasting and heavenly tabernacle, in which we will see him face-to-face, know as we are known, and forevermore taste that the Lord is good. It is the promise, the assurance of which we have in his word, spoken from the beginning of the world to and through patriarchs and prophets who heard the word of God and reported it to God's people; spoken through the Son, Jesus Christ in the flesh, Immanuel, God with us, who is the central realization of the promise; and spoken by faithful witnesses of his who preached the gospel of the promise unto us.

The history of salvation and revelation is the realization of that word of the promise. Always there was some measure of realization, yet always it remained the promise. Finally the promise was realized. The Word became flesh; the Lamb who takes away the sin of the world was slain; God was in Christ reconciling the world unto himself; and Jesus was raised from the dead and glorified at the right hand of God. The promise— atonement and reconciliation, forgiveness of sin and adoption, the breaking of the power of death, and the manifestation of life eternal —is realized in Christ Jesus. God has judged his people and justified them forever. The resurrection is an accomplished fact in Jesus Christ.

And still the word is a word of promise.

Still we possess only the firstfruits, and we long for the final harvest, for "the moment," the twinkling of an eye, when mortality will put on immortality and this corruptible will put on incorruption, when the trumpet will sound and time will be no more.

The definite and sure word of promise.

This promise is also definite with respect to those for whom the promise is intended. It is not a promise to all, but to the heirs. These are mentioned by name. They are the weary and those who labor, the hungry and those who thirst after righteousness, the poor of spirit who mourn, the meek and merciful and pure of heart, the penitent sinners and believers in Christ Jesus their Lord. They are the servants of Jehovah, whom he has called out of darkness into his marvelous light, who walk in his way, who delight in his precepts not in the things of the world, who have a small beginning of the new obedience that causes them to long and to strive to live not only according to some, but according to all the commandments of their God.

To these servants the word of promise is addressed.

And they hear.

For still it is Christ, the Son of God, who speaks his word in the Father's name, through his Spirit to all the heirs of the promise, assuring them that the promise is theirs, witnessing with their spirits that they are the sons of God, and if sons, then heirs.

They receive his word.

To them it is as if the word of the promise were addressed very intimately and personally.

And they respond, "The word unto thy servant, upon which thou hast caused me to hope."

❖

The servant of Jehovah hopes for both the content of the word of his God and upon that word as the ground of his hope.

To hope is to wait.

Hope is earnest expectation. Those who hope have their vision steadfastly fixed upon the future, not upon the present; upon the things above, not upon the things below. The "moment" engages their attention, occupies their souls, and dominates their lives.

Hope is personal assurance, for hope is certainty. It is the certainty that hope makes not ashamed because the love of God is poured into our hearts. It is the certainty that the object of our hope, though we see it not, is eternal reality as it is promised to us personally, and that eternal reality will far exceed in glory our boldest expectations.

Hope is patience, not that we do not earnestly long for the object of our hope, but that we wait for it. We stand waiting, our eyes steadfastly gazing up into heaven, and as we wait we let the things of the world pass by. Mockers and scorners deride us for our waiting attitude; the world invites us to abandon our position and to enjoy the lust of the flesh and the lust of the eyes and the pride of life. But we decline and remain waiting. The powers of darkness oppose us, threaten us, persecute us, and deprive us of name and place, of position and honor, yea, of our very life. But we remain waiting.

Hope is a strong and earnest longing for the final realization of our hope, for the firstfruits of the Spirit are ours. Possessing the firstfruits, we groan within ourselves, waiting for the adoption, that is, the redemption of our bodies. It is the looking forward, the earnest expectation, the stretching forth of the firstfruits unto the day of the final harvest.

The "moment" dominates our hearts and minds and souls and all of our strength.

In the light of that "moment" we see and evaluate all things.

Sub specie aeternitatis! (Under the aspect of eternity!)

❖

We count all things as dung for the excellency of Christ Jesus.

That hope is founded upon the word unto thy servant. Upon no other word can it rest.

No word of man can have anything to say about the object of this hope, for it belongs to the things unseen. Man's word is always from below. It cannot lift us above death and darkness. But the word of God came from above. It is the testimony of him who descended from heaven and is now in heaven and is able to speak of heavenly things. No word of man can serve as a basis of assurance upon which we can safely wait for the realization of the promise, though all things are against us. But the word of God is faithful and true.

Upon it we wait all the day.

Yet not ourselves. Thou hast caused me to hope!

By nature we do not and cannot hope upon the word of God, for we are children of wrath and under the judgment of condemnation. Neither do we by nature have an eye for the things of the kingdom of God and long for them. We are earthly, from below, carnal, and we delight in the things of the flesh.

How then can we hope upon his word?

Not only the promise, but also our hoping is of God.

For God pours out his love into our hearts by the Spirit he has given to us, and thus he causes us to hope in his mercy.

He made us partakers of the resurrection life of Jesus Christ and made us long for the "moment."

He causes us to count all things as dross for the glory of God that will be revealed in us.

He causes us to wait with patience.

To forsake all things and to suffer all things in hope.

Thou hast caused me to hope.

❖

Remember.

The word is thine, and my hoping is thine.

For thou hast spoken thy word, and thou hast caused me to hope. It is all thy word. Thy work it is that I stand here waiting and glorying in the "moment"; thy work it is that I forsake all things and suffer the loss of all things rather than to abandon my waiting attitude.

Remember then thy word unto thy servant, for else I stand ashamed, and thy name is blasphemed.

But is not the psalmist bold in his petition? Surely, the Lord is faithful and true. He will never forget his promise. What is more, he does not occasionally recall, but the promise is constantly before his mind from everlasting to everlasting. Having his promise to Christ and his church eternally before his mind, he is constantly actuated by it, and all his government of the universe, in heaven and on earth and in the abyss, tends toward the realization of the promise, so that all things work together for good to those who love God. Surely the Most High remembers the word unto his servant.

Is the psalmist's prayer born of doubt and infirmity?

God forbid!

He who comes unto God must believe that he is a rewarder of those who diligently seek him. Prayer that is rooted in doubt and fear that the Lord might forget his word unto his servant is no prayer.

And what is the true prayer of the servant of Jehovah? What else could it possibly be than the laying hold of the sure word of God, of the promise that cannot fail; to lay hold of it in the firm assurance that it will never be found faithless, and then to say, "Remember, O Lord"?

The psalmist needs God's answer. In the midst of trouble and affliction, of sin and death, of things that witness against the hope of the servant of Jehovah, he needs and seeks the answer that will surely resound upon his prayer of faith, "Be at rest, my child. I will surely, I always do, remember my word to you."

Always the church repeats this prayer, "Remember thy word. Come, Lord Jesus!"

And always the reassuring answer comes, "Behold, I come quickly! Amen, yea, amen!"